The Turkish Revolution 1960-1961

WALTER F. WEIKER

The Turkish Revolution 1960-1961

Aspects of Military Politics

GREENWOOD PRESS, PUBLISHERS
WESTPORT, CONNECTICUT

Library of Congress Cataloging in Publication Data

Weiker, Walter F
The Turkish Revolution, 1960-1961.

Reprint of the ed. published by Brookings Institution, Washington, D.C.
Includes index.
1. Turkey--History--Revolution, 1960. 2. Turkey. Ordu--Political activity. I. Title.
DR593.W44 1980 956.1'01 79-27852
ISBN 0-313-22303-3 lib. bdg.

Reprinted in 1980 by Greenwood Press,
a division of Congressional Information Service, Inc.
51 Riverside Avenue, Westport, Connecticut 06880

Printed in the United States of America

10 9 8 7 6 5 4 3 2 1

THE BROOKINGS INSTITUTION is an independent organization devoted to nonpartisan research, education, and publication in economics, government, foreign policy, and the social sciences generally. Its principal purposes are to aid in the development of sound public policies and to promote public understanding of issues of national importance.

The Institution was founded December 8, 1927, to merge the activities of the Institute for Government Research, founded in 1916, the Institute of Economics, founded in 1922, and the Robert Brookings Graduate School of Economics and Government, founded in 1924.

The general administration of the Institution is the responsibility of a self-perpetuating Board of Trustees. The Trustees are likewise charged with maintaining the independence of the staff and fostering the most favorable conditions for creative research and education. The immediate direction of the policies, program, and staff of the Institution is vested in the President, assisted by the division directors and an advisory council, chosen from the professional staff of the Institution.

In publishing a study, the Institution presents it as a competent treatment of a subject worthy of public consideration. The interpretations and conclusions in such publications are those of the author or authors and do not purport to represent the views of the other staff members, officers, or trustees of the Brookings Institution.

Foreword

THE MODERNIZING REVOLUTIONS which are giving rise to rapid political, social, and economic change in virtually every developing nation of Asia, Africa, and Latin America are being watched carefully by both American policy makers and scholars. In recognition of the importance of the problems and progress of these nations for the foreign policy of the United States, the Foreign Policy Studies Division of the Brookings Institution has embarked on a program of research on the political development of the emerging areas.

As part of this program, Mr. Weiker's study of some political problems of Turkey concerns itself with a country whose revolution occurred a generation earlier than those in most Asian and African countries, and whose difficulties in the 1960's, and the solutions attempted to meet them, may have much relevance for nations which will face similar situations in the future. The object of the study is to identify several of these problems and to relate them and various proposed or attempted solutions to the experience of the first generation of revolution in Turkey. Attention is also given to the relationship of the Turkish military revolution of 1960 to military revolutions in other developing nations, and to implications of the Turkish case for United States policy.

The author, Walter F. Weiker, was a Research Assistant in the Foreign Policy Studies Division of the Brookings Institution in 1961-62. He is now an Assistant Professor of Political Science at the Newark College of Arts and Sciences of Rutgers University. He received his B.A. from Antioch College, an M.A. from the Johns Hopkins School of Advanced International Studies, and his Ph.D. in politics and oriental studies from Princeton University. Research for this monograph was done in part during the author's residence in Turkey from December 1959 to April 1961, under the Foreign Area Training Fellowship program of the Ford Foundation.

In preparing this monograph, the author was advised by a committee composed of Roderic Davison, George Washington University; Robert Miner, Department of State; Kerim Key, Department of Commerce; H. Field Haviland, Jr., Robert E. Asher, Dankwart A. Rustow, and Laurin Henry, the Brookings Institution. The author and the Institution are indebted to this group for many constructive suggestions. Thanks are also due to Vakur Versan and Fahir Iz of Istanbul University for valuable factual information; A. Evelyn Breck for her editorial assistance; Virginia Haaga for preparing the index; and his wife, Miriam, for much patient and helpful assistance.

Brookings is indebted to the Ford Foundation for general support which has helped to make this study possible.

The views expressed in this study are those of the author and do not purport to represent the views of the other staff members, officers, or trustees of the Brookings Institution.

ROBERT D. CALKINS
President

The Brookings Institution
1775 Massachusetts Avenue, N.W.
Washington 6, D.C.

April 1963

Contents

The Turkish Revolution 1960-1961

1

The Background of the Revolution

THE UNITED STATES has understandably taken much interest in Turkey since the end of World War II. American programs of economic and military assistance there have achieved many of their aims. It is thus not without justification that American aid to Turkey since the proclamation of the Truman Doctrine in 1947 has amounted to around three billion dollars.

Turkey was a charter member of the United Nations even though it had remained neutral until the final months of World War II. Longstanding enmity with Russia made it clear where Turkish interests in the cold war lay, and in 1952 Turkey formally became a member of the North Atlantic Treaty Organization, giving that alliance a strong anchor on the Russian southern flank. In 1955 it also became the western anchor of the Baghdad Pact, now the Central Treaty Organization. An American-equipped standing army of 500,000 gives both of these alliances impressive additional muscle, and the record of Turkish troops in Korea leaves little doubt about the fighting qualities of these forces.

The United States also has a large stake in Turkish domestic health. The end of World War II brought liberalization in the authoritarian government through which Kemal Atatürk and his successors had begun to modernize the nation politically and economically. In 1950 the first free election swept the opposition into power and saw an event all too rare in the life of "emerging" nations, a smooth acquiescence of the government party and an orderly transfer of power. The 1950's were not without grave economic and political difficulties, to be sure, but for much of the period of multiparty politics, Turkey testified to the hopes of American policy makers that it was indeed possible for American aid to be an important factor in enabling economic development to proceed in a democratic, multiparty environment, an effective answer to Russian counterclaims.

The Turkish Revolution of 1960-61, which temporarily interrupted multiparty politics, has provided some important lessons for the United States about the difficulties that are sure to be encountered on the road to continued economic and political progress in the rapidly modernizing nations of the world. The Turkish experience can provide American policy makers with valuable guidance so that similar situations, which are sure to arise in other "emerging" nations, may be met constructively.

The roots of the revolution lie deep in the history of the westernizing reform program of Kemal Atatürk, who founded the Turkish Republic in 1923.[1] Underlying all the Atatürk reforms were the issues of secularism, of rapid social change versus the status quo, of political influence based on achievement, and democratic compromise versus that based on traditional status and relationships. The building of democratic, secular institutions of government was done by a single political party until in 1946 a combination of external and internal factors led Turkish leaders to believe that the time was ripe for multiparty activity. In 1960 it was widely felt in Turkey and abroad that the government of the Democratic party leaders, President Celal Bayar and Prime Minister Adnan Menderes, had strayed far from the path of the Atatürk revolution, and it was to return Turkey to democratic, secular politics that the armed forces took power on May 27, 1960. In October 1961, the armed forces kept their promise and turned power back to an assembly chosen in a free election.

The following chapters will deal with political problems which assumed importance during and/or because of the military take-over. To understand and appreciate these problems and the Turkish revolution of 1960-61, it will be useful to sketch briefly the background of multiparty government since 1923, the events that immediately preceded May 27 and that were important in shaping the political problems of the National Unity Committee (NUC) period, and the main events of the NUC period itself.

Birth of the Republic

In 1923 the Lausanne Treaty marked the successful conclusion of the War of Independence which the Turks had fought against the victorious Allies of World War I. The costs in human and material devastation incurred in driving out British, French, Italian, and especially Greek invading armies had been high, the more so when added to the debilitation that had resulted from an almost continual state of war since 1911. The War of Independence had been carried on chiefly by Turkish nationalists in Anatolia, led by Mustafa Kemal (Atatürk). Simultaneously

[1] Many people will contend that its roots go back much further than Atatürk. There are, to be sure, many connections between the Atatürk Revolution and the history of the Ottoman Empire. The best effort to date to describe those connections is Bernard Lewis, *The Emergence of Modern Turkey* (Oxford University Press, 1961). To discuss these subjects would be far beyond the field of this monograph, however.

with fighting the foreign invaders, the nationalists also had to contend with the government of the Ottoman Sultans in Istanbul. The Istanbul regime was charged with collaboration to the point of completely capitulating to the Allied demands and with signing the Treaty of Sèvres and other secret agreements. These divided Turkey into zones of occupation and provided for annexation by various Allied nations.

The war ended in victory for the nationalists both over the Allies, who were driven from Turkish soil, and over the Istanbul government. The Allies gave the nationalists important though involuntary assistance when the occupation of Istanbul reduced the Sultan's strength. As soon as hostilities ceased, Kemal used his military strength and political momentum to begin to bring into the open his plans for westernizing and modernizing Turkey. Even before the Lausanne Peace Conference, he abolished the Sultanate, ending the rule of a dynasty that had dominated a large part of Asia and Eastern Europe for over five hundred years. In 1923 Turkey became a republic. Over the next fifteen years Atatürk inaugurated many drastic reforms, seeking to destroy old institutions and power structures and to re-mold Turkey as a modern, western, democratic state. The dramatic reforms of substituting the hat for the fez, working to change the status of women in Turkish life, substituting Latin letters for the Arabic script, adopting a set of legal codes from those in use in European countries, the disestablishment of Islam, are well known and will not be discussed here.[2]

The Atatürk Reform Program

The ideological bases of the reform program were six tenets which, when they appeared together for the first time in 1931, became known as the Six Arrows of Kemalism—republicanism, nationalism, secularism, populism, étatism, and revolutionism. The Turkish State was declared to be irrevocably a republic. Nationalism was intended to focus attention on the Turkish nation inside its present frontiers rather than on the far-flung domains of the Ottomans. It was also the basis for working to exclude "internationalist" ideologies like communism.[3] Secularism

[2] For a discussion of the Atatürk reforms see Geoffrey Lewis, *Turkey,* revised ed. (Praeger, 1960); Lewis V. Thomas and Richard N. Frye, *United States and Turkey and Iran* (Harvard University Press, 1951); and Donald E. Webster, *The Turkey of Atatürk* (American Academy of Political and Social Science, 1939).

[3] In addition it became the take-off point for a large-scale program of revival, reinterpretation and some rewriting of the history of the Turkish people from the time of their origin to the modern period. The history reform sought among other things to link up the Hittite and Sumerian peoples with the Turks. Still another program sparked by nationalism was the language reform, which sought to substitute "pure Turkish" words for the large number of Persian and Arabic terms which had infiltrated Ottoman Turkish through the centuries.

was one of the most central planks of the Atatürk revolution. It was interpreted by Atatürk to mean virtually total exclusion of religious influence from public life, and in many cases meant discouraging private religious observance as well. After Atatürk's death, and especially since the rise of opposition parties in 1946, the role of religion in Turkish life has become one of the most important public issues.

Populism basically meant equality of all citizens before the law, and has usually been taken to include the principle of representative democracy as well. Major controversy has centered around étatism, that is, the role of the state in economic development. Government policy between 1923 and 1946 put great emphasis on the idea that the state had a useful and necessarily large role in economic activity of all kinds. Industrialization was carried on almost exclusively by state corporations and holding companies, and little private enterprise developed during these years. The Democratic party which emerged in 1946 was adamant in insisting that étatism must be succeeded by economic liberalism. Most authorities concur that étatism was necessary in the 1920's and 1930's, but beyond that there is little agreement on economic policy. Revolutionism has been taken to mean various things from an acceptance of the Atatürk reforms to a spirit of continuous rapid and radical change until westernization is complete.

The chief institution which Atatürk created to effect the reforms was the Republican People's party (RPP). It was organized in 1923 as successor to the Defense of Rights Society for Anatolia and Rumelia, the organization that had been the structural backing for waging the War of Independence. The RPP became the very personification of the revolution. From 1923 to 1946, with two exceptions, it ruled single handedly, and tolerated little resistance to its policies of rapid social, economic, and political change. The two short periods when opposition parties existed, however, already showed the seeds of the issues that were to divide the nation increasingly after 1946.

The loose structure of the Defense of Rights Society, devoted more to unifying the nation behind the war efforts than to controversial domestic actions, had been able to contain all of the Turkish leaders who for one reason or another opposed the foreign invaders and the collaborationist policies of the Sultan's government in Istanbul. But the disciplined structure of a political party was quite another matter. In 1924 a group of Atatürk's close collaborators in the War of Independence, of almost equal prominence but with more conservative views on the subject of social reform, resigned and formed the Progressive Republican party *(Terrakiperver Cumhuriyet Fırkası)*.[4] It lasted only a few months, for when it began to acquire a significant volume of support in the nation,

[4] On the Progressive Republican party see Tarik Tunaya, *Türkiye'de Siyası Partiler* (Istanbul, 1952), pp. 606-22; and Dankwart A. Rustow, "The Army and the Founding of the Turkish Republic," *World Politics*, Vol. 11, no. 4 (July 1959), pp. 513-52.

Atatürk saw it as an obstacle to rapid reform, though not comparable to the resistance, active and passive, of anti-Republic elements.

The closing of the Progressive party, and the exile or retirement of most of Turkey's conservative leaders of ability and experience, led to a period of virtually unhindered RPP power which lasted until the second opposition party emerged in 1930. During this five-year period most of the tradition-wrenching reforms took place. The RPP devoted its energies to indoctrinating the nation in the new ideas of secular, democratic politics and to pushing aside all possible barriers to change. Because of the one-direction flow of energy—the idea of seeking out the interests and needs of the people was still foreign to Turkish politicians—and because the closing of the Progressive party had eliminated the most effective channel for keeping track of the attitudes of important groups, the RPP deluded itself into thinking that reform was widely welcomed and absorbed by the Turkish nation.

The year 1930 brought what was one of the most important events in Turkish political modernization, the Free party,[5] an opposition party created by Atatürk from among his closest colleagues. The Free party lasted 99 days before it dissolved itself after having become the rallying ground for dissidents of all complexions. It is not insignificant, however, that the Progressive and Free parties raised the three issues that after 1946 came to dominate the bitter strife of Turkish politics. The Progressives' grievances were a pace of reform they thought too rapid and a secularism they thought too drastic. The Free party had concentrated on demands for more political and individual freedom, and on attacking the RPP's policy of a large state role in the economy.

The failure of the Free party was important for Turkey in that it revealed shortcomings which became the basis of a whole new direction for Atatürk's reform policies in the 1930's. It revealed how inadequate the efforts of the previous periods had been in preparing Turkey for multiparty government. The political elite had accepted the idea of the Republic and made a firm commitment to its institutions. But the stress on indoctrination, combined with the lack of controls on party domination, had resulted in failure to add to that commitment the political skills which would be needed to operate in a multiparty situation. The Free party failed partly because the elite proved unable to cope with the requirements of tolerating "loyal opposition." It was accustomed only to dictating to the people, not attempting to serve the people's interests so that they might win support in a free election, and it was unable to mobilize popular energies in the way needed to make real progress in economic and social improvement. The Free party adventure also revealed that the mass of the people had been practically untouched by

[5] The following paragraphs summarize material in the author's doctoral dissertation, "The Free Party of 1930 in Turkey, Loyal Opposition in a Rapidly Modernizing Nation" (Princeton University, 1962).

the reforms and that they were as ready to follow reactionary opportunists flocking to the Free party as they had been to follow earlier opposition groups.

During the 1930's primary stress was put on teaching the elite the techniques of democratic government and on building links between the urban and peasant sections of the nation, which might be the means of winning the mass of people to modernization. The basis of the new policies was to create public challenge to political leaders at several levels and to provide incentives for them to work with the people, solving local problems as well as paying attention to broader matters of national politics and ideology. To teach the deputies to take criticism, several "independent deputies" were introduced into the Grand National Assembly to challenge deputies and ministers. This would not risk another Free party debacle in the nation at large. A network of People's Houses was organized (and People's Rooms in villages), to serve as community centers. These were used for practical education in agriculture and homemaking, to be centers of group activities, libraries, and movies, as well as for political education in the bases and advantages of a modern republic. The RPP itself was turned into a flexible rather than a rigidly organized party, and concerted efforts were made to decentralize and to improve relationships with other elements in the community.[6] By 1935 difficulties of mobilizing the nation through such a loose structure had appeared, and there was some retrenchment, which reached its height in 1936 when the Minister of the Interior was concurrently made RPP Secretary-General and the governors of all provinces were given the additional job of province RPP chairman, "to increase cooperation and benefit from the work of both party and government."

The Multiparty Period

The situation went on largely unchanged after Atatürk's death in 1938. Increasingly, however, the liberal elements in the RPP emerged to support Ismet Inönü, Atatürk's successor as President of the Republic. Inönü was a partisan of liberal policies vis-à-vis the authoritarian sectors of the party which envisaged a long period of continued single-party tutelage. Inönü gave encouragement to the growing group of young party leaders who were fully committed to modernization, skilled in the techniques of democratic, secular politics, and increasingly impatient with the strictures of single-party discipline. In 1946, almost as soon as the international situation allowed a return to normal politics, opposition parties were permitted.

[6] The importance of all these events in shaping the current RPP will be dealt with in Chap. 5 below.

The Democratic party (DP), like the Republican People's party, came to possess an organization that penetrated every corner of Turkey. Indeed superior organization and grass-roots campaigning were in large measure responsible for the victory of the Democratic party in the 1950 elections. The basis of the DP's strength was the large portion of the nation either neglected by or dissenting from the policies of the RPP. The opposition's support included most of Turkey's conservative peasants, much of the business community, and a significant number of intellectuals who were eager to make Turkey a truly multiparty nation. Most of the early Democratic leaders had got valuable training and experience in the RPP. The four founders of the party, Celal Bayar, Adnan Menderes, Fuat Köprülü, and Refik Koraltan, were all deputies and RPP members before they rebelled in 1946. The election of 1946 was held before the Democrats had time to make a real race, but by 1950 they put up candidates in all provinces. To everyone's surprise, the 1950 election was really free. When the returns gave the Democrats an overwhelming majority of 416 out of the 487 Assembly seats, the RPP transferred power to them in a calm, orderly manner.[7]

The DP concentrated its fire on the RPP's étatism, on the restrictions on civil liberties which had been imposed during the single party period and accented during World War II, and on the alleged widespread corruption in the government. The first two areas were those on which the DP continued to concentrate during its entire existence. Both struck responsive cords. The core of the disagreement between the two parties, however, was not so much the merits of étatism versus free enterprise or complete versus restricted political freedom, but rather the relationship of these ideas to the larger framework of the Atatürk revolution. Etatism had been one of the RPP'S basic policies, reflecting among other things a distrust of the ability or willingness of private entrepreneurs to undertake the economic activity needed to develop the nation as a whole. It is true that Turkey lacked—and still lacks—a sufficiently large and experienced group of entrepreneurs to perform the multitudinous tasks of economic development. But it is also true that over the years étatism had become almost an end in itself to many political leaders. The RPP gave lip service to confining the economic role of the state to only what private enterprise could not do. But the lure of continued control of large resources had made many officials reluctant to practice what they preached. In 1946 the business community had, consequently, become increasingly hostile to the RPP and took advantage of the opportunity to gain a foothold in politics by supporting the Democrats.

More potent still was the freedom issue, and more dangerous. Political freedom was circumscribed during the RPP's rule, but the authorities thought for good reason. It had long been deemed necessary to exclude

[7] For a discussion of the 1946-50 period see Kemal Karpat, *Turkey's Politics, The Transition to a Multi-Party System* (Princeton University Press, 1959).

from the political arena those persons acting from nondemocratic motivations, including chiefly the opponents of secularism. The period of RPP rule was authoritarian but by no means totalitarian, though when a direct conflict developed between those who did and did not want to press forward rapidly with social reform, it was the former who always prevailed. When the DP called for more freedom, therefore, a fundamental issue was raised. The Democrats could claim, with considerable justification, that by giving voice to the people they were more democratic than the RPP. The Republicans countered with the accusation that the Democrats were betraying secularism by permitting "reactionaries" to usurp the freedom that was meant only for those honestly differing in the view of how to perpetuate the revolution.

Organizationally both the RPP and the DP were mass parties. Each had branches in every part of Turkey, including a large proportion of Turkey's 40,000 villages. It was estimated that in 1960, village and county branches of the three largest parties together totaled 154,000.[8]

Party organization worked up through county, district, and province branches to the central organization in Ankara. There were also youth branches and women's branches. In addition, the DP during the latter part of its existence, built up a "Patriotic Front" (*Vatan Cephesi*) which was closely coordinated with the party's regular organization.

The Decline and Fall of the Democratic Party

The decade from the formation of the Democratic party government in May 1950 to its overthrow on May 27, 1960, was characterized chiefly by a constantly growing polarization between the Republicans and Democrats. The fever pitch of irreconcilable hostility that was reached in 1960 began to build up within a short time after the Democrats came to power. The two main issues were the role of religion in Turkish life, and the maintenance of political freedoms. Almost as important was economic policy.

That some relaxation in the pressure for total secularization of Turkish life would come during the Democratic period was to be expected. Indeed the RPP itself had made certain concessions under pressure of the opposition in 1948 and 1949. The Democrats had been elected on a platform tending to be conservative and had based much of their appeal on representing the wishes of the people, in implied contrast to the imposed reform of the RPP. And a large part of the Democratic vote came from conservative rural areas. Thus though the RPP could

[8] A report in *Cumhuriyet* on June 24, 1960, when the NUC ordered dissolution of the local and county branches of all parties, gave the following figures: DP, 60,000 local and 6,000 county branches; RPP 50,000 local, 5,000 county; Republican Peasants Nation Party 30,000 local, 3,000-4,000 county.

hardly complain about the principle of relaxation of anticlerical pressures, it began to be increasingly upset at the complexion which specific Democratic policies took.

In the area of secularization, the RPP had agreed in 1949 to allow religious instruction in schools, if parents requested it for their children in writing. The Democrats altered this arrangement to read that all Muslim children would receive religious instruction unless their parents requested in writing that the children *not* receive it. The RPP had authorized the creation of a Faculty of Divinity in Ankara, and the training of *imams* by private individuals, in order to meet the well-taken objection that if no new religious leaders were trained, either Islam would die out altogether, or fall into the hands of the uneducated and the covert. The Democrats expanded the number of institutions for training *imams* and allowed them to take on a conservative tinge. In 1950 the Democrats also abolished the 1928 law prohibiting the use of the Arabic form of call to prayer. The entire country immediately dropped the Turkish translation which the earlier law had substituted.[9] Other areas of relaxation were more unofficial. Ramazan, the Moslem holy month, began to be celebrated more publicly. Religious publications began to reappear. The remnants of various mystic sects began tentatively to show their heads, although it must be said that the activities of the more troublesome sects like the Nurs were severely dealt with in 1959-60. Probably the most concrete criticism the Republicans could make was of the large amount of government funds used for building new mosques in cities, towns, and villages. One estimate by officials in the Directorate of Religious Affairs was that 5,000 new mosques were built between 1950 and 1960. This was approximately the same figure given by the Ministry of Education for the construction of new schools in the same period. As one correspondent put it, "...This silent struggle for scarce resources seems highly symbolic of the greater struggle between the forces of secularism and Islam in Turkey."[10]

There will be arguments in Turkey for many years about whether the Democratic party period was one of the betrayal of secularism, the exploitation of religion, the restoration of freedom of worship, or the beginning of a new period of "modernized Islam." The pertinent fact is that the Democrats and the RPP made the interpretation of secularism an ever-growing issue. It dovetailed with other issues and served to add fuel to a fire which will continue to smolder.

The second main issue, and the one which caused the most uproar in international as well as Turkish political circles and ultimately brought the downfall of Menderes, was that of political freedom. It was not long

[9] On this point see Paul Stirling, "Religious Change in Republican Turkey," *Middle East Journal* (Autumn 1958), p. 400.

[10] David Hotham, "Turks Turn Again to Religion," *The Times* (London), Feb. 23, 1960.

after their election victory of 1950 that some of the leaders of the Democratic party began to show a marked sensitivity to criticism. From 1953 on, a series of laws was passed which eventually placed severe restrictions on the press, the universities, and the opposition parties. None of these laws were, of course, overtly against freedom for these sources of criticism. Most of them were framed in a way that could be rationalized within the framework of the Atatürk revolution. It was the interpretation of enforcement of the laws which was the real rub.

In 1953, for example, a law provided for compulsory retirement of judges after twenty-five years of service, opening many judgeships for political appointees. Professors were banned from political activity, a reaction to the already noticeable tendency of professors to drift away from the Democrats. A law banning the political use of religious propaganda brought RPP fears that it would be used against the opposition. And late in 1953 the government confiscated most of the assets of the RPP, on the grounds that they had been illegally acquired with public funds during the single-party period.

In 1954 the government acquired the right to oust civil servants without giving them the right of appeal. Tighter curbs on electioneering included banning political propaganda from the state radio, a subject which entered the Yassıada trial of the Menderes regime in 1960, when it was charged that the DP had in fact monopolized the radio for its own partisan ends. In 1954 some of the first physical violence appeared between the parties in the Assembly; the RPP was openly backed by many university professors; and a Democratic election victory reduced the opposition to only 31 out of a total of 541. It was the year of the first restrictive Press Law, punishing the spreading of false news or insulting or invading the privacy of public officials. Before the year was out, three journalists had been jailed and four others dismissed from their jobs.

The year 1955 brought the arrest of RPP Secretary-General Kasım Gülek for insulting the government while on a speaking tour; the jailing under the Press Law of Metin Toker, journalist and son-in-law of RPP leader Inönü; and the suspension of five newspapers, including the RPP organ *Ulus,* for violating censorship about the Cyprus problem. Riots in Istanbul on September 6 and 7 against the Greek minority in that city were believed to have been deliberately encouraged by the government to press its point in the Cyprus dispute.[11] Some internal Democratic party difficulties also occurred in 1955, when nineteen deputies resigned over the administration of the Press Law. A small new opposition, the Freedom party, was formed in 1955 by some university and business elements, many of whom had formerly comprised the liberal wing of the Democratic party.

More of the same came in 1956. A second press law added to the

[11] The charges at the Yassıada trial on the instigation of the riots are discussed in Chap. 2.

offenses for which papers could be closed and newsmen jailed for "damaging public confidence in or the prestige of the government." Political party meetings were prohibited except during a forty-five day period before the general election. The same prohibition was applied to any type of electioneering, and the police were given authority to fire on crowds at "unlawful political gatherings." Under this law Kasım Gülek was arrested for hand-shaking activities on his visits around the country.

The first direct interference in university affairs took place when Turhan Feyzioğlu, Dean of the Ankara University Faculty of Political Sciences, was suspended for bitterly criticizing the government's refusal to promote a faculty member who was critical of government policy.[12] During part of 1956 the opposition boycotted the Assembly.

The impending election of 1957 gave rise to a new election law which, among other things, prohibited coalitions, a factor that worked to prevent the opposition from putting up a united front. Another election law provision awarding to the party winning the most votes in a province —even if not a majority—that province's entire number of deputies, was important in assuring a Democratic victory. Nevertheless the opposition increased to 186, 178 of these being RPP. In 1957 the government introduced restrictions on the Assembly itself, limiting the number and scope of questions deputies could ask of ministers, tightening the regulations for parliamentary immunity, and forbidding the press from reporting on "subjects of an offensive nature" even if these were debated publicly in the Assembly.

From 1958 on Turkey moved steadily toward the edge of violence. Charges that the 1957 election had been rigged were given more credence by the failure of the government ever to publish official results. The number of journalists in Turkish jails rose regularly. Menderes' support among the urban intelligentsia dwindled to virtually none. In the Assembly the two chief parties were hardly on speaking terms.

In 1959 came the first serious violence. In May RPP leader Inönü visited heavily Democratic southwest Turkey and was met at Uşak by a pro-Democratic demonstration during which he was cut in the head by a rock thrown from the crowd. Three days later, as Inönü entered Istanbul on his return trip, he was met by large numbers of Democratic partisans, and according to the evidence brought out at the Yassıada trial, would have been "accidentally" killed had it not been for the interference of soldiers after the police had looked the other way.[13] Censors banned publication of news about the incidents, setting a pattern which was to be followed frequently in 1960.

One other event of 1959 should not be forgotten. In February Prime Minister Menderes walked away from an airplane crash that killed fifteen other members of the Turkish delegation going to London to sign

[12] The Feyzioğlu case is discussed in Chap. 3 on problems of Turkish higher education.
[13] Details of these two cases are presented in Chap. 2 on the Yassıada Trials.

the Cyprus agreement. As a result of this escape, he was viewed as almost superhuman by many superstitious Turkish peasants. This considerably reinforced his already large peasant support, and was an important consideration in the National Unity Committee's decision not to commute the death sentence passed on him at Yassıada.

In addition to political affairs, a great deal of controversy centered around the economic policies of the Menderes government. The opposition was vindicated on this score when it was revealed, soon after the 1960 revolution, that the fallen regime had left Turkey with a huge internal and foreign debt. Figures released to the newspapers on June 17, 1960, were as follows:

Estimated Turkish Debts, June 1960
(Thousands of Turkish Lira)

	Internal	Foreign	Total
Regular budget	1,417,781	2,882,767	4,300,548
Annexed budgets and state economic enterprises	2,949,768	1,872,747	4,822,515
Total public debt	4,367,549	4,755,514	9,123,063
Private sector and miscellaneous debts			3,068,379
Grand Total			12,191,442

At the official exchange rate of 9 lira to the dollar, the total debt was equivalent to $1,354,604,636.

Few will dissent from the view that Menderes performed some valuable services for Turkish economic development. Road building and other "infra-structure" projects went forward at a rapid rate, and more attention was paid to agriculture than had been the case earlier. He seriously overextended his activities in relation to available resources, however, with the result that inflation became a serious problem.[14] His seeming phobia about any aspect of planning made for additional difficulties.

[14] Menderes did in fact appear to like nothing better than a great public works project. He frequently traveled around the country personally directing construction activities. Possibly one of his most noteworthy undertakings was improving roads and arteries in the city of Istanbul. On the negative side, the Istanbul projects were open to heavy criticism because certain historical sites were destroyed and because of Menderes' habit of requisitioning land and buildings with no or inadequate compensation. But it was Menderes who probably was responsible for at least starting to rescue the city from strangulation. Menderes' biggest project, the Bosporus Bridge, was again being actively considered just before May 27, despite strong criticism from financial experts. The NUC promptly canceled all plans for it.

But he did succeed in continuing to get massive foreign aid, especially from the United States.

In 1958 the situation almost reached a breaking point, and in order to get himself bailed out with a substantial amount of financial assistance, Menderes agreed to the terms of a Stabilization Program set down by the International Monetary Fund, the chief partner in a composite loan totaling some $359 million. These conditions were: (1) effective devaluation; (2) inauguration of a system of global import quotas to replace bilateral agreements; (3) consolidation and orderly repayment of a foreign debt of about $1 billion; (4) restriction of domestic credit; (5) abolition of price control; (6) abandonment of deficit financing; (7) striving toward financial balance in state and semistate organizations; (8) closer coordination of investment.[15]

Menderes' implementation of both the letter and spirit of the Stabilization Program was sluggish, however. By 1960 many of the shortages of consumer goods—including, for an extended period, an almost total absence of Turkish coffee—had eased, but the NUC also found that Menderes had already run through practically the entire Stabilization Loan.

The End of the Menderes Regime

The sequence of events leading finally to the revolution of May 27 began about six months earlier. The opposition began to devise new ways of defying the government, and the latter was forced to more and more drastic measures.[16] Probably the greatest Menderes' blunder was bringing the army in to quell political disturbances. The Chief of the General Staff, Rüştü Erdelhun, seems to have convinced the Prime Minister as well as himself[17] that the army would remain loyal to the government. Even had the army not been brought in directly, however,

[15] Economist Intelligence Unit, London, *Three-Monthly Economic Review, Turkey,* Annual Supplement, June 1961. This series of publications is also the source of much of the data below.

[16] One clever tactic took place when the government suspended the weekly news magazine *Kim* in December 1959. The following week a magazine appeared identical to the suspended one, except its name was *Mim.* The advertisements read "What is *Mim?* Everybody knows what *Mim* is!!"

[17] Among those who were apparently convinced that everything would be all right was the staff of the American Embassy. According to a *New York Times* story datelined Washington, May 27, "It was the view of the [American] Embassy [informed sources in the State Department said], that a coup by the army was unlikely. In support of this belief, it was understood, the Embassy pointed out that General Rüştü Erdelhun, Chief of Staff of the Turkish Army, was apparently standing firm behind Premier Menderes, and that a military coup was most unlikely unless it was led by, or had the blessing of, General Erdelhun." Most other observers in Ankara had abandoned this interpretation well before May 27.

it is unlikely that it would have remained aloof much longer in the midst of the steadily worsening political situation.

Early in 1960 the rumor began to circulate in Ankara that the government would call new elections in the spring, although they were not legally required before 1961. The opposition quickly converted the rumor into a pledge, and Menderes did nothing to dispel the idea. Thus the element of pre-election politicking was added to the already boiling pot. In February the RPP succeeded in bringing to the Assembly floor eleven motions for investigation of alleged irregularities and profiteering by cabinet ministers. Some charged that illegal gains ranged as high as $750,000 for one former minister. The debates, lasting several days and nights, were not unexpectedly expanded to include opposition charges of rigging the 1957 election and other sources of dissatisfaction over the previous several years. Before the Assembly voted to reject all of the motions, there had been fist-fighting on the floor, and a field day for the newspapers which reported the debates in every detail, with illustrations. The budget debate a short time later was almost as violent, and it was only because the Assembly recessed in March that the crisis abated.

But the interlude was short. Menderes continued to make speeches around the country, and Inönü began to follow suit. On April 2, Inönü and several RPP deputies were traveling to the city of Kayseri in central Anatolia when their train was stopped by rows of soldiers blocking the tracks. The governor of Kayseri entered Inönü's railroad compartment and informed him that the people of Kayseri were excited to the point of endangering public order, and that the authorities were ordering him to return to Ankara. Inönü tore up the written order which the governor handed him and refused to budge.

The scene which took place while the governor frantically telephoned Ankara for fresh instructions should have given Menderes something to think about. As Inönü sat in his compartment, numerous officers, soldiers, and civilians came to pay their respects by kissing his hand. They made it clear that blocking the road was only to avoid being court-martialed for insubordination. The governor made several other fruitless attempts to turn the party back to Ankara, but Inönü persisted and continued to Kayseri, passing through ranks of saluting officers and soldiers as if he were still wearing general's stars as he had during the War of Independence forty years earlier. When on the following day Inönü's return by car to Ankara was halted by four army trucks blocking a bridge, the RPP leader took matters into his own hands, left his car, and strode firmly toward the obstruction. Before he had reached the bridge the soldiers drew back, saluted, and the auto caravan continued to Ankara without further incident.

The Kayseri incident was the most direct public confrontation to date between the two sides. Although it is unlikely that this event set in motion the activity of the officers who acted on May 27, the incident probably convinced many of them that it would hardly be possible to keep aloof if the situation continued to worsen.

And worsen it did. On the morning of April 18 the news spread in Ankara that the Assembly session of that afternoon would be an important one. The journalists and spectators who jammed the galleries hours before the opening were not disappointed. The business of the day was a motion by two Democratic deputies to establish a Committee to Investigate the Activities of the Republican People's Party and a Section of the Press. The session opened with a scathing speech by Inönü denouncing the proposal as dictatorial, unconstitutional, and violating human rights. Several Democrats then proceeded to attack the opposition, the most violent speech being a personal hour-long assault on Inönü by Samet Ağaoğlu, who listed the RPP leader's "crimes" dating from the War of Independence period. Not even the most partisan presiding officer could deny Inönü the right to rebut this, and the veteran statesman made his now-famous assertion that "If you continue on this road, even I will not be able to save you."[18] At this point the cheering and booing from various groups of deputies gave way to fist-fighting. A Democratic deputy brandished a pistol (in violation of Assembly bylaws), but was prevented by his colleagues from doing any harm. When a Republican, instead of the Democratic pistol-waver, was expelled from the Assembly for fighting, the entire Republican delegation followed Inönü out the door. In an obviously well-planned action, the Investigating Committee was set up minutes after the Assembly vote. Headed by Denizli deputy Ahmet Hamdi Sancar, it consisted of fifteen Democrats known for being among the most partisan and unscrupulous.[19] Simultaneously the committee issued decrees suspending all political activity in the nation and banning publication of anything whatsoever concerning the investigation.[20] The following day, April 19, the first public disorder took place when a large crowd gathered to cheer Inönü as he passed through Ankara's main square on his way to RPP headquarters. At this point, though, neither side forced the issue, Inönü's banquet in honor of some RPP deputies was not disturbed, and he made no further public appearances which could have become disorderly.

The incident needed to touch off the revolt was soon produced, how-

[18] The texts of both Inönü speeches, and a report of much of the debate of April 18, are printed in *Ulus,* April 19, 1960.

[19] Other members were Nusret Kirişçioğlu (Sakarya), press spokesman; Nuzhet Ulusoy (Samsun), secretary; Vacıt Asena (Balıkesir); Kemal Biberoğlu (Çorum); Turan Bahadır (Denizli); Bahadır Dülger (Gaziantep); Sait Bilgiç (Isparta); Hilmi Dura (Kastamonu); Osman Kavuncu (Kayseri); Himmet Olçmen (Konya); Kemal Ozer (Kütahya); Necmettin Onder (Neyşehir); Selami Dinçer (Sakarya); Ekrem Anıt (Samsun).

[20] By the time police arrived at the printing plant of the RPP organ *Ulus,* RPP deputies in their private cars had already taken several thousand copies. These were sent to the provinces, and copies were distributed free the next morning on the streets of Ankara. *Ulus* was, of course, suspended indefinitely.

ever, in the form of a law formally conferring wide authority on the Investigating Committee. The powers granted it on April 27 included forbidding all publications tending to impede the investigation; closing newspapers for definite or indefinite periods if they violated this prohibition; seizing all documents and property necessary for the investigation; forbidding all political activity as the committee deemed necessary; imposing summary penalties of from six months to three years imprisonment on persons violating any of these prohibitions; and suspending operation of civil service, penal, and judicial laws.[21] When Inönü vehemently protested, he was expelled from the Assembly for twelve sessions.

The repercussions of the new law and the expulsion of Inönü led directly to the bloody clashes on April 28-29 at Istanbul and Ankara Universities, dates which are now commemorated each year in mourning. A professor in Istanbul University's Faculty of Law told his class "My subject today is the Constitution. But it is forbidden, and being violated, so you are all dismissed." The massing of students in the square in front of the University gate quickly brought the police. Rector Siddik Sami Onar was summoned. He tried to separate the combatants by having the students return to the supposedly inviolate University grounds, but received a slight head injury when the police attempted to take him to headquarters. Open fighting between students and police ended in gun-fire by the latter, police jeeps also being driven zig-zag fashion through the student ranks, which broke and reformed inside the campus. The police who followed through the gate were driven out, but when the students began a silent march to the governor's office, cavalry were used. Rumors of the toll of killed, injured, and arrested ran completely wild.[22] Martial law was declared that night in both Istanbul and Ankara. This incident also was the first to receive publicity in the strange form of being banned from the press. Numerous times up to May 27 the public learned of an incident when the newspapers gave large headlines to the decree forbidding publication of news about the incident. As for details, they came freely through other channels.

Ankara University followed the next morning. Students gathered in the courtyards of the Political Science and Law Faculties, met this time by soldiers of the martial law authorities as well as by the police. Defying all attempts to disperse them, the students built barricades, hurled stones and other objects, and at one point captured a fire engine and turned it on the police. Then occurred the now-famous incident of the

[21] Text of the law is found in *Zafer*, April 27, 1960. The Investigating Committee affair is discussed in more detail in Chap. 2.

[22] The death toll was only one, which is what Menderes said on the radio shortly afterward. Few believed him, of course, until a later investigation by the military government confirmed the figure. The number of injured has not been definitely determined. A large number of students were arrested, some staying in custody until after May 27, others having been taken to army camps and released after short periods.

order to fire. The senior military officer on the scene was the Ankara Martial Law Commander himself, Lieutenant General Namık Argüç. As the situation grew more and more tense, Argüç ordered the cavalry commander on the scene, Major Vehbi Ersü—later a member of the National Unity Committee—to open fire. Ersü refused, and was promptly placed under arrest by the general. After several fruitless attempts to place junior officers in charge, Argüç gave the order himself, after which police and soldiers charged the Political Science Faculty building, and pitched battles took place both inside and outside.[23] No fatalities but an undetermined number of injuries resulted from the disturbance. More students were carted off to detention camps, and the universities were closed for a month.[24]

From then on there were riots almost every night on the main boulevard of Ankara. It must be said, however, that after the first few times the rioting was gentlemanly in comparison with that in some other troubled nations, and mild in comparison with Korea, from which the Turks took their most immediate inspiration.[25] Demonstrations usually took place between five and seven in the evening, when there were "natural crowds" of after-work strollers who could serve as support and concealment. Police and troops lolled on side streets at peak traffic hours, waiting for the choruses of "freedom, freedom, Menderes resign!" to arise from somewhere on the boulevard. They would cordon off the street, some tear gas might be used, a few students arrested, and then the crowds watching from the street and from windows and balconies on all sides would break up and go to dinner. There were some exceptions to this general pattern, however. One was the bizarre incident of 555-K.

On the morning of May 5, word spread through Ankara that a demonstration of special interest would be held that day—the fifth day of the fifth month, at 5 p.m. in Kızılay Square. Everyone gathered, including the police who had also been advised. About 5:45 the crowds were puzzled when the usual choruses were ignored by the police, but shortly their attention turned to a black Cadillac moving down the hill from the presidential residence. President Bayar and Prime Minister Menderes, it seems, had been the origin of the call for a show, to demonstrate that they too had partisans. But the small group of Democrats who turned out were no match for the mass of antigovernment students. When Menderes stepped out of his car, he promptly had his hair mussed and tie knocked askew. When he threw his chest forward toward the students and shouted "then kill me!" he was met with the deflating answer: "We don't want to kill you. Just resign!" With difficulty Menderes man-

[23] In the Yassıada trials Argüç received a sentence of ten years for this incident.

[24] The students were sent to their homes, where they were beyond most control and were probably influential in spreading opposition to the regime in provincial towns and cities.

[25] Student demonstrations in Korea had just resulted in the downfall of the Syngman Rhee government, a downfall which Turkish newspapers exploited to the utmost.

aged to get into a journalists's car which had been accidentally trapped in the crowd. Now he was not only the villain of Ankara, but also its laughing stock.[26]

Foreign policy was never more than a peripheral subject in the political strife,[27] but two events the timing of which was unfortunate had international repercussions. One was the meeting of NATO Foreign Ministers held in Istanbul on May 2-4. What was to have been a great prestige occasion for Turkey turned into an airing of dirty linen before a large contingent of Western newsmen. As one correspondent reported it: "The streets are lined with Turkish soldiers in battle regalia. The extraordinary all-day curfew has halted civilian traffic. Visiting foreign ministers and delegates drove about by virtue of bright yellow stickers honored by the army commanders."[28] Menderes canceled his speech to the meeting in order to stay in Ankara on top of developments. Foreign Minister Zorlu was forced to give an abjectly apologetic press conference. A student march got all the way to the doors of the hall where the ministers were meeting before troops turned them back within full view of the visitors, and a silent march of one hundred lawyers got almost as far.

The second ill-timed event was a state visit by Indian Prime Minister Nehru. Deaf to the Turkish government's private requests for a postponement, Nehru arrived in Ankara on May 20, as luck would have it at 5 p.m., so that his ride through the city from the airport with Menderes took place at the height of the evening rush. The crowd took full advantage of the opportunity to boo Menderes directly. The most interesting incident of the visit, though, was the press conference. None had been

[26] There has been much discussion of whether Menderes was mentally unbalanced. Probably the most that could be said is that he had strong psychological pre-dispositions for and against certain ideas like economic planning. Many observers also contend, however, that personal pride was such a large factor in his make-up that it is unlikely he could ever have brought himself voluntarily to resign.

[27] Since 1950 there have been no important differences between the parties on matters of foreign policy. Menderes had been criticized, however, for his planned visit to Russia in July 1961, a trip which, of course, never took place. Domestic affairs had also caused at least four postponements of a state visit to Greece, with the result that some Greek sources began to complain that Turkey was little interested in good relations with its Western neighbor. Unconfirmed stories after May 27 charged that Menderes had made plans for large concessions from Russia in exchange for "selling" to the Soviet Union the area around Kars which had been claimed by both Russia and Turkey during the decades since current boundaries were fixed in 1921.

A more important foreign policy problem was the fact that many Turkish intellectuals were displeased with the United States, it being contended that the large amounts of American aid had been one of the chief supports of the Menderes government. Had the United States demanded better uses of its aid, these intellectuals continue to maintain, Menderes would never have been able to go as far as he did in using it for partisan advantage. They also feel that the United States had considerable leverage to induce the government to inaugurate planning, and to govern more democratically. Turkey is a country, they point out, where the possibility of a nation going over to the Communists if massive aid is not forthcoming cannot be used as an excuse.

[28] *New York Times,* May 2, 1960.

scheduled, but on Saturday afternoon someone called all the correspondents in town and invited them to one. Nehru came into the room quite surprised, but agreed to answer questions as long as everyone had gathered. He talked mostly about the recent collapse of the Summit Conference, but eventually was asked leading questions, such as whether *he* put journalists in jail during India's critical days. He parried the questions nicely, but it was enough for the newspapers to do a big spread. It never was made clear who started calling the correspondents, for the Indian press attache denied it. It was a clever victory for the opposition.[29]

In mid-May, Menderes set out on a tour of Turkey's Aegean region which was his home area, and one of the centers of his greatest strength. Speaking to a sizable crowd in Izmir, he said that "elections are very near," thus making at least a faint move toward meeting the demands of the opposition. Later in Istanbul he repeated his statement, obviously buoyed by the demonstrations of support on his recent tour. The tense atmosphere made it unlikely, however, that early elections would have been orderly even if they had been fair, which few opponents believed possible based on their experiences in 1957. These hesitating feelers were too little to stop the spiral of tension. Youth Day, May 19, found the traditional sports demonstrations and other events prohibited and in their place major demonstrations at Atatürk's Mausoleum in the morning and on Atatürk Boulevard in the evening.

Only one round remained. The Investigating Committee continued its work, generating stories of third degree interrogation methods and of plans to arrest large groups of professors and Republican deputies. Censorship of letters and telephones had been authorized, all foreign publications were stopped at the border if they contained any criticism of the Turkish situation, and most Turkish newspapers and magazines had been suspended. When news of the arrest and alleged beating of several army officers was added to this, the cadets of the Military College gave what turned out to be the last warning Menderes received. On May 21 about 1,000 cadets marched toward the presidential residence, accompanied, but not led, by their officers—Military College Commander Sitki Ulay was later a prominent member of the National Unity Committee—and followed by a large crowd of officers and civilans. The Ankara Martial Law Commander personally pleaded with the cadets,

[29] An amusing sidelight was the presentation to Nehru by a Turkish woman journalist of one of Atatürk's shirts for, as she said, "Nehru and Atatürk were both fighters for freedom." In the pocket was concealed a note saying "I am a Turkish journalist, but due to restrictions I can approach you only as a representative of a foreign press agency." She said later that she was not sure whether Nehru had seen the note, but that at a later reception "he clasped my hand warmly." When Nehru said he would put the shirt into a museum, one Western correspondent quipped to his neighbor, "Well, what should he have said, that it doesn't fit?" The last act in the drama was when the Turkish Women's Society later asked Nehru to return the shirt for a Turkish museum.

but only after he had given a pledge that there would be no reprisals, and after the cadets had stood their ground and sung military marches long enough to make their point very clearly, did the demonstrators move off to other parts of the city and back to their quarters.

The government's reply was to extend the one-month closing of universities, instruction to resume only in the fall. The Assembly recessed on May 25 after another bitter fist-fight. The Prime Minister went to the city of Eskişehir, where he announced that the Investigating Committee had finished its work in one month instead of the projected three. But by this time only far more substantial concessions, probably including the resignation of the government, would have headed off the events of May 27.

The National Unity Committee Period

The revolution of May 27 was completed within four hours. Strategic spots were secured, the President, Prime Minister, and cabinet taken into "protective custody," and military commanders placed in charge of the areas in which they were stationed. At 4 p.m. the curfew in Ankara was lifted, and the city witnessed a celebration such as it had not seen since the victory in the War of Independence. Istanbul was also the scene of wild celebrations. The rest of the country was less excited, partly because most of the disturbances had been confined to Ankara and Istanbul (and to a small extent Izmir), partly because there were still many Menderes sympathizers in the nation, and partly because few people had any idea what to expect from the armed forces. Most of those who initially hesitated were quick to get on the band wagon. Celebration and ceremony continued for the better part of a month, no day going by without several groups laying wreaths at the Atatürk Mausoleum.[30] Then Turkey began to settle down and to realize the difficulty of the work ahead.

In mid-morning on May 27 the armed forces broadcast a message to the Turkish nation and to the world:

> Honorable Fellow Countrymen: Owing to the crisis into which our democracy has fallen, and owing to the recent sad incidents and in order to prevent fratricide, the Turkish armed forces have taken over the administration of the country.
>
> Our armed forces have taken this initiative for the purpose of extricating the parties from the irreconcilable situation into which they have fallen and

[30] Undoubtedly the junta itself encouraged many of these ceremonies, as a means to keep the nation from losing its momentum now that the immediate objective had been won. Among the largest ceremonies was a great state funeral on June 11 for the two soldiers and two civilians killed in the revolution or in events connected with it. The sports festival which had been banned on May 19 was held in great enthusiasm on June 26.

for the purpose of having just and free elections, to be held as soon as possible under the supervision and arbitration of an above-party and impartial administration, and for handing over the administration to whichever party wins the elections.

Our initiative is not directed against any person or class. Our administration will not resort to any aggressive act against personalities, nor will it allow others to do so.

All fellow countrymen, irrespective of the parties to which they may belong, will be treated in accordance with the laws and all the principles of law.

For the elimination of all our hardships and for the safety of our national existence, it is imperative that it should be remembered that all our fellow countrymen belong to the same nation and race, above all party considerations, and that therefore they should treat one another with respect and understanding, without bearing any grudge.

All personalities of the Cabinet are requested to take refuge with the Turkish armed forces. Their personal safety is guaranteed by law.

We are addressing ourselves to our allies, friends, neighbors and the entire world: Our aim is to remain completely loyal to the United Nations Charter and to the principles of human rights; the principle of peace at home and in the world set by the great Atatürk is our flag.

We are loyal to all our alliances and undertakings. We believe in NATO [North Atlantic Treaty Organization] and CENTO [Central Treaty Organization] and we are faithful to them.

We repeat: Our ideal is peace at home, peace in the world.

The body formed to govern the nation became known as the National Unity Committee (NUC). For several days neither the names nor the number of officers composing the junta was officially known, other than that of General Cemal Gürsel, former Commander of Land Forces, who became Chairman of the NUC, President, Prime Minister, and Chief of the General Staff. A few days later the official list of thirty-eight officers was published. One of the first acts of the NUC was to bring to Ankara a group of professors from the Law Faculty of the University of Istanbul, to write a new Constitution and Election Law. On May 28 the junta appointed a seventeen-man cabinet, of whom fifteen were civilian "technicians" who had not been identified with any political party.[31]

In mid-June the Cabinet forwarded to the NUC a list of fifteen matters which required urgent attention: (1) establishing a planning board for investments; (2) reviewing investments which had not yet been implemented; (3) fiscal reform without raising taxes; (4) floating a "freedom loan"; (5) transferring the International Cooperation Bureau from the Foreign Ministry to the Ministry of Finance; (6) preparing the formula for taking declarations of wealth of NUC and Cabinet members; (7) inserting into the Constitution a provision to deal with problems of afforestation on a nonpartisan basis; (8) placing in the Constitution measures

[31] The making of the Constitution is discussed in Chap. 4; the cabinet is discussed in Chap. 5.

strictly prohibiting the exploitation of religion; (9) assuring that there be no reduction in newspaper circulation; (10) improving efforts of the Ministry of Monopolies for the import of coffee; (11) reviewing anew the decisions to build a second steel mill and other major projects; (12) easing the prohibition on Turks leaving the country; (13) allowing resumption of property transfers except for property belonging to persons arrested by the NUC or to their families; (14) easing conditions of financial transactions by private citizens; (15) speeding up consideration by the NUC of proposed laws.[32]

This was followed on July 11 by issuance of the government's program. It concentrated on foreign policy and economic problems, and in most respects seemed almost to be a detailed indictment of the Menderes regime as well as a declaration of future intentions. Its main points were:

A Constitution on fully democratic bases, including adherence to the spirit of the United Nations Charter and the Declaration of Human Rights.

A foreign policy "worthy of the respect and trust shown Turkey by other nations." Turkey's hand will "be offered to all who show the desire for true friendship." The program specifically mentioned the desire for friendship with Turkey's neighbors, singling out strengthening friendship with Greece after the Cyprus dispute as one of the most urgent tasks.

Establishing a truly balanced budget, and ending the resort to inflationary methods in order to meet budget deficits. Trade policy must be one of the foundations of economic stability, with volume and quality of Turkish goods increased so as to be able to command good prices. The goal of free imports and exports should be reached as soon as possible. Absolutely no possibility can be left open for transactions circumventing the process of open competition through circulars and bulletins. Steps must be taken to reorganize the state economic enterprises "which due to internal political considerations over a long period have become state uneconomic enterprises." Efforts must be continued to obtain Turkish admission to the Common Market.

Construction and public works to be guided only by need and importance, always within the realms of financial possibility. Measures must be taken for land reform.

Education is one of the most urgent national problems.[33]

[32] *Cumhuriyet*, June 21, 1960.

[33] The NUC soon published the report of the National Education Commission which had made a thorough study of the Turkish education system in 1959. Chaired by Professor Fahir Iz of the Istanbul University Faculty of Letters, the commission had visited several foreign countries and had made far-reaching recommendations for reform. Apparently displeased with its conclusions, Menderes had refused to publish the report. In addition to this, the NUC convened an Education Commission of its own, which also made many recommendations for reform at all levels of schooling in Turkey. Several of the proposals were put into effect during the NUC period.

Health problems to receive early attention; specifically, improving the situation of health service personnel, meeting the needs of neglected regions of Turkey, and generally raising the standards of Turkish medicine.

The establishment of a truly nonpartisan administrative apparatus is one of the most urgent needs. "One of the basic conditions of preventing degeneration of our democracy is the cleaning out of an administration which over the past 10 years has become highly partisan, and the taking of measures to prevent this situation from recurring."[34]

In September the NUC issued considerably more detailed instructions to the Cabinet, covering virtually all areas of policy but leaving the means toward the stated ends largely to be worked out by the Ministers. The committee summarized its overall goal as:

> To realize the goal of the National Unity movement and take in hand Turkey and the Turkish nation as a whole; to found an impartial and superior administration based on the Atatürk revolution; to solve the short-range problems of our day; and to begin as far as possible in the time available to solve long-range problems by laying down the bases for their solution; to take the administrative measures needed in order to transfer to a new administration at latest in autumn of 1961.[35]

In this framework the National Unity Committee worked for seventeen months until it gave way to a government chosen in a free election on October 15, 1961. During those seventeen months many things occurred which will be of great importance in Turkey's future. In August 1960, 5,000 officers were retired as part of a "rejuvenation" of the Turkish armed forces. In October the NUC dismissed 147 university professors just before passing a new University Autonomy Law. On October 14 there opened the trial of over 400 leaders of the Democratic party government, a trial which lasted eleven months and ended with the execution of former Prime Minister Menderes and two of his cabinet members. In November the NUC purged from its ranks fourteen "radicals" who had allegedly worked to postpone elections for an indefinite period. After that, Turkey moved with ever-increasing speed, though not always without tribulation, to a return to civilian government.

In January 1961 a Constituent Assembly was convened, composed of representatives of many economic, professional, and other private organizations as well as of the political parties. The Assembly prepared a new Constitution and Election Law, which were accepted with great ceremony on May 27, 1961, the first anniversary of the revolution. In January new parties were allowed to organize, and they developed quickly enough that the national referendum on July 9 to approve the new Constitution already had the atmosphere of a campaign in which the parties

[34] The partial text and summaries of the program are found in most newspapers of July 12, 1960.

[35] *Cumhuriyet*, Sept. 11, 1960. The extent to which various of these objectives were achieved is discussed in Chap. 6 below.

were the centers of public attention. After the referendum approved the Constitution, affairs moved steadily toward the election of October 15, and the end of the formal existence of the NUC.

The first Grand National Assembly of Turkey's Second Republic convened in Ankara on October 25, 1961. Twenty-two of the original members of the National Unity Committee took their places as ex-officio members of the Senate of the Republic. On October 27, General Gürsel was elected Turkey's fourth President. After protracted negotiations a coalition government was formed by the Republican Peoples Party and the Justice Party, the two largest parties in the Assembly, and RPP Chairman Ismet Inönü became Prime Minister. In May 1962 the government resigned over the issue of amnesty for the convicted Democrats, and in June a second coalition was formed between the Republicans and the smaller Republican Peasants Nation and New Turkey parties, again with Inönü as Premier.

2

The Trial of the Fallen Regime

AMONG THE MANY difficult problems with which the National Unity Committee (NUC) had to deal, one of the most thorny was what to do with the leaders of the overthrown Democratic regime. But several important considerations led to the decision that they would receive a fair trial. First, the statement which the NUC broadcast on May 27 had said that the revolution was not for or against any group, but only to rescue the nation from the impasse between parties. This position meant that the NUC could not now proclaim itself judge over the ousted leaders. Second, it soon became apparent that the peasants were cool to the revolution, and it was hoped that a revelation of the misdeeds of their former hero (Menderes) would impress rural Turkey. Third, the armed forces had to legitimize the revolution for themselves and for the world, which had looked to Turkey as one of the bastions of multiparty government in an underdeveloped country. Fourth, the best opportunity to eliminate the leaders of the Democratic party (DP) passed when the army publicly imprisoned them instead of shooting them on the spot as has been done in revolutions in some other nations.

The eleven-month trial of the Democratic leaders should prove of great interest to legal as well as political observers.[1] Charges were brought not only against those officials individually charged with corruption, crime, or specific political misdeeds, but also against almost the entire Democratic party membership in the Grand National Assembly, who were accused of approving and voting for laws that contravened the Constitution. The nature of the charges presented a host of legal complications for which precedents were lacking both in Turkish law and in any international documents to which the judges might have been able to look.[2]

The handling of the trial and the selection of cases, methods of publicity, etc., were influenced by both domestic and foreign political con-

[1] The problem of trial by a successor regime is among the legal-political questions discussed by Otto Kirchheimer, *Political Justice, The Use of Legal Procedure for Political Ends* (Princeton University Press, 1961).

[2] The trials were conducted strictly according to Turkish law and in terms of Turkish constitutional and penal law provisions. But both witnesses and newspaper analyses often stated the opinion that the repressive acts of the Menderes government had also violated things like the Declaration of Human Rights.

siderations. Great care was taken, however, not to prejudice the legal correctness in any way. One happy result of this care is that while there is plentiful dispute over the political wisdom of various actions, no significant question has been raised, either inside or outside of Turkey, about the overall legality and impartiality of the trial itself—albeit there were some questionable procedural aspects. This chapter will attempt to bring together the relevant information about the trials, and to assess their current and future impact on Turkish domestic and foreign affairs.

The Setting of the Trials

The trials of the former Turkish leaders opened on October 14, 1960, four and a half months after the revolution, on the island of Yassıada in the Sea of Marmara within sight of the great mosques and the luxury hotels of Istanbul, hotels in which the fallen leaders had spent many gay hours. The island was a virtual fortress. Persons going to Yassıada were permitted to board the special boat only after rigid security checks. Before its departure from Istanbul each morning, the boat itself was checked by frogmen to prevent possible sabotage by fanatic sympathizers of the former regime. A constant watch by naval units kept all boats well away from the island. This was supplemented by barbed wire, anti-aircraft, and machine gun emplacements surrounding the areas where the defendants were housed. The defendants themselves were closely guarded and escorted by heavily armed soldiers whenever they were taken to or from the court building. The latter precautions were probably taken as much to prevent the defendants from attempting suicide[3] as to prevent sympathizers from rallying around them. In the courtroom itself squads of husky soldiers kept constant watch over the defendants and the spectators. The changing of these guards every hour was conducted in full military fashion with the loud clump of boots and the clanking of rifles.

The defendants numbered 592. They included former President Celal Bayar, former Prime Minister Adnan Menderes and former Assembly President Refik Koraltan, the entire cabinet, all except one of the Democratic party deputies in the Grand National Assembly,[4] several former provincial governors, the former Chief of the Army General Staff, local officials and police officers involved in the cases of restricting freedom of

[3] The suicide of former Interior Minister Namık Gedik shortly after his arrest deprived the government of one of its prime culprits as well as a key witness.

[4] The exception was Ali Fuat Cebesoy, a retired general, hero of the War of Independence, and one of Atatürk's closest collaborators for many years. Under the Turkish electoral system it was almost impossible for an independent to be elected to the Assembly without party support. Consequently on many occasions one of the major parties included on its ticket prominent persons—soldiers, diplomats, poets, etc.—whom it wished to see in the Assembly. Cebesoy did not join the meetings of the DP Assembly Group, and never supported the activities of the Menderes government.

movement and the shootings at the universities, and a number of businessmen involved in corruption cases. Most had been confined on the island since early June.

The pretrial investigations were carried on by a special High Investigation Commission of thirty-one members selected by the military regime. They selected as their chairman an experienced lawyer, Hayrettin Perk. Working day and night, the commission attempted to sift the evidence and prepare cases for the prosecution. One of the reasons the trial was delayed more than four months was the overwhelming size of many of the dossiers. In some instances the High Investigation Commission finished work on a case only shortly before it was scheduled to be heard.

The prosecution was handled by a team of prosecutors headed by the former public prosecutor of the province of Izmir, Altay Omer Egesel. Most recently a member of the Supreme Court of Appeals *(Yargıtay)*, Egesel had wide experience both as a judge and as a prosecutor. Though his manner of presentation and analysis of the strengths and weaknesses of the evidence sometimes left something to be desired, on the whole Egesel handled his duties competently.

Probably the key figure in the entire proceedings was the head of the High Council of Justice, Salım Başol. This fifty-five-year old jurist whose professional abilities were described by a western correspondent as "altogether remarkable,"[5] brought with him over thirty years of experience and an outstanding record for fairness and honesty. His last post had been as head of the Penal Division of the Supreme Court of Appeals. Başol's handling of the trials was exceptional. Foreign legal observers at the trials at various times were unanimous in their praise and in their amazement that in the heavily charged political atmosphere Başol was able to keep the trials orderly, surprisingly fair, and with a minimum of political propaganda from any quarter. Indeed in the opinion of some more impatient Turks, it was much too fair, a rigamarole too good for the defendants. The tribunal consisted of nine judges, including Başol, picked by the NUC. Of these, six were civilian and three were experienced military judges. In addition there were six reserve judges. Prosecutors, investigators, and other personnel were also selected by the NUC from the established body of civilian and military jurists.

Over one thousand witnesses appeared at the trials. Many were eyewitnesses to the events in question or technical personnel such as those who had audited accounts in corruption cases. A large group consisted of persons who had knowledge of political actions or opinions of the defendants. These presented difficulties in that few had direct evidence that riots or disturbances had been deliberately planned, as was charged in some cases, or that Menderes had stated directly his aims in matters where constitutional rights of the opposition were violated. The fact that many of these witnesses also might have had personal motives for

[5] *The Economist*, Feb. 25, 1961, p. 771.

testifying in certain ways had to be taken into account by the court. A notable omission was the failure of the prosecution to resort to promises of immunity from prosecution for defendants who would testify against other defendants.

Some relevant statistics of the trials from the opening, October 14, 1960, to the closing, September 15, 1961, are given in the table that follows.

Number of:	
Sessions	202
Spectators	150,000
Hours of trials	1,033
Secret sessions	5
Defendants	592
Witnesses	1,068
Defendants dying during trials	6
Times death penalty was asked	228
Verdicts:	
Death sentences by unanimous vote	4
Death sentences by majority vote	11
Executions	3
Commutations	12
Life imprisonment	31
Lesser jail terms	402
Defendants acquitted	133
Defendants with charges dismissed	5

The Legal Aspects

The trials were conducted under the Turkish Penal Code, based on an older Italian model, and called for trial procedure as follows: (1) reading of the indictment, with each defendant invited to comment as reference was made to him; (2) questioning of the defendants by the judges; (3) presentation of the case for the prosecution; (4) hearing of prosecution witnesses; (5) the defense. Other than creating the High Council of Justice as a special court, the National Unity Committee made only two changes in the penal code: it repealed the article providing that the death penalty could not be imposed on anyone over sixty-five years old, an obvious reference to former President Bayar; and it declared that verdicts handed down by the court would be final, with the exception of death sentences, which had to be approved by the NUC itself.

Two procedural matters disturbed many American observers: the use of hearsay evidence, and the prominence given to political opinions of both judges and witnesses. Turkish law, like much European law, recognizes two categories of evidence. In civil cases, only "material evidence" plays a role, and it must be detailed and precise. In penal cases, however, there is also "personal *(vıcdan)* evidence," which covers any matters the judges choose to take up. They are free to ask anything and accept or reject it at their own discretion. Since the judges are not compelled to state what evidence they have accepted or rejected, an evaluation of the proceedings must in this regard be based on other considerations. The evidence in many cases at the Yassıada trials was primarily circumstantial. It was usually sufficiently strong however, to be convincing in the eyes of many foreign observers, even if the latter felt that some items of hearsay should have been thrown out.

The judges did not hesitate to make it clear that politically they had little sympathy for the defendants. An example was chief judge Başol's exchange with former premier Menderes during the case charging illegal use of the state radio for partisan purposes. To Menderes' assertion that in the election campaign of 1954 the violence of opposition attacks made it important for the nation that the Democratic party's position be fully publicized, Başol countered that in his opinion the behavior of the opposition had certainly not been bad enough to warrant the violent language the Democrats used—"we all lived through those days."[6] On other occasions when Menderes asserted that various restrictive measures were necessary to keep the government from being ousted, Başol demanded to know why, if the regime was that unpopular, Menderes did not resign.

The holding or expressing of political opinions, of course, does not per se prejudice the decision of a judge in a political case. On the contrary, the very nature of such a case makes it important that the judge bring to deliberations experience in and perspective on the social and political affairs of his society. A judge in the midst of a political crisis of the magnitude of the Turkish one who was completely neutral politically would likely lack these qualifications as well. What is of primary importance—even in the context of a revolution—is that the judge be willing to consider the merits even of unpopular viewpoints and be able to render his decision on the charges brought. The Yassıada trials generally fulfilled these conditions. The acquittal of various defendants, including several cabinet members, in some cases was certainly not politically popular, even though the flimsy nature of the evidence left the judges no grounds on which convictions could have been based.

A far more serious shortcoming than the holding of political opinions by the judges was the treatment of defense attorneys. The time allotted to meetings between defendants and their attorneys was severely restricted, sometimes to as little as one hour per case. Such meetings were always monitored by a military officer. There were also strict controls over the attorneys' activities, and several were arrested or barred from the trial for certain tactics that the government considered to be influencing the trials unfairly. Some instances were abuses of privilege, such as the attempt by some attorneys for Menderes to distribute thousands

[6] *Cumhuriyet*, Nov. 30, 1960.

of copies of a pamphlet outlining the defense case. But many instances of intimidation can only be deplored.

The nineteen cases tried can be divided into three categories: (1) three cases involving criminal charges, including murder, inciting to riot, and wilfully causing injuries and property damage; (2) nine cases of corruption of government officials: illegal extension of state credits to personal friends and for personal gain, foreign exchange violations, illegal use of discretionary funds, illegal expropriation of property, and forcing the government to buy for a zoo a dog that had been given to former President Bayar;[7] (3) seven cases of a political nature involving violation of various guarantees in the Constitution. The cases can be summarized as follows:

1. *The Dog* (Oct. 14-24). Bayar, former Minister of Agriculture Okmen convicted of forcing zoo to buy dog Bayar had received as gift.

2. *September 6-7 Incidents* (Oct. 20-Jan. 5). Menderes, Zorlu, one local official from Izmir convicted of causing injuries and damage by deliberately inciting riots against Istanbul Greeks over Cyprus dispute in 1955. Bayar, Köprülü and six others acquitted.

3. *The Baby* (Oct. 31-Nov. 22). Menderes, Dr. Atabey acquitted of killing Menderes' illegitimate baby.

4. *Vinileks Co.* (Nov. 4-26). Former Finance Minister Polatkan convicted of illegal extension of government credits to personal friends.

5. *Fraud* (Nov. 8-Dec. 3). Former ministers Erkmen and Mandalinci acquitted of failing to return unused expense money from a trip to the United States.

6. *Vacant Lots* (Nov. 11-26). Former Agriculture Minister Okmen convicted of forcing government to buy at inflated prices properties belonging to his wife.

7. *Ali Ipar* (Nov. 15-Jan. 19). Menderes, Zorlu, three former ministers, and shipping magnate Ipar convicted of foreign exchange violations.

8. *The Mills* (Nov. 18-Dec. 3). Charges against former Trade Minister Yircali and mill owner Demirkan, for illegal extensions of credit for personal profit, dropped because of Statute of Limitations.

9. *Barbara* (Nov. 21-Dec. 20). Polatkan, Koraltan convicted of foreign exchange violations in bringing a young German girl as "servant" to Koraltan under guise of "medicines."

10. *Secret Payments* (Nov. 25-Feb. 2). Menderes and his under secretary Korur convicted of illegal use of Prime Minister's discretionary funds.

11. *Radio* (Nov. 29-Dec. 26). Menderes, Zorlu, and six former ministers and radio officials convicted of using state radio for partisan political aims

[7] It might be asked why the really big corruption cases were not brought up at Yassıada. This omission can probably be explained by the psychological motives involved in much of the trial. That is, the desire to get at defendants whose cases would have greatest political impact; and the lack of time, either to prepare the extremely complicated cases, or to introduce new cases into a proceeding that was already promising to drag out and seriously delay any other steps toward elections and the end of military rule.

and prohibiting same to opposition, in violation of Turkish Constitution. One former radio official acquitted.

12. *Topkapı Incident* (Dec. 2-Apr. 17). Bayar, Menderes, fifty-eight other former ministers, deputies, and police, charged with inciting riot with intent to harm a deputy, opposition leader Inönü, in Istanbul on May 4, 1959. Forty-three acquitted, seventeen, including Bayar and Menderes, convicted.

13. *Çanakkale Incident* (Dec. 27-Mar. 10). Menderes and three former deputies convicted of impeding freedom of movement of two opposition deputies, Sept. 19 and 23, 1959.

14. *Kayseri Incident* (Jan. 9-Apr. 20). Bayar, Menderes, and eleven former deputies and local officials charged with impeding freedom of movement of a deputy, opposition leader Inönü, April 2, 1960. Eight acquitted, Bayar, Menderes, three others convicted.

15. *Demokrat Izmir* (Jan. 12-May 5). Menderes and twenty-three former Izmir officials charged with inciting destruction of printing plant of anti-government newspaper in Izmir, May 2, 1959. Sixteen convicted, eight acquitted.

16. *University Incidents* (Feb. 2-July 27). 118 former government, army, and police officials charged with illegally entering university grounds (Istanbul April 28, Ankara April 29, 1960), firing on citizens without cause, and declaring martial law in illegal manner and without cause. Eighty-four including all major defendants convicted, thirty-four acquitted.

17. *Expropriation* (Apr. 17-June 3). Menderes and nine other former officials charged with expropriating property for construction in Istanbul without proper compensation, forcing citizens to sign releases. Menderes and two others convicted, eight acquitted.

18. *National Front* (Apr. 27-June 21). Bayar, Menderes, and twenty former government and party officials charged with using National Front organization to impose the rule of one class on another. Nineteen convicted, three acquitted.

19. *Subversion of Constitution* (May 11-Sept. 15). 397 former deputies and government officials accused of violating constitutional guarantees of property rights, judicial autonomy, freedom of association, free elections, etc., through seven specific unconstitutional laws. Almost all convicted.

Most of the political cases were brought under Article 146 of the Turkish Penal Code, which states that "attempts to alter, despoil or annul by force the Constitution of the Turkish Republic or any part of it, or to forcibly silence the Grand National Assembly established by the Constitution or prevent it from carrying out its duties shall be punishable by death."

Lawyers will probably argue for many years on the legal validity of applying Article 146 in the Yassıada trials. One point of controversy is the conflict with Article 17 of the Constitution, which states that deputies cannot be held legally accountable for their votes. Another is the interpretation of the word "forcibly" and the question whether voting for a committee that then acted illegally (which is what took place in the matter of the Committee to Investigate the activities of the Republican

People's Party and a Section of the Press), makes one liable under this article. The question had never really been considered in Turkey before the Yassıada trials, although there are many other laws, passed under both the Republican and Democratic governments, which could easily be interpreted as unconstitutional. In the Yassıada cases, both the prosecution and defense asked advice from the universities but received no clear-cut answers.

The primary difficulty lay in the Constitution itself. The Assembly was given virtually unchecked legislative and executive power, and there was no provision for judicial or other review of the constitutionality of any Assembly action. The Constitution could be amended simply by a two-thirds vote of the Assembly. Many important subjects were also left "to be determined by special law." Thus, for instance, the law giving the government the right to retire at its option judges with over twenty-five years of service, a law on which charges of violating judicial autonomy were based, could well fall within Article 56 of the Constitution, which said that "the qualifications of magistrates, their rights and duties, as well as their salaries and the manner of their dismissal, shall be determined by special law." Given these legal complications, the Constitution Case was perforce based largely on the question of intent. The strengths and weaknesses of the evidence itself will be discussed below.

The Dog, Barbara, and Baby Cases

These three cases were in large part designed to tarnish the image of the fallen leaders for those of the Turkish people who still saw them as good men.[8] The dog case charged former President Bayar with forcing the government to buy from him a dog which he had received as a gift from the King of Afghanistan. Bayar's defense was that he had wanted the money used to build a fountain for a village near Izmir.[9] Though the court found him guilty, indications were that this defense made more impression on the peasantry than did the legal niceties.

The Barbara case involved former Assembly President Refik Koraltan, who was charged with foreign exchange violations in importing a young German girl under the guise of a private nurse as part of the "medicine" for a certain illness. The job of tarnishing the reputation of the corpulent Koraltan—known in Ankara circles as Refik the Drum, big, noisy and empty—was easy because he had neither a powerful defense nor was he personally identified with policies the peasants approved. On the other hand, there was far less interest in him than there was in Bayar or Menderes, and the psychological impact that was achieved was not significant.

[8] The impact of corruption and repression had been felt only remotely among the peasants.

[9] Bayar did not actually get the money. It was transferred directly from the Ministry of Agriculture to the village authorities.

The baby case was the most spectacular of the three, not because of its legal aspects but because of the revelations about the personal life of Adnan Menderes. The former premier, married and the father of three children, was accused of ordering the killing of a child he fathered by Turkish opera star Ayhan Aydan. The prosecution failed to refute the assertion of Menderes' co-defendant Dr. Fahri Atabey that the baby had been born dead (and thus both defendants were acquitted), but for weeks the newspapers seemed little more than scandal sheets. Neither Menderes nor Miss Aydan denied their affair, in fact the soprano tearfully protested that she still loved Menderes and lived only for him. In this and subsequent cases there were details of other "affairs" between Menderes and various women.

Sharp differences in the images of Bayar and Menderes emerged from the trials. The former president's defense was essentially "I did it and I'm glad." Though just prior to the opening of the trials he had attempted suicide, he maintained his dignity and proud manner throughout the entire proceedings. Referring to the dog case, he said "let the decision be for or against me, it is not an important matter."[10] Even the urban groups which had been responsible for his overthrow eventually expressed a certain admiration for the spunk of the "old guerrilla fighter," as Bayar liked to refer to himself. Menderes, on the other hand, soon changed from a confident, hard-driving Prime Minister into a sniveling, cowardly figure. The newspapers eventually lost count of the times he asserted that he could not remember or had never heard of an incident. Through the early cases he had maintained the sharpness of mind which had kept him in office for ten years, but as the proceedings wore on he more and more often attempted to throw the guilt on his subordinates, and increasingly addressed the court in pleading, almost weeping tones. The change from the man who many superstitious peasants once considered almost superhuman for walking unhurt away from a plane crash could hardly have been greater.

The Case of the Anti-Greek Riots

The case probably attracting the most international interest was the one charging ten former government officials with inciting riots against the Greek population of Istanbul on September 6-7, 1955, as a means of pressing the Turkish viewpoint on the Cyprus dispute. Bayar, Menderes, and former Foreign Minister Zorlu were accused of ordering the riots, former Deputy Prime Minister Fuat Köprülü of having supported the plan and of having defended the government's illegal actions in the Assembly, the former Turkish Consul in Salonica and a Turkish student studying there at the time of having aided in causing an incident useful

[10] Bayar referred to himself as a "Komitadji," which in Turkey meant a member of a secret revolutionary society during the end of the nineteenth and beginning of the twentieth centuries.

for sparking the riots. Several former local officials from Istanbul and Izmir (where lesser disturbances took place at the same time) were charged with having failed to perform their duties of safeguarding lives and property. The inclusion of Köprülü among the defendants aroused concern among academic circles in several countries, as Köprülü had, before entering politics in 1946 as a co-founder of the Democratic party, been a world-renowned authority on the early history of the Turks. Köprülü's position at the trials was eased by the fact that he had resigned from the Democratic party in 1957 saying that he saw "no hope for the future of the party."[11]

The facts of the case were that in the summer of 1955 the Cyprus problem had entered a critical stage. While the Turkish and Greek Foreign Ministers were in London for talks on the matter, a bomb exploded on the grounds of the Turkish Consulate in Salonica, Greece, allegedly damaging the house in which Atatürk, the founder of modern Turkey, was born. An Istanbul DP paper printed the news in large headlines, whereupon riots broke out which heavily damaged the property of that city's Greek population. The police stood by and watched. Bayar and Menderes were, at the time the riots broke out, on their way back to Ankara after having attended some meetings in Istanbul where the Cyprus situation was among the matters discussed. They returned to Istanbul on receiving news of the disturbances, and martial law was declared, the army then moving in to master the situation. Smaller-scale demonstrations had taken place in Izmir almost concurrently.

The charges about the events in Salonica were not proved, nor were the charges against Köprülü and former Istanbul Governor Gökay. Charges against Bayar were dropped on technical grounds.[12] In reference to Menderes and Zorlu, the prosecution was able to present considerable circumstantial evidence that a small demonstration had indeed been planned to press the Turkish cause on Cyprus (evidence was presented that Zorlu had telephoned from London urging that "a little activity would be useful" to his negotiating position), and that the police had received orders not to interfere with the marchers. What seems to have happened is that the demonstration rapidly got out of hand, and the police being under orders not to interfere, did not take on themselves the responsibility for acting even in the new and more

[11] *New York Times,* Sept. 8, 1957.

[12] The charges against Bayar in this case were dropped in accordance with Article 41 of the Constitution which said that the President is responsible only in cases of high treason or for matters of a personal nature, but not for specific acts of the government.

In the Constitution Case, Bayar was charged under the concept present in continental penal codes of "execution by negligence," i.e. why he did *not* use his veto power. The principle is doubtful in penal law, and probably even more so in constitutional law. In the Turkish situation it should also be pointed out that the veto power is not final, and that in the entire history of the Republic there has never been a case where the veto has been used.

serious circumstances. Undoubtedly many of the police sympathized with the anti-Greek rioters, for Turkish hostility against the Greeks dates back many decades. Although there was testimony that rioters were apparently well-briefed regarding which houses belonged to Greeks and which to Turks, few of the witnesses were able to do more than give their "personal conviction" that the riots had been incited. Refik Tulga, former aide-de-camp to Bayar and later military governor of Istanbul, could not state definitely that he himself had heard any officials plan the riots, though he persisted in his opinion that Bayar and Menderes knew of the plans for the smaller demonstration. The Greek Orthodox patriarch of Istanbul told of being visited by officials who said that there would be a small demonstration, but nobody would be hurt. However, he refused to support the inferences by the prosecution that this was only a cover for more sinister plans. Evidence on the allegation that Menderes hid his handiwork by suppressing discussion of the incidents in the Democratic party group of the Assembly was also obscure, depending largely on an interpretation of the often sketchy minutes of several meetings.

The verdict was a popular one in several ways. Conviction of Menderes and Zorlu, two of the main culprits in the eyes of the anti-Democratic elements, vindicated "what everybody knew" about the riots before the trial had even opened. Acquittal of the others was seen as a testimony of the fairness of the trials, important to Turkey's position in the civilized world. By the end of the case even those Turks most strongly opposed to Menderes admitted that most of the evidence had been flimsy and would never stand up to scrutiny by Western standards.

The Radio Case

It is no accident that the new Turkish Constitution of 1961 provides in Article 121 that "all radio and television broadcasts shall be made along the principles of impartiality." One of the chief reasons advanced for the revolution against the Menderes regime was its flagrant persecution of the opposition press and use of the state radio for partisan purposes. The main facts were not really in dispute. Though done under the guise of various laws and the interpretation put on them by the government, it was undeniable that the opposition had since 1954 been denied all use of state radio facilities,[13] while the notorious "Radio Journal" had regularly broadcast the most violently partisan attacks by government party spokesmen. As Menderes became more and more desperate in the months before his regime was overthrown, he resorted to other tactics as well, including ordering long lists to be read of persons who had resigned from the Republican party to join the Democratic party or its National Front organization. When it became clear, how-

[13] There are no private radio facilities in Turkey.

ever, that most of the names were invented, repeated many times, or included people who had died, the effect—at least among intelligent listeners—was the opposite of what he had envisioned.

There were two issues before the court: For legal purposes, had the defendants written, ordered, or knowingly sanctioned the broadcasts? There was little doubt that the defendants had been responsible for at least tacitly supporting partisan radio activities. All denied writing broadcasts, but they liberally accused each other of sending notes to subordinates ordering scripts to be written and altering texts to increase their violence. Menderes frequently resorted to "I didn't know," and "I can't remember" tactics.

The political issue was more difficult. When was a broadcast giving unfair advantage to the party, and when was it a legitimate statement of government policy? One of Menderes' defenses was that it was his responsibility as Prime Minister to present to the nation the information necessary to aid in understanding and helping to carry out government policies. He justified the violence of the attacks on the opposition by asserting that opposition newspapers and speakers had so distorted the true facts of many situations that it was vital to the national interest that the distortions be denied in terms that nobody could fail to understand. These defenses would have been much stronger had not all the facts of radio administration and press persecution of the previous several years stood against them. Eight of the nine defendants were found guilty. A verdict of acquittal was handed down in the case of Altemur Kılıç, capable long-time official of the Turkish Information Office in New York, who had returned to Turkey to become Director of Press and Publication in the Menderes government. The lack of evidence of Kılıç's direct participation in illegal activities led to his legal acquittal, but not to his reinstatement to good standing among his fellow journalists.

The Topkapı and Kayseri Cases

The charges against Bayar, Menderes, and others in these two cases had solid legal backing, but main interest centered on the fact that the actions involved had been directed against the leader of the opposition himself, former Prime Minister and President Ismet Inönü. The popularity of Inönü, the man who had been the chief collaborator with and successor to Atatürk, was significantly increased as the Democrats in these two incidents unwittingly made him appear more and more as a martyr for freedom and democracy.

The Topkapı case charged sixty defendants (ministers, deputies, and police officials) with organizing and abetting an attempt to kill Inönü as the latter entered Istanbul through the Topkapı district on May 4, 1959. Besides attempting to do bodily injury to a citizen, the indictment also charged violation of Article 146 prohibiting interference with a deputy carrying out his duties. A pro-Democratic demonstration during Inönü's visit to the Southwest Turkish City of Uşak on May 1 ended with his being hurt by a stone thrown at his head by one of the demonstrators. The Istanbul incident only three days later could possibly have been merely a contagion, except that there were many indications that it was planned. As in other cases, however, no direct evidence was produced that the planning had been actually instigated by Menderes. The plan allegedly was to have Inönü's car drive through an area in which Democratic partisans had been gathered, arrange that the car would get stuck in the heavy traffic, and have the car "spontaneously" attacked and Inönü "accidentally" killed.

There was considerable evidence presented that such a plan did in fact exist. The defense assertion that it was no more than a spontaneous demonstration was difficult to believe in view of the many "questionable" actions of police and government officials to which witnesses testified at the trial. These officials had been warned several times that the crowds along the Topkapı road were becoming unruly, but they apparently chose to interpret the situation as a normal, peaceful show of political feelings. Inönü was saved only by the intercession of soldiers brought to the scene by army officers—the major commanding the unit testified at the trial—even though these officers had previously been ordered not to interfere and to leave the situation to the regular civilian police.[14] Of the sixty defendants, forty-three were convicted, including all the important figures involved.

The Kayseri case concerned violation of the clause in Article 70 of the Constitution which guaranteed freedom of travel to Turkish citizens, as well as the above-mentioned Article 146 of the Penal Code. On April 2, 1960, the government attempted to prevent RPP leader Inönü and several RPP deputies from traveling to Kayseri for a political meeting.[15] The chief complication in the case was that there was a law on the books forbidding political campaigning except during the forty-five days preceding an election, and though it was generally believed that an election would come soon, and Menderes was making speeches sounding like campaign talks, no election had yet been called. It is probably because the government acted while Inönü and his party were on the road instead of waiting until he had begun to take part in a political meeting, that the case ended in the conviction of Bayar, Menderes, the governor of Kayseri, a retired general, and a former Inspector of National Security. There was no real doubt about the prosecution's contention that the governor of Kayseri would hardly have acted in such a fashion without orders from Ankara. Eight Kayseri deputies accused of complicity were acquitted.

[14] It is likely that this incident was an important turning point in the eventual involvement of the army in politics which culminated in the May 27 revolution.

[15] The details of the incident have been described in Chapter 1.

The real importance of the Kayseri incident was its role in the rising level of political tension. Inönü showed all the shrewdness of a veteran Turkish politician in making sure that Menderes went too far. If Menderes had waited until Inönü got to the Kayseri meeting, it might have affected the legal outcome of the matter at Yassıada, although undoubtedly Inönü would have been able to make a good case that the meeting was the same kind of "nonpolitical" meeting Menderes himself had been holding recently. Politically probably the best that Menderes could have done in relation to Inönü's Kayseri trip would have been to let it go on and attempt to keep it as quiet as possible, but there was no way at that point in the development of political hostility by which he could have prevented the effect of the trip altogether. The Kayseri incident is generally accepted as the beginning of the series of events, described in Chapter 1, which ended less than two months later with the ouster of the Menderes regime. The incident's importance was also paramount in that for the first time the government itself brought the army into politics. As reflected in the Topkapı and Kayseri incidents, both the focusing of opposition around the figure of Inönü, and the involvement of the army directly in a political controversy, were to a significant extent the work of Menderes himself.

The University Incidents Case

Of all the cases heard at Yassıada, the one involving the firing by police and soldiers on students at Istanbul and Ankara Universities on April 28-29, 1960 was the one that brought on the highest degree of public indignation. The 118 defendants included Bayar, Menderes, and most of the cabinet, the former Chief of the General Staff Rüştü Erdelhun, the former Ankara martial law commander, the former governors of the provinces of Ankara and Istanbul, the mayor of Istanbul, and a long list of Ankara and Istanbul police officers. It was the last named who were the targets of the public's loudest cries for blood—former Istanbul police official Zeki Şahın, frequently referred to as "Gestapo Zeki;" Bumin Yamanoğlu, accused of bludgeoning Istanbul University Rector Onar and of deliberately firing at and driving a jeep into groups of students. No tears were shed at the nineteen and sixteen year sentences respectively meted out to them. The charges against the principal political figures were that they had directly or indirectly been responsible for illegally invading the grounds of Istanbul and Ankara Universities in violation of university autonomy; of deliberately firing on citizens without sufficient cause; and of declaring martial law in an illegal way and for insufficient reasons.

The facts of the case, the organization of the Committee to Investigate the Activities of the Republican People's Party and a Section of the Press on April 18, the granting of extraordinary authority to that committee on April 27, the expulsion of Inönü from the Assembly on the same date, and the bloody incidents at Istanbul University on April 28 and at Ankara University on April 29, have already been described.

The nature of the case was such that several important matters could not be subjected to strict legal analysis. Many key points turned on the reasonableness of the actions of the defendants. A good example was the question whether and/or when the authorities were justified in opening fire. Once the authorities are brought in to restore order—leaving aside for the moment the question of the legitimacy of declaring martial law—the decision about when and how to act to keep order must be made on the spot and according to the best judgment of the commander, who has presumably been chosen for his competence in evaluating such situations. In the absence of clear-cut malfeasance of duty, it is questionable whether a court can seriously question the fine points of what is in many ways a professional determination.

Even in more clear-cut matters the situation was confused. There was, for instance, the declaration of martial law. The prosecution based its case on the allegation that the cabinet had acted illegally when they had approved in general terms the declaration of martial law, but left it to Menderes to decide on the timing. Testimony from various ministers regarding what occurred was contradictory, and no records existed to help establish the facts. The situation at Yassıada was further complicated by the fact that communications about the incident had apparently been channeled through Interior Minister Namık Gedik, and that this key figure had died by hurling himself out a window of the Military Academy shortly after his arrest on May 27. The circumstances of the suicide are not fully clear, but it is probable that Menderes and others knew that the absence of Gedik's testimony would considerably weaken the cases against them.

Another unclear point was how much effort the Istanbul police made in trying to contact the university rector before entering the university grounds without permission. Indicative of their not having made much effort was the protestation of one policeman, "but the students were out there and were not going to class," whereupon Judge Başol ended the exchange by demanding just how that should concern the police. On one point there was a great deal of certainty. This was the matter of police brutality. The actions of certain individuals were vividly documented in pictures as well as words.

The crux of the University Case was assessment of the motives of the main defendants. There was considerable evidence that Menderes saw the universities mainly as a part of the Republican opposition. The evidence of codefendants, who probably would not hesitate to throw as much guilt as possible on Menderes, must, of course, be taken with caution. But the testimony of various former ministers—one reported Menderes to have raved that he would break up the Republican party, destroy Inönü, and abolish the universities—was backed by considerable documentary evidence, such as the minutes of meetings of the Democratic party group in the Assembly, as well as by the context of progressive deterioration of the political situation and movement toward the major crisis that ended with Menderes' overthrow. On the basis of lack of evidence for certain specific acts (the bullet which killed the Istanbul student could not be traced to the gun of any policeman, and the allegation that another bullet was substituted during the autopsy could not be proved) thirty-four defendants, mostly police, were acquitted. Though lawyers might dissent from the convictions of the remaining accused, most political observers will probably agree that the evidence was sufficient to indicate at least that the major defendants were not displeased at the incidents, had done nothing to prevent them, and saw them as politically justified.

The Constitution Case

The leading case at the Yassıada trials, subversion of the Constitution, opened on May 11, 1961, almost a year after the revolution and the confining of the defendants on the island. For the many prisoners who had not been involved in any previous cases, even the nerve-racking experience of being a defendant must have been a welcome relief. In the dock were 397 former Democratic deputies, including President Bayar and the entire cabinet. Death sentences were demanded for 37, up to twenty years imprisonment for the remainder, with reduced terms for some 90 deputies who had in some way tried to get the Menderes government to resign.

Eight specific violations of Article 146 of the Penal Code were enumerated in the indictment. They were: (1) confiscation of the property of the Republican party, 1951 and 1953; (2) downgrading the city of Kırşehir and its vicinity from a province to a district because of its heavy vote for the Republican Peasants Nation party, in effect punishing citizens for political activity, 1954; (3) violating judicial autonomy by passing a law giving the government the right to retire at its option judges with over twenty-five years of service, 1953; (4) making undemocratic changes in the election laws, 1954 and 1957; (5) passing restrictive and undemocratic legislation regulating meetings and demonstrations, requiring prior permission from the government for meetings of any sort, 1956; (6) the decision, and the reasoning behind it, to set up the "Investigating Committee" to look into the activities of the opposition, April 18, 1960; (7) conferring extraordinary authority on the Investigating Committee, authority which the Assembly did not have power to give,

April 27, 1960; (8) intending with this extraordinary authority to abrogate and nullify the Constitution.

The eight items enumerated above largely summarized the series of major political disagreements since 1954. The first five had provoked violent dispute between the government and the opposition, and left the growing legacy of bitterness that accented the violent character of the final struggle before the military took over. But it was the Investigating Committee incident, which had set in motion the rioting and persecution that immediately preceded the fall of the regime and was dramatic and fresh in the public mind, that was the main focus of the Constitution Case at Yassıada.

Testimony at the trial indicated that the committee had used its authority freely. Journalists and others told chilling stories of being called before the committee and questioned for hours without rest and of being arrested and jailed without any attempt to inform them of charges against them. Excerpts were read from the committee's report, which accused the RPP of instigating the student riots and aiming by these means to come to power without elections. "This is an attempt to prepare rebellion and a coup d'état. Inönü has even announced his intentions from the floor of the Assembly. All necessary measures must be taken at once." A long list of proposed steps was appended. Additional damaging evidence was taken from the diaries that many of the former officials had rather naively kept. An excerpt from that of former Defense Minister Ethem Menderes, for instance, noted that at a party in 1957 Bayar had said to several deputies, "If need be, I would not hesitate to send Inönü to the gallows. . . . If necessary we will run the nation through dictatorship."[16] Still other evidence came from tapes made by telephone operators monitoring conversations between the former leaders.

The legal complications of the Constitution Case brought under Article 146 and the difficulties created by the word "forcibly," have already been discussed. Given the arguments for and against the legal validity of charges on the basis of this article, the matter of intent became crucial. While the reliability and the conclusiveness of much of the evidence brought out at the trial was open to doubt, the overwhelming volume and the fact that it originated with some of Turkey's most respected individuals, were sufficient to create a strong presumption of the intent of the defendants. Added to the evidence about the specific events of the Investigating Committee were tales of Menderes saying that the Assembly could do anything it wanted, even to bringing back the Caliph! That Menderes was well aware of the problems in this area was testified to by lawyers who had been involved in the arguments on this point in the period before the revolution.

An important part of the case was the determination of the degree

[16] *Cumhuriyet,* May 19, 1961.

of guilt of each individual defendant. There were several possible categories: those planning, encouraging, or performing unconstitutional acts; those sympathizing with the actions to one degree or another; and those who were in some degree opposed, but who in the name of party discipline or for other reasons went along. The first category was not hard to distinguish—death penalties were demanded for the cabinet, members of the Investigating Committee, and others. For many other defendants, however, it was difficult to establish individual responsibility; thus the ignominious spectacle in the court room of many former deputies desperately trying to prove that illegible signatures on documents opposing Menderes were theirs. An additional difficulty was the fact that votes in the last days of the Assembly had frequently been taken by voice or rammed through in some other way. The sheer magnitude of the Constitution Case largely prevented the court's consideration of each case individually, even if more evidence had been available.

The Verdicts

After spending almost a month preparing its decisions, the court delivered its verdicts on September 15, 1961, eleven months and one day after the trials had opened. They were as follows:

Four death sentences were passed by unanimous vote of the judges: Bayar, Menderes, Foreign Minister Zorlu, and Finance Minister Polatkan. Menderes was sentenced to death eight times in eight different cases, Bayar in three. Eleven other defendants were sentenced to death by majority vote. These included former Assembly President Koraltan, two other Assembly officers, three members of the Investigating Committee, four leaders of the Democratic party group in the Assembly and former army Chief of Staff General Erdelhun. The death sentences of all except Menderes, Zorlu, and Polatkan were commuted to life imprisonment by the National Unity Committee.

Thirty-one defendants were sentenced to life imprisonment: four cabinet ministers, eight members of the Investigating Committee, six Democratic party group leaders in the Assembly, the three deputies who introduced the Investigating Committee law, the former governor of Istanbul, and nine other deputies.

Shorter prison sentences of from two to twenty years were passed for 402 lesser figures, and there were 133 acquittals.

Many of those acquitted were minor figures against whom no individual wrong-doing could be proved. About thirty-five deputies were acquitted. Apparently some psychological considerations played a part in the latter, for some deputies who proved they had not been at the session where the Investigating Committee had been voted were convicted, while some who had been at that session, but who had records of opposing the actions of the regime, were freed. A deputy who was a retired admiral and was still popular with naval officers, was also freed. On the whole, however, the verdicts appear to have been well related to individual cases.

Political Aspects

The chief importance of the trials for Turkey is their impact on the domestic political scene. There is no doubt that the execution of Menderes and two of his ministers had an important effect on the elections which took place less than a month later. One of the first questions to be brought up in the new Assembly—and which almost wrecked the effort to organize an effective successor government to the NUC—was that of amnesty for the Yassıada defendants.

An important question that confronted the National Unity Committee was what kind of public involvement in the trial to encourage. On the one hand there was the need to keep the trial impartially focused on legal points so that the judges would not be swayed by the reactions of public opinion either in or outside the courtroom, a situation that would have seriously prejudiced the proceedings in the eyes of Western nations. On the other hand was the desire to draw the attention of the Turkish people to the crimes of the former regime, and drive home a lesson that such behavior in the future would again be met with summary action.

The junta's actions were apparently guided a little by each consideration. Attempts to keep the judges from being swayed by daily politics included keeping them and the prosecutors in semi-isolation in a resort hotel on a nearby island, carefully screening trial spectators, and forbidding spectator demonstrations of sympathy or hostility in the courtroom.[17] The public was kept aware of the trials, however, in a manner which often was almost calculated sensationalism. Shortly before the trials opened the government released a series of pictures of the defendants, showing them being interrogated, exercising, eating, and sitting on their bunks, all in the atmosphere of strict surveillance by soldiers. The disturbing aspect of the pictures was that they were sold at auction to the newspapers, which then competed to present the biggest and most bizzare layout. The government later backhandedly acknowledged that the sale had been a mistake, but the sensation was achieved nonetheless.

Press coverage of the trials was extensive, though it was notable that less sensational proceedings soon were relegated to the inside or back pages of most papers. Probably the most effective means of publicity was the radio. Tapes of the proceedings were aired each night for an hour during "prime listening time," with portions selected that were judged to be of "most public interest." Listeners to Yassıada Hour included a

[17] Even with stern warnings from the judge, however, there was often spontaneous applause or booing from the audience which left no doubt that most of the spectators heartily disliked the fallen regime.

large portion of the nation. In the cities people listened out of interest, in the villages partly from interest and partly from the fact that listening to the radio was often the only thing to do on long winter nights at the coffee house. Supplementing the radio and press were two full-length movies of the trials shown throughout the country. The trials were also witnessed by approximately 150,000 spectators under a system of ticket allotment designed to bring visitors from the provinces as well as from Ankara and Istanbul.

The major psychological difficulty was that even after being overthrown, Menderes was still popular with a large percentage of Turkey's rural population.[18] Despite opposition claims to the contrary and evidence that Menderes had probably not got a majority in the 1957 elections, the opinion of most detached observers was that his chances for re-election in 1960 would have been very good. What made him a hero to the peasants was precisely what made him a villian to the urban intelligentsia—relaxation of pressures for rapid secularization, building mosques as well as roads and without particular care to meeting the payments, concentration on economic problems of the rural population at the expense of urban groups, and an excellent personal speaking manner. The chief opposition to Menderes, the Republican People's party, was in turn identified with relentless and rapid reform, and with the authoritarian rule that not surprisingly had developed over the span of continual and unchallenged power monopoly between 1923 and 1946—the gendarme is still the symbol of the RPP to many Turks in Anatolia.

The psychological impact of the trials on the peasantry has probably been largely the reverse of the hope of the National Unity Committee. Though, as mentioned earlier, the legal aspects of the trials were generally satisfactory, politically it was said in Turkey that if the Republican party had conducted the trials it could not have done a better propaganda job. Most observers agree that the rather crude attempts to tarnish the images of Bayar and Menderes through the dog and baby cases were dismal failures. The corruption and political cases appear to have had only minimal effect on rural Turks, many of whom are still psychologically and physically so remote from Turkish city life that they have little of either interest or understanding of the issues involved.

Apparently the trial also failed to impress a considerable number of political leaders when they set about organizing new parties as preparations continued for elections which would return power to civilian hands. While Menderes and his colleagues were on trial for their lives, three political parties were only thinly veiling their attempts to capture the popular support Menderes had recently enjoyed. The Republican

[18] The mystical character attributed to Menderes by the peasants after the plane crash was evident in a rumor that became widespread during the trials that Menderes rode each night on a white charger across the water from Yassıada to the mosque in Istanbul's Eyup district.

Peasants Nation party (RPNP), a small conservative party which was the only one other than the RPP to have survived the Menderes period; the newly formed Justice party (JP) of retired General Ragip Gümüşpala, which was phenomenally successful in the areas of western Turkey where Menderes had had his strongest backing; and the New Turkey party (NTP), successor to the Freedom party of 1957 which had opposed both the Democrats and the RPP. So bold did these parties become that the NUC frankly condemned the actions of the Justice party in urging the voters to vote against the Constitution in the referendum of July 9. Few people dissented from the view that the referendum was more a vote in favor of or against the NUC than anything else.

Over 38 percent of the voters rejected the Constitution. Of the ten provinces voting against it, eight had been in the group giving the Democrats a high percentage of the vote in the 1957 election. The lesson was not lost on the NUC as the trials neared their end. On August 22, after the trials had ended but three weeks before the verdicts were handed down, the NUC prohibited all publications "which could influence the Yassıada verdicts or which could arouse public opinion."[19] And early in September, at a Round Table Conference of the NUC and the leaders of the major parties preparing to contest the election now firmly set for October 15, a "National Declaration" signed by these leaders and later by the representatives of the Turkish press, included a promise "not to do or say anything to influence the Yassıada verdicts, or to exploit or dispute them."[20]

This was the setting, then, for what was probably the single decision most fraught with political implications, the National Unity Committee's action on the fifteen Yassıada death sentences. There were powerful arguments both for and against carrying out the executions. In favor were some of the arguments that largely motivated the trials in the first place: the need to drive home the idea that attempting to subvert Turkey's democratic political system would be met with drastic action. The show of strength by former Democratic party supporters in the referendum and disturbing reports of growing dissatisfaction with the military regime weighed heavily. Finally, there was the argument that if Menderes' life were spared, the peasants would again think of him as supernatural—"they found him guilty and even the Army can't kill him."

On the negative side there was the international image of the Turkish military regime as one which was "different" and would avoid bloodshed. The ambassadors of several European nations did in fact make representations to the junta to refrain from carrying out any executions. The old European image of the "terrible Turk" raised its head for a brief moment. Domestically there was the possibility of making Menderes an

[19] *Ulus,* Aug. 22, 1961.

[20] *Cumhuriyet,* Sept. 6 and 7, 1961. More details on the "National Declaration" are given in Chap. 5 below.

even greater martyr than he already was and further deepening the division between supporters and opponents of the former government. This argument was somewhat softened, however, by the image of a cowardly and sniveling man which Menderes had created for himself by his behavior during the trials.

After an all night session the National Unity Committee decided to approve three executions. Foreign Minister Zorlu and Finance Minister Polatkan, both guilty on many counts, hated by the intelligentsia, and neither with enough popularity to make trouble among the peasants, were sentenced to death by unanimous vote of the Yassıada judges. They were executed the same morning. Menderes went to the gallows the next day after recovering from what was said to have been an overdose of sleeping pills. Turkish law provides that a man cannot be hanged if he is unable to walk to the gallows under his own power. Menderes' ignominious end came after pictures had been published showing him with tubes in his nose and arm, evidence that everything was being done to restore him to health and to forestall rumors that he had been beaten. The committee commuted to life imprisonment the sentences of the eleven whose death sentences had been given only by majority vote of the judges, as well as that of former President Bayar, whose age and dignified bearing throughout the trial probably saved him.

The long-range significance of the trials has both positive and negative aspects. There were defects in procedure, weaknesses in evidence, and psychological miscalculations, but basically the Turkish armed forces kept their pledge that they did not take over the government to favor or condemn any particular group, and did not themselves pass judgment on their predecessors. The executions, however, somewhat diminished these other gains.

The negative results have already proved of great importance in the future of Turkish domestic politics. Activity since the NUC period has shown that the trials have not helped to bridge the gulf between the supporters of the former Menderes regime and the former opposition personified by the RPP. Almost immediately after the new Assembly was elected in October 1961, Justice party deputies demanded amnesty for the Yassıada defendants as a tacit condition for most other political cooperation. Almost no other subject was discussed in the Assembly, and on February 22, 1962 the government was narrowly able to avert a new coup d'état by a group of young officers around the Military College. Meanwhile the convicted former Democrats, incarcerated in various jails around the country, have remained in the headlines, their supporters taking full advantage of the liberal visiting and communication privileges granted by the authorities. A group of citizens in Kayseri, for instance, where the chief prisoners are being kept, gathered contributions to provide them with a gala New Year's dinner. Within eight months the pro-Menderes forces were able to force acceptance of a significant part of their demands, and a part of the protocol issued late in June 1962 in connection with the formation of a second coalition government provided for amnesty which took effect in October for all those sentenced to six years or less and reductions in the sentences for most others.[21]

Meanwhile the leftovers from Yassıada remain to be disposed of, and Turkish courts are busy trying corruption cases of lesser figures. The impact—or lack of it—will continue to be a factor in Turkish politics for some time to come.

[21] All papers, June 25, 1962.

3

Problems of Academic Freedom and Higher Education

THE NEWS FROM ANKARA on October 28, 1960, that the military junta had summarily dismissed 147 faculty members from Turkey's six universities was a severe shock to academic circles both inside and outside of Turkey. This seemingly arbitrary act was out of character for what was supposed to be a "different" type of army rule than in other countries that had recently seen civilian government shunted aside. And adding insult to injury, the universities had been the very center of the activities precipitating the revolution. It was those same universities that were one of the military junta's chief sources of support, as well as the pool from which talent was constantly being drawn to help the soldiers in the complicated operations of government.

The action of the National Unity Committee was, however, neither one of ingratitude nor of spite. It was the culmination of long-standing concern in many quarters of Turkish society about the status of university education in Turkey. The action did show that it was ends rather than means which might make the Turkish junta different from others. Before considering the details of the "147 incident" therefore, it would be well to look at the nature and background of the problems of higher education in Turkey.

University Autonomy

"Higher education" in Turkey, which was at least minimally along Western lines, dates from the first half of the nineteenth century. The earliest schools offering nominally modern curricula were in the military and naval fields, that is, those areas in which the Ottoman Empire's need to match Western power was most obvious, and which were least likely to lead to objections by conservatives. The soldiers soon found it necessary to have available modern medical personnel, and a school of military medicine followed. As the influence of the Ottoman reformers grew, higher schools were established in public administration (the *mülkiye,* a training center for civil servants, established in 1859), finance (1878), law (1878), fine arts (1879), commerce (1882), customs (1892), and an improved new medical school (1898). After three fruitless attempts (in 1846, 1870, and 1879) a university, the Darülfunün, was established in Istanbul in 1900.[1]

The university was reorganized and expanded during the Young Turk period (1908-18), including such an innovation as opening its doors to qualified women. Under the Republic higher education was further reorganized and expanded, and Turkey today has six universities and a number of teacher training, vocational, commercial, and other specialized higher schools. The universities include Ankara University (with faculties of law, medicine, agriculture, science, history-language-geography, divinity, and political science, the last-named the modern outgrowth of the *mülkiye*); Istanbul University (law, economics, letters, medicine, sciences, forestry); The Aegean University at Izmir (medicine, agriculture, commerce); Istanbul Technical University (sciences and engineering); the newly founded Atatürk University in Erzurum, which will eventually be a major cultural center for all of Eastern Turkey; and the new Middle East Technical University in Ankara (sciences, engineering, public administration).

The history of university autonomy since the founding of the Republic in 1923 falls into three periods. For the first ten years the universities enjoyed a large measure of autonomy. In 1933 the government undertook to thoroughly overhaul higher education and began to exercise close control over the universities. One step of the reorganization was closing of the old Darülfunün and the opening of the modern Istanbul University. Modernizing the faculty was accomplished by rehiring only 59 of the original 151 professors and by importing a large contingent of German professors who had recently fled from the Hitler regime. Though legally the action was in order, this could constitute a precedent of sorts for the firing of the 147. It must be pointed out, however, that except for clearly anti-revolutionary activities or statements (communism or Turanism, for instance) the government had considerable respect for academic freedom.

The third period began with the new Universities Law of 1946. It conferred on the universities the right to elect their own rectors, and created University Senates and an Inter-University Board (also elected by the faculties themselves) with the exclusive right to judge and penalize faculty members for their actions or views.[2] Approval by the Ministry of Education continued to be required for budgets and professional appointments, but the increase in university autonomy was nevertheless considerable. In 1948 when the government wanted to discharge professors accused of harboring Marxist views, it had to resort to more subtle

[1] Bernard Lewis, *The Emergence of Modern Turkey* (Oxford University Press, 1961), pp. 177-78; Roderic Davison, "Westernized Education in Ottoman Turkey," *Middle East Journal,* Vol. 15 (Summer 1961), pp. 289-301.

[2] Kemal Karpat, *Turkey's Politics* (Princeton University Press, 1959), p. 158.

methods, finally abolishing the budget provisions for the courses of four Ankara University professors after the Inter-University Board had refused to effect the dismissals.[3]

The 1946 law organized the universities according to the German system—around chairs in separate subjects, with a cadre of junior faculty to supplement the *ordinariyus* professor who held the chair itself. Combined with the absence of a mandatory retirement provision, this method of organization severely limited the possibilities of promotion except through the creation of new chairs, a rare event. The saying that someone had to die before a junior man could be promoted was not far wrong. The situation deteriorated with the formation of cliques, the retention of unqualified teachers, and the steady worsening of university discipline and morale.

One of the manifestations of this situation was the inability of the universities to see to it that professors maintained a minimal separation between academic and political activity. Not that professors should have taken no part in politics, but the phenomenon of literature professors talking politics in their lectures and seminars overstepped both the bounds of propriety and the limits of prudence in a sensitive political environment. Menderes' Democratic party had since its founding in 1946 and for the first years after coming to power in 1950 been one of the strongest partisans of university autonomy (and had played an important role in getting the Inönü government to pass the 1946 law). But in 1953, as elections approached amid growing university criticism of the government, the Democrats began to have second thoughts. The issue of professors in politics became continually more important and partisan, as the general political atmosphere grew more and more strained.

The first real break between Menderes and the universities came in 1953 when the government passed three laws which the universities interpreted as unacceptable invasions of academic freedom. Law 6185 further restricted the universities' authority over their own budgets; Law 6422 established compulsory retirement at the government's option of all civil servants after twenty-five years of service; and Law 6435 provided that all government employees could be dismissed by the same authority which appointed them, with no right of appeal. In addition, the government laid down as one of the qualifications for teaching positions in higher education that a professor should confine himself to "scientific, educational writing," as contrasted to becoming involved in "active partisan politics." The government was careful not to say directly that it did not want professors commenting adversely on matters of public policy.

[3] *Ibid.*, pp. 372-73. The professors involved were Pertev Naili Boratav, Niyazi Berkes, Behice Boran, and Adnan Camgil. Some observers have contended that the real reason for firing these four was hostility to modern sociology and anthropology, in which Berkes and Boran were specialists.

In the period after 1954 the authority of Law 6435 was applied in at least four important cases. In October 1954 Bulent Nuri Esen, who had been calling the Menderes government a "cacocracy" rather than a democracy was dismissed. In September 1955, Osman Okyar, an economist at Istanbul University, was suspended for a magazine article entitled "American Aid Capacity may have a Limit." In 1958 Istanbul University law professor Huseyin Nail Kubali was dismissed. While attempting to be careful not to mix politics into his academic activities, he had nevertheless been a constant and outspoken commentator on national affairs.

The most spectacular case came in the fall of 1956, when at Ankara University, Political Science Faculty Dean Turhan Feyzioğlu was suspended for his speech opening the new academic year, in which he assailed the government for refusal to approve the promotion of economics docent Aydın Yalçın. The University Senate's recommendation that Yalçın be promoted to the rank of professor had lain on the Education Minister's desk for over a year, and frequent inquiries had produced no reply. There is no doubt that the government's refusal to promote Yalçın was a political act. Since 1954 Yalçın's wife had been the owner and publisher of FORUM, a bimonthly journal commenting on Turkish economic and political affairs. FORUM's criticism of government economic, social, and political policies had been severe and outspoken, and among the journal's editors and regular contributors were Yalçın and many other of Ankara University's foremost critics of Menderes, though this did not mean that they were necessarily adherents of former President Inönü's Republican People's party, the main parliamentary opposition. As was to be expected, FORUM's attacks on the government had become more severe as the Menderes government made moves against the autonomy of universities, the press, and the opposition.

The reaction of the universities to the Feyzioğlu case was mixed. There were protests to the government from both faculty and student groups and a small wave of student strikes, but FORUM's call for mass resignations was heeded only by Yalçın himself, and four other regular FORUM contributors. Probably the most notable general protest was the omission of the Ankara University opening ceremony for the 1957-58 academic year, the first anniversary of the affair. Four of those involved in the affair went into politics, Feyzioğlu and Muammer Aksoy joining the RPP (the former was elected to the Grand National Assembly in 1957), Yalçın and Şerif Mardin choosing to take part in organizing a new opposition group called the Freedom party. The latter choice, based on Yalçın's opposition to the RPP as well as the Democratic party, proved fruitless, and after the Freedom party was badly routed in the 1957 elections, Yalçın and Mardin went to the United States, where they remained until after the fall of the Menderes regime.

By 1960 the universities of Ankara and Istanbul had become virtual opposition fortresses. The Menderes government had drifted into a policy of repression of all criticism, with numerous journalists languishing in jails. When in April 1960 the government opened an investigation of the opposition by suspending political activity, the students took to the streets. Except for several professors who individually made blunt public statements that the government's actions were unconstitutional, however, the majority of the faculties gave the students only moral support, most preferring to continue their activity of discussing and petitioning even when it was clear that it would not be long before a final test of strength would make these methods obsolete.[4] The faculties did serve as a kind of center for disseminating information, since the professors' connections extended to many corners of Ankara and Istanbul, and because the universities received a steady stream of otherwise censored news through their subscriptions to foreign newspapers.[5]

When the army overthrew the Menderes regime on May 27, 1960, it immediately began to call on the Ankara and Istanbul faculties for personnel to run many of the complicated operations of government, and as advisers in many government offices. The first civilian cabinet, formed within a few days after the army took power, included several professors from among those not closely identified with any political party. Others were selected to write the new Constitution and to organize a State Planning Board. The Ankara and Istanbul public looked at the universities as saviors of Turkish democracy second only to the armed forces themselves.

It was into this environment, then, that there came the shock of the 147 dismissals. In the remainder of this chapter three questions will be considered. (1) What caused the "147 incident"? (2) Why was the problem not settled and at least some of the 147 returned to their universities before the NUC went out of power? (3) What are some of the major problems facing Turkish higher education; what are the prospects for solving them?

The Dismissal of the 147

The decision to take direct action to clean dead wood out of the universities reflected no one political view, but rather a general desire in the armed forces for speedy and efficient reform to prepare the nation for a return to civilian government. Most of the NUC was desirous of

[4] Some 400 faculty members submitted written protests to the rector of Istanbul University on May 26, endangering themselves when the martial law authorities got wind of the action and began seeking the names of the protestors. The public actions and risks taken by the students, however, were far more instrumental in bringing Menderes' downfall.

[5] The government had stopped the flow to newsstands of all foreign newspapers and magazines which carried articles about the incidents in Turkey, but did not interfere with mail deliveries of these items.

removing the military from politics with all possible speed, which meant that certain reforms would have to be made quickly. Though they had taken power mainly to end the threat of civil war among the civilian politicians, there was also a good deal of impatience among the soldiers with the failure of Turkish political parties to effect some obviously long overdue reforms. General Gürsel at one point remarked that the difference between civilian politicians and the military regime was that the latter did not need constantly to look over its shoulder to make sure it was still loved. Among the actions the military took which the civilians had shunned for years were the introduction of a tax on income from agricultural products and the abolition of the right of all high school graduates to receive automatic army commissions.

The immediate precedent for the "147 incident" was the forced retirement of more than 5,000 military and naval officers, including 235 of 255 generals and admirals, described as a "rejuvenation." That the retirements were in principle justified is clear—both Turkish and foreign military experts had been saying for some time that the Turkish army was excessively top-heavy. There was not, as there would be in the case of the 147, public pressure for a return of the 5,000 to their posts, but the problem of the latter to an important extent complicated reconsideration of the 147 decision as well.

It is significant that simultaneously with Law 114, firing the 147 professors, Law 115 was issued—a revised and strengthened University Autonomy Law. The NUC's chief contention in firing the 147 *before* the new University Law became effective was that the universities had failed over a long period to make the necessary reforms by themselves, and that there was no prospect that with renewed university autonomy the situation would be any different. The reforms had allegedly been prevented by the 147 variously putting their own interests above those of the nation—doctors and lawyers holding university positions but teaching seldom or not at all and using their titles for private advantage; lacking academic qualifications but building up seniority and blocking the advancement of younger teachers; and holding political views not in the best interest of the nation. The new University Law included provision to correct various of these alleged abuses by, for instance, forbidding any professor from being physically away from the university more than ten hours per working week,[6] and guaranteeing docents a voice in university administration.

What was, and remains today, a mystery is the basis of the decision on who was to be dismissed. There were rumors about how each name got

[6] This provision worked a special hardship on part-time faculty, and on those whose academic activities were better performed away from the university itself. None were exempt from the law. Enforcement of the provision of the previous law, that non-university activities were limited to no more than 8 hours a week for each faculty member would have been much more sensible. The 10-hour rule is a good example of a military solution to a nonmilitary problem.

on the list, but no definite reasons were ever established. The most persistent report was of jealousy among certain faculty members who induced the NUC to accept their suggestions, and one newspaper reported a statement by two NUC members about help from a "scholarly delegation."[7] The NUC maintained that it had gone over the names one by one, but it is doubtful that the soldiers had sufficient acquaintance with the universities to work independently. Most puzzling was the heterogeneity of the list. One prominent and respected Istanbul University professor voiced the opinion that at least 100 of the dismissals were justifiable, but no common denominator could be found which would include all 147.

Some dismissals were clearly political, such as Istanbul Law Professor Tarik Tunaya and Docent Ismet Giritli, who had recently been fired from the commission writing the new Constitution because of violent arguments with the commission's chairman; or Law Professor Ali Fuat Başgil, whose political views were classed by most observers as "reactionary." A large number of those dismissed were doctors and lawyers holding part-time teaching appointments. It was agreed that there were many who were unfit to hold such posts, but the list also included some who carried out their duties with great competence and enthusiasm. A few cases in Ankara could be put down to dislike of a father, husband, or other relative also holding a teaching post. But as soon as grounds for dismissal of one of the 147 were found, it became possible to say the same things about some professors not fired.

The most prevalent theory in Turkey has been that the action was instigated mainly by "fourteen radicals" on the NUC. It has been asserted several times, and never denied, that the action itself was approved by all the members of the committee, but it is impossible to avoid associating the purge of the radicals from the NUC two weeks later with the great and largely unexpected outcry over the 147 incident.[8] It should also be noted that when the university Senates later asked for the files on the 147 in the course of negotiations to restore some of them to their posts, it was stated that whatever files existed had been destroyed or carried off by the fourteen. The question of what were the bases for the list remains an enigma.

The Problem of Reinstatement

The firing of the professors evoked an immediate and loud outcry from almost the entire Turkish intellectual community. The protests included the most critical editorials to date of the NUC's actions, a student boycott of the October 29 Republic Day ceremonies, and the resignations of the rectors of all six Turkish universities. Though some members of the NUC asserted that "we anticipated the reaction, but this is May 27,

[7] *Vatan*, Oct. 29, 1960.
[8] See Chap. 6 below.

and the rocket age,"[9] it was clear that at least the degree of reactions was not foreseen, and on November 1 General Gürsel issued a statement saying "If we have made mistakes, we will work together with the universities to correct them as soon as possible. To correct mistakes is excellence."[10] Talks were begun between the NUC and the universities on the problem, but they soon stalled, for two principal reasons. First, the 147 problem became entangled with other parts of the NUC program. Second, the principle of academic freedom was not the only consideration that influenced the policy of the universities on the problem.

The difficulties of undoing the act became apparent quickly. Before anything could be done, new rectors and Senates had to be chosen for the universities. On the strength of the NUC's conciliatory statements all the rectors accepted re-election. This took a week. Another ten days went by until the NUC sent a formal letter to the universities asking what they suggested be done. Istanbul and Ankara Universities made their views known to the NUC on November 24. By this time new factors had begun to enter the situation. One was the need to assign other faculty members to take over the courses of the 147, at least for the immediate future. Some departments of the Istanbul Faculty of Medicine, for instance, had lost up to 90 percent of their teaching staffs.

Another was the growing restlessness of the 5,000 retired officers, who soon realized that the fate of the professors would have an important effect on their own status. Despite the official position of EMINSU, the Association of the Retired Officers of the Revolution, that the case of the professors was different from their own and that EMINSU backed the readmission of the former, this was by no means the unanimous opinion among the officers. In view of the strength of the NUC's feeling on the retired officers' return to the army, the spectre of demands that "if one professor returns, we will put on our uniforms again," was a formidable barrier to solution of the problem of the professors.

An important complication was the position of the universities themselves. The considerations of what to suggest to the NUC were not simple. On the one hand there was the principle of academic freedom. On the other was the political situation of the day, the fact that the dismissals had taken place in the circumstances of a revolution. There were also the questions whether the universities did in fact want all of the 147 back, and if not, whether Law 114 was not the best opportunity to get rid of the unwanted ones.

In its answer to the NUC, Istanbul University called for repeal of Law 114 in its entirety. Ankara University chose the milder alternative of asking only for repeal of Article 5 (which provided that the 147 could never return to the universities), and letting each of the dismissed professors apply to his own University Senate for reinstatement. The former had the advantages of maintaining the principle, and also avoiding the

[9] *Vatan,* Oct. 29, 1960.
[10] *Cumhuriyet,* Nov. 1, 1960.

prospect of grave political complications in having to rejudge each case. The latter idea was most likely to win approval of the NUC, but ran into serious difficulties over the disappearance of the dossiers, access to which was felt to be necessary in any such review. A third suggestion was made by the Education Minister, Bedrettin Tuncel—and summarily rejected by the universities—that the universities prepare a new list according to their own criteria, a list which might also include names which were not on the original and which would then be considered by the NUC.

Finally there was the effect that continuing public pressure about the 147 was having on the members of the NUC. Not all were as magnanimous as General Gürsel in admitting a serious mistake, for this was, after all, a revolution. The feeling grew among the soldier-rulers that the issue was fast becoming one of prestige. Their resistance to the return of the 147 gradually grew, and after several months had passed, it was openly admitted that the majority of the NUC had come to the conclusion that Law 114 was part of a group of basic reforms which had recently been put into effect, and that to undo one would be to endanger all of them. When an attempt was made in the spring of 1961 to introduce an amendment to Law 114 into the Constituent Assembly, not one NUC member could be found who would provide the necessary countersignature.

Despite continuous pressure from many sides the NUC remained firm.[11] It was only after the most careful scrutiny of all aspects of the question that the civilian government which followed the military regime repealed Article 5 in March 1962, making it possible for the 147 to apply for reinstatement by the Senates of their respective Universities. The chief reason given for not repealing the entire law was that it would violate the constitutional guarantee of university autonomy in hiring faculty. It is safe to say, however, that the considerations discussed above also played an important role in determining the shape of the readmission. The immediate issue was then solved, when the universities decided to take back all of the 147. More difficult problems such as reintegration of the 147 have resulted so far in at least one court proceeding: members of the Istanbul University Medical Faculty have been unable to agree on who should occupy clinic directorships where replacements for the 147 had been appointed. The effect of the 147 incident on the universities solving of their more fundamental problems of reform remains to be seen.

Major Problems of Higher Education

Turkish universities hold up Western universities as their ideal. It is by Western standards, then, that they should be appraised. The 147

[11] The 147 formed their own association, an aid fund was set up with much fanfare for those whose salaries had been suddenly cut off and who had no other source of income. Hardly a week went by without some public discussion of the matter.

incident has once again emphasized the magnitude of the problems facing Turkish higher education. They include not only problems of quantity and quality of students and instructors, but also the need to make basic—though difficult and probably unpopular—decisions on the direction and underlying philosophy of Turkish higher education. The following discussion will try to illuminate some of the areas where important problems of both principle and practice arise.

Students—Quantity, Quality, Motivation

One of the most serious problems is that of a vast number of students, many of them unqualified and often enrolled for other reasons than the desire to learn. This situation arises from a number of specific administrative causes, but also from a basic philosophical dilemma which Turkey has never faced up to, mass versus quality education.

It is generally accepted in Turkey that all lycee graduates have the right to go on to higher education—it is said that to restrict the right to learn is incompatible with the principles of a democracy. The continuing acceptance of this philosophy is a manifestation of the habit of Turkish governments to take the easy way out and accept all comers. Thus the spectacle each fall of lycee graduates who fail to pass the entrance examinations demonstrating in the streets, engaging in sit-down or hunger strikes, and finally being admitted by the hundreds into classes already at least twice the size of even the biggest lecture halls in Ankara or Istanbul. Thus also the phenomenon of a student taking the entrance examinations for schools as diverse as law, medicine, engineering, or literature, in the hope that he will be successful in one. An attempt several years ago to force students to choose one field by scheduling all entrance examinations on the same day was unsuccessful—the large number of failures had immediate political repercussions.

Many students take full advantage of this situation to reap the fringe benefits attendant on student status in Turkey. For example, a student card entitles the holder to a reduction of 50 percent or more on public transportation, movie and theatre tickets, and other purchases. Also not to be ignored is the prestige factor of being able to write home to an Anatolian village that one is studying at a great Istanbul University. The situation is not helped by the provision that students who fail examinations can repeat courses as many times as they like—cases of students repeating a class nine times are not unheard of. The estimate of one professor at the Istanbul University Law School is that less than 10 percent of first-year students in that faculty go on even to the second year.

In this context the current clamor by leaders of many Turkish cities for new universities has great political advantage. If based on a well-founded estimate of Turkey's future needs for trained personnel in various fields, the opening of new faculties could effectively channel able young people into those fields as well as help to alleviate the overall surplus student problem. The great difficulty, however, is that precisely these fields, technical, scientific, agricultural, are those in which the greatest staffing difficulties are currently being encountered. It was recently reported that Istanbul Technical University had vacancies for 233 professors, 86 docents, and 127 assistants, and that Istanbul University was seeking 53 professors, 64 docents, and 67 assistants.[12] The problems of staffing the new Atatürk University at Erzurum have also proved far more serious than anticipated. The recommendation by the 1960 Turkish National Education Commission that new universities be opened "only after there is assurance of sufficient number and quality of teachers"[13] indicates that many problems still lie ahead.

Discipline problems also plague Turkish universities. The role of heroes in the 1960 revolution has had an exhilarating effect on Turkish students, who found that boycotting classes and holding street demonstrations have a multitude of uses. In 1960-61 students of various schools walked out to protest teachers politically unpopular to them, the standards of certain courses and examinations, shortages of books, and poor food in university canteens. The disturbing factor is that even in cases where the protest was due to disagreement between students and faculties on how high the requirements of acceptable academic performance should be, it was almost always the students who prevailed. The attitude which this has fostered inside the classroom is seriously distressing many excellent professors.

Teaching Staffs

Despite the fact that university professors are among the highest status groups in Turkish society, Turkish higher education has a serious problem in both quantity and quality of teaching staffs. In the Istanbul Law Faculty, for example, approximately forty professors and docents (assistants do not teach) face a student body of about 8,000, a situation further aggravated by the fact that classes are relatively small in the advanced courses, often leaving instructors in the beginning classes with 2,000 to 3,000 students. The problems encountered at examination time, for example, are too obvious to need comment. Individual help for students is virtually impossible most of the time.

It is fair to say that the quality of teaching in most Turkish universities is substantially below that of most Western universities, though there are many capable and conscientious teachers. Typically a faculty consists of a small core of excellent people, and a large number which can

[12] *Akis*, Nov. 13, 1961, p. 25.
[13] *Milli Eğitim Planının Hazırlıgı Ile Görevli Komisyonun Raporu*, Ankara (1960), p. 39.

be rated only mediocre. The causes of this situation must be sought partly in terms of the low pay levels, an important factor in a nation where the demand outside of the universities for educated talent is high. Not only do many of the best people shun teaching positions, therefore, but those who do stay in the universities spend a large part of their time on outside work. The vast majority hold two or even three jobs. Other factors affecting teacher quality are poor promotion possibilities, and the fact that it is almost impossible to appoint at middle levels persons from other walks of life who have not worked their way up from the bottom of the academic ladder.

Probably the most important cause of poor teaching quality, however, is inside the universities themselves. Whatever fame professors have, in the past as well as the present, has generally come from activities other than teaching. Lectures are often no more than a recital of material in textbooks, books which are often the instructor's. Even in small classes the serious use of reports, papers, and comments by students is still a comparative rarity. Young western-trained instructors often seem to find it either impossible or impractical to transfer modern teaching methods to their own classes. Problems of low pay and of attracting more people to university teaching can be solved, and steps are being taken along these lines. Whether the faculties will then raise their teaching standards will be watched with interest in many quarters.

The Use of Existing Resources

One reason the problems have not been at least reduced in magnitude is the failure to make maximum use of some existing resources. One is time. An important Education Commission recommendation is that the academic year be lengthened and the examination system reformed.[14] The current academic year lasts nine months, but three of those are entirely given over to examinations. In many faculties examinations are almost entirely oral, a method wasteful of the time of both students and professors, as well as failing to make use of assistants who could grade written examinations.

Another underused resource is libraries. Most Turkish students spend the greatest amount of their study time poring over the textbook—often reading it as many as twenty times. This means, of course, that few have time for reading anything else. An example is the use made of the public administration collection given to the Ankara University Faculty of Political Sciences several years ago. Despite the existence of Institutes of Public Administration at both the Faculty of Political Sciences and the Middle East Technical University, and the stiff formal requirements

[14] *Ibid.*, p. 38.

of both of those institutions for knowledge of English, a recent check of the books revealed that less than 10 percent had ever been consulted. The library problem is complicated by the high cost of books and the resulting high propensity to fail to return books, by the frequent practice of professors of keeping library books in their fields as a semiprivate collection in their offices, and by the general shortage of Turkish translations of Western materials. Efforts are being made to remedy some of these faults, for example, the Political Science Faculty's translation program. But the problems in this area, as elsewhere, will require solutions affecting important philosophical and methodological premises of Turkish higher education.

Considerable use has been made of foreign exchange professors and students. Turkey ranks among the highest in the world in the percentage of students sent to study abroad. Exchanges of teaching faculty, both foreigners coming to Turkey and Turks going abroad, have also been at high levels. Besides a large Fulbright program, important relationships exist or have existed between Columbia University and Istanbul University, New York University and the University of Ankara, University of Nebraska and the Atatürk University at Erzurum, Georgetown University and many Turkish institutions engaged in English language instruction. British, German, and French educators are also prominent on the Turkish scene. The results of these contacts have been uneven. In some cases they have stimulated impressive improvement in Turkish higher education. Some efforts at curriculum reform, on the other hand, have failed to produce satisfactory results. Both Americans and Turks can be blamed for disappointing results in some projects. Not all the Americans sent to Turkey were of top calibre, and many sometimes failed to take into account Turkish circumstances or cultural characteristics. Turks on the other hand, in certain instances proved more interested in being relieved of heavy teaching loads or sending professors abroad than in effecting basic changes. Resistance by older professors to invasion of their prerogatives or serious challenge to traditional viewpoints also contributed to the difficulties. It is to be hoped that the new pressures for educational reform will in the future make better use of these potentially significant opportunities.

The Problems of Robert College and the Middle East Technical University

Two institutions of higher education in Turkey are potential leaders in university reform, though only if solutions can be found to important difficulties currently besetting both. One is Robert College, the Turkish-

American institution in Istanbul now preparing to celebrate its centennial. Having survived numerous political crises and threats to its continued existence in Turkey, its problems today are finding ways to realize its full potential both as a high quality teaching institution, and as a leader in improvement of other Turkish higher education.

The most urgent problem is the establishment of better relations with Turkish universities. Istanbul University rector Siddik Sami Onar, for instance, recently acknowledged that he had never once in his long career in Turkish education been on the Robert College campus. Aloofness by Turkish university professors stems partly from the allegedly low standard of teaching at Robert College (the College has many able and dedicated faculty members, but also a distressingly large number lacking these attributes), the fact that young American instructors are paid far more than many senior Turkish university professors (a problem for Turkey more than for the college which has trouble attracting able staff even at prevailing pay scales), and predominance of non-Turkish influence in the college curriculum. Part of the difficulty comes from the college side as well, most conspicuously from a tendency toward clannishness, and only few efforts to make contact with Turks not associated with the college. On the other hand, there are potentially far-reaching projects like the Joint Humanities Course which attempts to consider both Turkish and Western cultures on a comparative basis. If the considerable resources of the college and its potential value as a laboratory for improving higher education in Turkish institutions are to be fully used, much more effort will have to be expended along these lines. It is noteworthy that one of the first acts of Patrick Malin, who took over as President in 1962, was to install a Turkish Vice President, former Communication Minister Orhan Mersinli, a man with outstanding academic, administrative, political, and personality qualifications.

The other opening wedge to education reform is the Middle East Technical University. Founded during the Menderes period, it concentrates on the sciences, sociology, and public administration, all its teaching being in English. Its most controversial feature is that it is run by its own board of trustees rather than being under direct government control like other Turkish universities. METU was originally conceived of as serving the entire Middle East, but the number of non-Turkish students and teachers has not become significant. It is not inconceivable, however, that it may achieve regional prominence if it proves successful in becoming a center of high academic achievement. Major contributions have been made by American foundations, and several Americans and Europeans occupy important teaching and administrative posts. By offering substantially higher salaries, it has been able to attract the nucleus of an excellent Turkish staff, though it has the same problems of personnel shortages which face other Turkish universities. If METU's relations with the Turkish government and with other Turkish universities can be put on a satisfactory basis, its modern administrative and teaching practices are a potentially powerful stimulus to reform and improvement elsewhere.

Conclusion

The question of academic freedom in Turkey has many sides. It is unlikely that the next few years will see a significant separation of universities from politics in Turkey. Like their counterparts in most of the rapidly modernizing nations, Turkish professors and students are frequently directly active in partisan capacities, and are likely to remain so as long as so many fundamental social and political problems of the nation remain unresolved. Nor is such a separation entirely desirable, for the contribution of university faculties to the solution of public problems is potentially very great. It is precisely in these circumstances, however, that the boundary lines of academic freedom become most difficult to draw. Granted that the situation under the Menderes regime was unusual, it is still the case that in the past Turkish universities have often been unable to enforce on their own members many of the standards of propriety in regard to privileges under academic freedom which the Western academic world generally accepts. Whether Turkish faculties can participate in partisan politics but be unwilling to let the rest of the political community partake in setting the boundaries of academic immunity should be watched with interest by academic groups everywhere.

The "147 incident" and all the uproar that was maintained about it for over a year emphasized once again the high status that university professors enjoy in Turkey. This high status, however, at the same time greatly increases the professors' obligation to serve their country; and for this reason alone, university autonomy in the Turkish context can be an important contribution to democratic government. Possibly an even more important problem is what the universities must do in a positive sense to justify that autonomy and create a situation in which autonomy will be of benefit to national development. There is much talk in Turkey about the sacrifices that will have to be made in order to reach the ambitious development goals which Turkish leaders—headed by the universities—maintain are required. It is the university faculties themselves that continually point out the importance of quality education in the development picture, yet in the past it is they, with some significant exceptions, who have been either unwilling or unable to undertake needed reforms on their own initiative.

If few professors can be found to accept long-term appointments to establish the new Atatürk University in Erzurum, it is understandable that other elements of the Turkish people see little reason to heed the intellectuals' exhortations to greater efforts. To solve political problems, pressure for incursions on academic freedom as well as for lower academic standards must be resisted. Similar situations in several other rapidly modernizing nations have forced choices between the principle of university autonomy and the need to gain maximum value from the nation's educational resources. It is to a large extent in the hands of the university faculties to see that this choice will not have to be made in Turkey.

4

Constitution Making for Turkey's Second Republic

THE PROMULGATION OF A liberal constitution for Turkey's Second Republic in 1961 was an important turning point in one of the twentieth century's significant examples of political development. In this day of many first and a growing number of second constitutions in "emerging" nations, it represents the systematic statement of what a modernizing elite with forty years experience feels is the most appropriate legal and structural underpinning for continuing development. The Turkish Constitution of 1961 is also significant because it may shed light on the important question of how appropriate a liberal Constitution is in a situation where it is felt that a one-party regime is no longer required, but at the same time much difficult reform remains to be accomplished.

The Constitution aims on the one hand at giving the government and the political parties maximum maneuverability, but insists with equal vigor on preventing a repetition of the concentration of power in the hands of a single party on the basis of only a small margin in the popular vote, as had been the case in the Menderes regime. The system of proportional representation, imposed on an electorate divided on fundamental political issues, has so well achieved the latter aim that there is now serious concern about whether the former can be fulfilled. The legacy of the First Republic is such that the four parties in the 1961 Assembly, none with a majority, are reluctant to work with each other, to resolve the mutual antagonisms which go deep into the Turkish body politic. Thus the chances appear slim for party discipline and coalition government sufficiently effective to achieve the reform needed for continued development.

The 1961 Constitution makers looked to the West for models, as had their predecessors. Turkey's first Constitution, the Ottoman Constitution of 1876, was modeled on the Belgian Constitution of 1831. It "combined the advantages of being liberal, monarchical, and written in French." But the Ottoman Empire was not Belgium, and "the [Belgian] Constitution, adapted into Turkish, was inevitably irrelevant, unrelated to Turkish conditions, and ultimately unworkable."[1] Suspended by

[1] Bernard Lewis, *The Emergence of Modern Turkey* (Oxford University Press, 1961), p. 356.

Sultan Abdülhamid II between 1878 and 1908, the Ottoman Constitution was not put into effect until after the Young Turk revolt of the latter year, and it was not long until the Young Turks had emasculated the principle of the sovereignty of parliament in favor of concentrating power in their own hands.

The principle of sovereignty of the nation was first formally enunciated by Atatürk in the Constitutional Act adopted by the Grand National Assembly on January 20, 1921. The National Assembly received all powers necessary to administer the nation, and although it was stated that these powers were being exercised in the name of the Sultan-Caliph until that personage was liberated from the Allied occupation of Istanbul, the substitution of the Assembly for the Sultan-Caliph was in effect a permanent one. On April 20, 1924, a new Constitution was adopted by the Grand National Assembly. It was this charter which was to be replaced in 1960-61.

The 1924 Constitution established a parliamentary republic, with all power concentrated in the National Assembly, although the judiciary was autonomous in the performance of its assigned duties. The enumeration of individual rights and freedoms was taken from the most liberal European constitutions. The reaction to the abuses of power by executives from the Sultans to the Young Turks was largely responsible for the failure to include any of the checks and balances found in constitutions in Europe and the United States. Atatürk's strong determination that nothing would hinder efforts at rapid and radical reform was also a consideration in this omission. It was a Constitution "drafted . . . primarily to meet the immediate needs arising from the special conditions of a regime in transition."[2]

In the years that followed, European models were used as the basis for civil, penal, commercial, and other codes, many taken over almost directly from the most advanced codes in the West. In 1960, then, the first job for the various scholars was to study all available western constitutions. Features were taken over, almost verbatim in several cases, from the American, French, German, and Italian constitutions. As was true in the 1924 charter, many of the 157 articles are designed to meet specific needs of the new political environment.

The Constitution-Making Process

The process of evolution of the Constitution lasted just over one year and involved four different printed versions,[3] a nationwide poll of intellectuals, a national referendum, and plenty of political dispute. One

[2] Kemal Karpat, *Turkey's Politics, The Transition to a Multi-Party System* (Princeton University Press, 1959), p. 248.

[3] *Yüksek Oğretim Uyelerinden Kurulu Anayasa Komisyonunca Hazırlanan Anayasa Ontasarısı,* Ankara, 1960 (cited hereinafter as Onar Commission); *Siyasal Bilgiler*

of the first acts of the National Unity Committee (NUC) on taking power was to appoint a commission of Istanbul University Law professors to write a new Constitution. In fact it was only hours after the takeover when several professors were flown to Ankara. The Constitution Commission chairman, Istanbul University rector and professor of Administrative Law Siddik Sami Onar, was one of Turkey's oldest and best-known personalities in the legal field. He had often been mentioned as a possible presidential candidate in the event of a Republican election victory. Onar had also become a public hero through suffering a head injury while protesting the illegal police invasion of the grounds of Istanbul University late in April.

Even before the commission got to Ankara, General Gürsel, chairman of the NUC, had announced that the new Constitution would provide for a bicameral instead of unicameral legislature, proportional representation, and a Constitutional Court, points on which there had been almost unanimous agreement among Turkish leaders (excluding the Menderes government) for several years. Within two days the commission issued its first report, re-affirming these points, pledging inclusion in the Constitution of human rights and of democracy for political minorities, and issuing a sort of latter-day after-the-fact *fetwa,* a long statement justifying the army coup in terms of the political ideals of the Turkish nation.[4] But at this point the smoothness of the process came to a halt as opposing schools of thought clashed again and again.

Onar had estimated that the new Constitution would be drafted in a month, with a similar period allotted to consideration of comments of bar, press, university, and other groups. What Onar apparently did not count on was emergence of basic philosophical divisions even within his own committee and the rapid resurgence of political parties on the national political scene, which then demanded and received a major voice in the making of the Constitution. The crux of the differences of opinion was between what may be tentatively labeled the legalistic school and the political school.

The Legalistic and Political Schools

The two positions may be summed up roughly as follows: The legalistic school favored incorporating into the Constitution all possible safeguards and restrictions, the absence of which had allegedly been useful to the

---

Fakültesi Idari Ilimler Enstitüsü'nün Gerekçeli Anayasa Tasarısı, Ankara Universitesi Siyasal Bilgiler Fakültesi Yayınları No. 116-97, Ankara, 1960 (cited hereinafter as Ankara proposal); *Türkiye Cumhuriyeti Anayasa Tasarısı ve Anayasa Komisyonu Raporu,* Temsilciler Meclisi S. Sayısı 35, 9 March 1961 (cited hereinafter as Karal Committee); *Türkiye Cumhuriyeti Anayasası,* Resmi Gazete Nr. 10810, 31 May 1961. English translation: *Constitution of the Turkish Republic,* translated for the Committee of National Unity by Sadik Balkan, Ahmet E. Uysal and Kemal H. Karpat, Ankara, 1961.

4 *Ulus,* May 29, 1960.

Menderes government in its attempts to subvert Turkey's democratic political system. As little as possible was to be left among the items which "will be specified by law." Not only were numerous councils, committees, and other semiautonomous regulatory bodies specifically provided for, but such detailed items as selection provisions for membership on all of these were specified. Proportional representation, seen by many Turks as one of the most effective panaceas for preventing despotism of the majority, was prescribed even for the election of secretaries of each of the houses of parliament as well as for selection by professional and business groups of their own representatives to a corporate upper house. More important, the legalists favored all possible limitations on the freedom of action of whatever political party came to power. This was reflected most prominently in the provision for a corporate upper house, the point on which the two schools eventually became deadlocked. The Onar Constitution called for an upper house made up of 1 elected deputy for each 500,000 inhabitants (the population of Turkey is approximately 25 million), plus 85 other members, of whom 5 would be veteran judges or prosecutors, 5 generals and admirals, 5 university professors, 40 delegates from bar, medical, or business groups, and 30 members from among teachers, the press, farmers, and other groups, all of which were to be selected by their respective organizations or professional groups. Party groups in the parliament were described as "organs of the parliament," and the Constitution carefully spelled out conditions under which members would be obliged to break party discipline. Discipline could be broken, for instance, if in the opinion of a deputy his party group made decisions contrary either to the Constitution, or to its own party program and by-laws. On the question of constitution-making itself, the legalists favored obtaining the criticisms of the commission draft by bar, press, university, business, and other groups and submitting the final version to a national referendum.

The political school took an opposite view on most of these issues. They believed in relying chiefly on "forward-looking" political parties for achieving the dynamics needed for rapid social, economic, and political development. Though urging that all possible hindrances to political innovation be avoided, they continued to support strongly the most important safeguards against a new despotism of the majority, that is, the bicameral legislature, proportional representation in national elections, and the Constitutional Court.[5] An important part of the thinking

[5] There was some debate about the merits of proportional representation as against single-member constituencies, but preponderance of opinion, including that of the army, was on the side of the former, which was often seen as an almost magical device for preventing the abuses of province-wide winner-take-all elections through which there had been much distortion of representation in relation to popular vote. The most spirited debate came between proponents of various systems of proportional representation, a debate which received much newspaper space but which few other than the experts understood.

of the political school centered on the idea of planning, and to this end their proposals included a provision for a permanent nonpolitical state planning organization. In this the political school had the strong backing of the Republican Peoples Party (RPP).

The political school strongly opposed the corporate form of upper chamber, and favored broad provisions which would permit a government to organize itself as it saw fit in most respects. They opposed the legalists' vast network of organizations, especially in the economic and financial sphere of government activity, as well as the idea of giving legal sanction to deputies to break party discipline in the legislature. On constitution-making, the members of the political school generally opposed the idea of a national referendum, claiming that the Turkish nation was not mature enough to vote intelligently on the complicated issues of various proposals for a constitution. Instead they urged convening of a Constituent Assembly representing the views of all responsible groups in the nation, including the political parties. This idea was in turn strongly opposed by the legalists. The division of opinion on the latter point was not clear-cut, however, and Ismet Giritli, an adherent of the political school, came out for both some form of Constituent Assembly and a referendum.[6]

The Onar Commission

Of the seven professors in the initial group flown to Ankara, at least four were strongly "legalistically" oriented. Siddik Sami Onar, Hüseyin Nail Kubalı, Hıfzı Veldet Velidedeoğlu, and Naci Şensoy were essentially products of the legal training of an earlier age, and of a conservative, legal orientation to the political process. Two other members of the commission, Tarik Tunaya and Ismet Giritli, plus some professors added later from the Ankara University Faculty of Political Sciences, were younger, and trained for the most part to rely on the political process rather than an elaborate legal framework for achieving both development and the preservation of basic political liberties. The younger group tended toward the political school also because they were generally more involved in politics than were their older colleagues. The proposal which came out of the Onar Commission was highly legalistic. So much so, that opponents of such an interpretation of the sort of a constitution that would best serve Turkey reacted by mobilizing all their political power to prevent the Onar proposals from being adopted.

The Onar Commission's estimate that one month would be sufficient for it to write a draft soon proved unrealistic, and it was not until mid-October that the document was finally given to the NUC. Even then it

[6] *Cumhuriyet,* Aug. 24, 1960. For a further statement of his views see Ismet Giritli, "Some Aspects of the New Turkish Constitution," *Middle East Journal,* Vol. 16 (Winter 1962), pp. 1-17.

had not been circulated to other organizations for comment. Earlier it had been envisioned that both writing and commenting would be done by the end of July.

One obstacle to writing the Constitution was that this was new to the commission's members, most of whom were specialists in other areas of law. It was the series of bitter internal disagreements, however, soon spilling into the press, which most complicated the work. The most dramatic incident in the growing rivalry between the legalist and political schools took place at the beginning of September, when Onar flew to Ankara to discuss "internal commission disputes" with the NUC. The chief areas of disagreement were the composition and authority of the second house, the place of political parties in the Constitution, the proposed High Economic Council, and the relations of Onar himself to the press. On the last-named subject, there had been growing complaints that the Onar Commission was operating like a secret organization rather than a public body deliberating the most vital national issues. The complaints were probably not wholly justified, in view of the fact that the nature of the work was often plodding technical research rather than newsworthy political decision-making. Toward the end of the commission's work Onar did somewhat increase his contacts with the press.

The result of Onar's trip to Ankara was the dismissal from the commission of its two chief political school representatives, Tunaya and Giritli. In a series of press conferences these two made a full publication of the areas of disagreement and charged Onar with firing them solely because they disagreed with his views.[7] Onar on the other hand denied any disagreements whatever, saying that appointments and firings were handled by the NUC only, and that the NUC had not even consulted him on the matter.[8] Even his staunchest supporters inside the NUC could not go this far, and a statement by NUC members Esin, Ozdağ, and Solmazer, while saying "we decided, acted and that is that," said also that it was indeed disagreement on the form of the second House which was delaying the work, though they referred to "a sort of 6th sense" when asked on what information the NUC had acted.[9] General Gürsel himself told the press that Tunaya's and Giritli's "too meticulous" habits had slowed down the commission's work when speed was of the essence, and that it had been necessary either to fire them or reconstitute the entire commission.[10]

An important outgrowth of this incident was an impetus for concerted

[7] *Cumhuriyet,* Sept. 2 and 4, 1960.

[8] *Cumhuriyet,* Sept. 3, 1960.

[9] *Vatan,* Sept. 5, 1960. All three of these officers belonged to the group of fourteen radicals who were purged from the NUC in November for allegedly opposing the decision to hold elections as soon as possible. The radicals, led by Col. Türkeş, appear to have shared the legalists' basic distrust of too much free play for political parties, though for different reasons.

[10] *Cumhuriyet,* Sept. 7, 1960.

attacks on Onar himself by the press, which was largely favorable to the RPP, and the emergence of a picture of Onar as a self-styled "emperor of the law." This tarnishing of his public image was undoubtedly a factor in the gradual decline of the sympathy of the press with the Onar Commission's efforts. By this time, however, other members of the political school had also begun to marshall their forces. First, the Executive Committee of the Republican party had drawn up a detailed response to a questionnaire it (among 2000 others) had received from the Onar Commission asking for suggestions for the Constitution. The RPP response stressed planning, flexibility, and rapid economic development with no reluctance to use state means wherever necessary. Second, a group of professors on the Faculty of Political Sciences at Ankara University, led by senior professors Tahsin Bekir Balta and Yavuz Abadan, drew up a proposed Constitution of their own. The Ankara professors not only dissented strongly from Onar's legalist views, but they also had reason to feel they were being given a subordinate position. Of the ten members of the Onar Commission only three relatively junior professors were from Ankara (Bahri Savcı and Muammer Aksoy of the Political Science Faculty, and Ilhan Arsel of the Faculty of Law), and these had been selected as an afterthought. The Ankara group soon won the support of much of the press. They also had the advantage of being physically much closer to the seat of the NUC's activities, and many from Ankara University were among those called on by the NUC to remedy its own obvious lack of political experience. The tension between the Ankara University group and the Onar Commission increased when Onar said that the published, annotated Ankara proposal would be treated no differently than any other of the several hundred answers to Onar's questionnaire.

The Ankara Group

The highly involved Onar Constitution of 191 articles was finally submitted to the NUC on October 17. By this time, however, whether or not the Ankara group aimed at countering the Onar proposals or merely at a neutral educational endeavor, it was moving at full speed along its own lines. The Political Science Faculty began holding a series of "Constitution Seminars" in which professors explained technical, theoretical, and political considerations on various aspects of the constitutions. The seminars were well attended by NUC members, journalists, and political and academic figures. In the course of these seminars most professors did not hesitate to bitterly denounce many of the ideas in the Onar proposal.

The precise influence of the various activities of the Ankara group is impossible to measure, but it is certain that the NUC members were exposed to considerable thinking of the political school. There probably was more than a coincidental relationship between this exposure and the NUC's decision at the end of October to accept the political school's opinion and convene a Constituent Assembly.

The Assembly's purposes were outlined as reviewing the Constitution, providing a legal basis for its acceptance, preparing a new election law, and generally strengthening national unity. A committee of five professors was appointed to draw up the Constituent Assembly's organizational statute. It was headed by Turhan Feyzioğlu, former Political Science Faculty dean and later Republican deputy. The other four members of the committee, including Aksoy and Savcı, also came from Ankara. Two were the political school's representatives on the Onar Commission. About all that the legalists were able to salvage was the inclusion in the Constituent Assembly of representatives of many national organizations and groups, though these were outnumbered by direct representatives of the political parties and delegates from Turkey's sixty-seven provinces. The legalists succeeded in getting a referendum on the Constitution, though by the time this was held in July 1961, the reasons which carried most weight in the decision to hold the referendum were political and unrelated to those earlier put forward by the legalist school.

The Karal Committee

The opening of the Constituent Assembly on January 6, 1961, was an important milestone in the return of political parties to the center of the national stage. Though ostensibly nonpartisan, the Assembly was overwhelmingly composed of RPP members, who besides having been allotted a sizable contingent of party representatives, had also managed to be elected as representatives of many provinces and from many nonparty organizations. The political school among the constitution makers now came firmly into control. The Assembly's twenty-member Constitution Committee included six from among the deputies representing the RPP directly, plus such leading political school personalities as Tunaya, Aksoy, and Savcı. The legalists were represented on the Assembly Committee only by Professors Sarıca and Velidedeoğlu.

The Assembly Constitution Committee was chaired by the respected head of Ankara University's Institute for the History of the Turkish Revolution, Professor Enver Ziya Karal. It labored for two months before presenting a draft to the Assembly early in March. In contrast to the Onar Commission, the Karal Committee maintained excellent relations with the press, and the texts of articles were released almost as soon as the committee had agreed on them. The contrast in the press relations of the Karal Committee and the Onar Commission served to emphasize even more the public image of Onar as a self-styled despot with out-of-date ideas. This comparison was probably somewhat unfair in view of the differences both in the composition and the tasks of the two groups. One of the results of the constitution-making process, however, has been that Onar has never since enjoyed the reputation he had before the revolution.

The NUC, in contrast to its attitude toward the Onar Commission, seems to have refrained from pressure on the Karal Committee,[11] with the understanding, of course, that certain features such as the two-house legislature and the Constitutional Court would remain in any proposal. The difference in the NUC's role toward the Karal Committee was probably due partly to the growing domination the parties had begun to exercise over the NUC, to the education carried on in the Political Science Faculty seminars by the same people who now sat in the Constituent Assembly, and to the elimination from the NUC the previous November of fourteen radical members who strongly distrusted political parties.[12]

The Karal Committee draft was far closer to the Ankara University proposal than to that of the Onar Commission. With minor changes, which will be indicated below, it was approved by the Assembly on May 27, 1961, the anniversary of the revolution. On July 9 the Constitution was approved by 62 percent of the voters in a national referendum, although the voting had only a remote relation to the issue of the Constitution since the referendum was almost universally interpreted as chiefly a vote for or against the military regime. The political school's opinion about a referendum on the Constitution itself was probably largely correct, and it is doubtful that even had the Constitution been the main focus, it would have created significant personal identification of voters with the new charter. As the political situation stood in July, however, the referendum provided a much-needed warning that neither general satisfaction with the military regime nor an RPP victory in the coming elections could be taken for granted.

The 1961 Constitution

In content, the Constitution reflects the ideas of multiparty democracy which, though not always observed in practice, have been present in Turkish political thought since the beginnings of the Atatürk modernization program. The changes from the 1924 Constitution fall into two general categories: (1) The political freedoms which during the First Republic were anchored chiefly in the charismatic leadership of Atatürk are given more permanent legal status, closing the loopholes that allegedly gave former premier Menderes opportunity to subvert Turkish democracy. (2) As far as possible, nongovernment checks that could restrict the scope of political leaders to innovate and experiment are removed.

[11] This was stated to the author independently by several members of the Karal Committee, some of whom had served on the Onar Commission as well.

[12] The relations between the NUC and political parties are discussed in detail in Chap. 6.

General Principles

The Constitution left to Turkey by Atatürk contained six principles: republicanism, nationalism, secularism, populism, étatism, and revolutionism. The new constitution retains four of these, in proclaiming that "The Turkish Republic is a nationalist, democratic, secular and social state." (Art. 2) Over the democratic, secular, and social bases there was no disagreement among the Onar, Ankara University, or Karal proposals, though the determination of just how much "social justice" should be incorporated into the Constitution itself was a matter of some controversy, as will be discussed later. The "revolutionist" plank was mentioned first in the Ankara University proposal, which described Turkey as "adhering to the revolutions." These were unspecified except in a commentary which noted that May 27 was a continuation of the national struggle begun by Atatürk.[13]

Revolutionism to Atatürk had, however, meant more than just a few basic acts of reform. It implied a continual application of thorough and rapid reform, something not universally popular among the Turkish electorate of 1961. In the context of a prospective election contest with the votes of several million disaffected Democrats at stake, it was probably prudence, therefore, that led the Constituent Assembly to specify exactly what was meant by "revolutions." Included are eight specific reform laws about which any dissent would be no less than treason in the eyes of progressive Turks: the unification of education; the Hat Law forbidding the fez; the closing of dervish orders; civil marriage; international numerals; the new Turkish alphabet; abolition of titles and appelations; and the prohibition against wearing religious garments in public. (Art. 153)

The inclusion of nationalism among the basic principles was not proposed in any of the three drafts, but it was among the first amendments offered in the floor debates of the Constituent Assembly. The failure to include nationalism specifically in the various drafts was probably due to the reluctance to appear too chauvinistic, to cast a shadow on Turkey's often-stated adherence to many international commitments within the free world, and certainly included a desire to maintain an atmosphere of assurance for foreign private capital. On the other hand, its omission is puzzling in view of the Turks' intense national pride. National unity was not forgotten, appearing in the preambles of each of the drafts, though not everyone made the theoretical distinction between these two ideas. When General Gürsel among others commented favorably on the Assembly proposal for incorporating nationalism in the Constitution, he equated it with national unity. What in fact emerged was a new definition of Turkish nationalism with which few Turks will argue: it is a

[13] Ankara proposal, Art. 89, pp. 19, 45. For Atatürk reform program, see Chap. 1.

spirit "which unites all individuals, be it in fate, pride, or distress, in a common bond as an indivisible whole around national consciousness and aspirations, and which has as its aim always to exalt our nation in a spirit of national unity as a respected member of the community of the world of nations enjoying equal rights and privileges."[14]

Etatism was not proposed in any of the drafts, and the politicians of the Assembly gave short shrift to this most controversial of Atatürk's six program points.

Fundamental Rights and Duties

The Constitution of 1961 guarantees Turkish citizens a wide variety of political rights and freedoms. They include all those now generally regarded as fundamental in Western nations. The notable aspect of this section is its reflection of the reaction to the most heavily felt abuses of the Menderes regime. Thus, for instance, special emphasis is placed on specifying the prohibitions against appealing to religious motives in political activity, including a provision that "no person shall be reproached for his religious faith and belief." (Art. 19) Religious education, always a subject of controversy in Turkey, is made "subject to the individual's own will and volition." (Art. 19) This has in the past been applied in different ways. At one time public school pupils were given religious instruction only at their parents' specific request, at another time they were excused only on individual application.

Another area in which special care is taken is freedom of the press. A provision that "media and facilities provided by the State and other public corporate bodies shall be equally available to all" (Art. 23) would seem to be a reaction both to the Menderes government's flagrant abuses of the state radio, and to the manipulation of state advertising (by far the biggest category of newspaper advertising in Turkey) to aid or penalize newspapers according to their political views. The protection of printing equipment from seizure or prevention from operation is singled out for special mention. (Art. 25) Emphasized as well is the right to controvert and rebut by individuals whose honor and dignity has been affected or "where they have been made the butt of unfounded statements in print," newspapers being obliged to publish such a rebuttal in the same position on the same page as the original item. (Art. 27) Still another specific reference is to the right to prove the truth of an allegation attacked as libelous (Art. 34), a right abrogated by the Menderes government, especially in press cases.

Specific recognition is given to political parties. Article 56 states the principle that "whether in power or in opposition political parties are indispensable entities of democratic political life." The parties are accountable to the Constitutional Court which has the power to review

[14] Preamble.

their internal affairs and activities to assure that they "conform to the principles of a democratic and secular republic, [are] based on human rights and liberties, and on the fundamental principle of the State's territorial and national integrity." (Art. 57) The parties are also accountable to the Constitutional Court for their sources of income and expenditures. There are no other conditions, and the Constitutional Court is barred from delegating its function in regard to political parties in any way to lower courts or other government agencies.

Economic and Social Provisions

The new Turkish Constitution is a welfare one in a broad sense. It assigns to the individual many rights and to the state many duties. Most of the economic and social provisions of the new Turkish Constitution are found in one or more of the West European constitutions, but as a whole the Turkish Constitution goes further than any of these.

Guarantees are given of property rights, freedom of work and contracts, and against nationalization or expropriation without compensation. As is the case in the German and Italian Constitutions, Turkey recognizes "the family as the fundamental unit of Turkish Society" (Art. 35) but stops short of the rather detailed provisions for its protection which are found in the Catholic-influenced charters of Italy and Germany.

Several points among the Constitution's economic and social provisions deserve special note. One is the specific inclusion of the State Planning Organization, on whose work economic, social, and cultural development is to be based. (Art. 129) The inclusion of such a specific provision went further than either the Ankara or Onar proposals. The Ankara draft had said only that "development proceeds according to definite plans," while the Onar Commission had made no reference to planning at all. Here is one area in which the military influence undoubtedly played a large part, for one of the NUC's first and most important actions was to establish such a Planning Organization, which by the time the Constitution was debated in the Constituent Assembly was a full-blown and busily functioning organization.

The strong Republican party predilection for planning was also partly responsible for the incorporation of the Planning Organization into the Constitution in specific and permanent nonpolitical form. Another important influence was the desire to keep in the favor of potential dispensers of economic aid. It was widely said that Menderes had an aversion even to the word "planning," and the Stabilization Program insisted on by the International Bank's mission to Turkey in 1958 notably demanded greatly increased coordination and rationalization if the Bank's development assistance was to continue.

The High Economic Council, though proposed by both the Ankara and the Onar drafts, was not included in the final version. The Ankara proposals had been for a group representing the universities and professional organizations which would advise the government on economic and social problems.[15] The Onar Commission had gone further and included in the Economic Council's duties the study of national problems, the submission of annual reports, and the proposing of laws. As it did with most of the other bodies it proposed to establish to help the government in many fields, the Onar draft also included the composition, terms of office, and complicated selection procedures for nomination and appointment of High Economic Council members.[16]

The Constitution includes land reform as a duty of the state. (Art. 37) Whatever activity is carried out in this regard, however, will undoubtedly be influenced more by political than constitutional developments. For land reform purposes "the law may define the size of tracts of land according to different agricultural regions and types of soil," and the Constitution includes an obligation of the state to assist farmers in the acquisition of agricultural implements. (Art. 37) The long-standing cry of Turkish and foreign economists about the neglect of agriculture, as well as the realization that Turkey's becoming a chronic wheat-importer is due to more than just unfavorable weather conditions, are probably largely responsible for the stricture of Article 52 which obligates the state to take necessary measures "to provide the people with adequate nourishment, to assure an increase in agricultural production to the benefit of society, to prevent erosion, to enhance the value of agricultural products, and the toil of those engaged in agriculture." One of the most widely voiced complaints has long been the alarming diminution of Turkey's forests. Thus Article 131 prohibits the state from turning forests over to private persons for any reason, mentions resettlement of populations in or near forests if this is required to improve the people's living conditions and to conserve the forests, and concludes by saying "no amnesty shall be granted for offenses involving forests; and no political propaganda likely to lead to the destruction of forests shall be permitted."

A final area under economic and social matters which deserves comment is working conditions for labor. Here it is not what is in the Constitution which is of main interest, for the Turks are not pioneers in inserting in their Constitution the right to paid week-ends, religious and national holidays, and paid annual leave. (Art. 44) What is notable is again the difference between the legalist and political school proposals. The former went so far as to include in the Onar proposals a guarantee to each worker of at least three weeks annual paid vacation,[17] something enjoyed even in the United States by only a minority of workers. The

[15] Ankara proposal, Art. 89, pp. 40, 83.
[16] Onar Commission, Art. 140.
[17] Art. 42.

Ankara draft, on the other hand, did not even mention the subject of "fringe benefits."

Article 47 formally recognizes labor unions: "In their relations with their employers, workers are entitled to bargain collectively and to strike with a view to protecting or improving their economic and social status." Although the right to strike has been promised to labor by the parties for many years, however, neither the NUC nor any important political party was willing to go further in the Constitution than to leave its specific determination to await further political developments. Article 47 also says "The exercise of the right to strike, and the exceptions thereto . . . shall be regulated by law." Another new provision is that "the rights of employers" are added to the things to be regulated by special law.

Government Organization

The 1961 Constitution establishes a bicameral Grand National Assembly, composed of the National Assembly and the Senate of the Republic. The 1924 Constitution, in contrast, had provided for only a single chamber, in which all legislative power was concentrated. The virtually unlimited possibilities of dictatorship over the legislative process through control of the majority party in the single chamber had been exploited to the fullest extent by Menderes, and one of the major aims of the 1961 constitution makers was to reduce the scope of these possibilities. To accomplish this, differences between the chambers in the new bicameral legislature were provided both in method of election and in length of terms of office, with the hope of avoiding domination by the same party in both chambers.

The National Assembly is composed of 450 members, elected for four-year terms. The number of deputies for each province is assigned in relation to that province's population, and within each province the number of deputies elected from each party list is determined by that party's proportion of the popular vote. The Senate of the Republic, on the other hand, is composed of 150 members elected for six-year terms, with one-third to be rotated each two years. The number of Senate seats for each province varies from one to six according to population. The party winning the most popular votes in each province receives all of that province's senatorial seats, except in the provinces of Istanbul and Ankara which because of their unusually large number of Senators, ten and seven respectively, have been divided into smaller electoral districts for this purpose. In addition to the 150 elected members, the Senate also contains 15 presidential appointees, the latter to be "from among people distinguished for their services in various fields." (Art. 72) The first Senate will also include the members of the National Unity Committee, who were retired from the army when the government was returned to civilian hands in October 1961. That the variations in method of election can in fact produce a different complexion in the two chambers was proved in the elections of October, when the Republican party emerged with the most deputies, but the Justice party returned the largest number of senators.

The Grand National Assembly must be in session at least seven months of the year. It may organize itself as it wishes, but with the stipulation that all parties must be represented in proportion to their strength in each chamber on the Chairmanship Council, committees, and investigative bodies. Another Menderes abuse is eliminated, incidentally, in the provisions that the salaries of members of the Grand National Assembly may not exceed the salaries of government officials in the highest civil service pay bracket, travel allowances may not exceed 50 percent of the salary, and to pay more than a three-month total of salary and travel allowance in advance is forbidden. (Art. 82) Among other things, this provision may help guarantee adequate civil service pay.

In the making of laws the National Assembly is the more powerful. It may, in fact, enact legislation over the rejection of the Senate. If a bill is approved by the National Assembly but rejected by the Senate, it goes back to the former which may then reapprove it (by absolute majority if the Senate rejection was at that level, by two-thirds if the Senate rejection had been by at least two-thirds), in which case it is considered enacted. (Art. 92) The President of the Republic has a right of veto, which can be overridden by the Grand National Assembly by simply re-enacting the legislation. (Art. 93) The National Assembly has the sole right to initiate motions of no confidence in the government (Art. 89), although the Senate shares in investigations, parliamentary inquiries, questions, and general debate. (Art. 88) A special procedure is provided for consideration of the annual national budget. It goes directly from the executive to a joint committee of both chambers, whose report is considered first by the Senate, whose recommendations are then given final review by the National Assembly. (Art. 94) The cabinet and all deputies and Senators have the right to introduce bills. (Art. 91)

The President of the Republic is elected by the Grand National Assembly in joint session, by two-thirds majority on a secret ballot. If no candidate receives the required two-thirds on the first two ballots, a simple majority suffices thereafter. The President is required to have received "higher education," i.e. be a college graduate or its equivalent. He serves a seven-year term and is not eligible for re-election. On election he must dissociate himself from his party, and his status as a member of the Grand National Assembly is terminated.

The President appoints a Prime Minister, and other ministers on the latter's recommendation. The President may, if he deems it necessary, preside over the Council of Ministers. The government must submit its program to the National Assembly for a vote of confidence within one week after the cabinet is formed. No approval is needed from the Senate.

A beneficial feature of the Constitution is that with the exception of the President and the Prime Minister, ministers may be selected from outside the Grand National Assembly. (Art. 102) Another worthy innovation is the provision that prior to national elections a Provisional Cabinet shall be formed of Grand National Assembly members from all parties in proportion to their representation, and that independent (nonparty) members shall be appointed to the caretaker posts of Justice, Interior, and Communications Ministers. (Art. 109)

Dissolution of the legislature was a controversial subject during the drafting of the first Republican Constitution in 1923-24, and this was one of the areas in which Atatürk lost out, failing in his determined bid to win the right of dissolution for the President. The 1961 Constitution again denies the President this right, and in a provision similar to that in the Constitution of the Fourth French Republic, limits dissolution to a situation in which the government has been unseated twice within eighteen months and thereafter receives a vote of no confidence. (Art. 108)

Some controversy also took place on the issue of the relationship of the armed forces to the government. The Onar Commission provided that the Chief of Staff be tied directly to the President. The Karal proposal and the final version of the Constitution, however, made the Chief of Staff responsible to the Prime Minister, who also received the power to recommend appointees to the President.

In the judicial field, the major change from the 1923-24 Constitution is the addition of the Constitutional Court. Its judicial functions are limited to reviewing the constitutionality of laws and the By-Laws of the Grand National Assembly. As was the case under the earlier Constitution, a Court of Cassation sits for final review of decisions and verdicts of lower courts, and a Council of State serves as an administrative court. The Constitutional Court is composed of fifteen members, of whom four are elected by the Court of Cassation, three by the General Assembly of the Council of State from among its own members, one by the Court of Accounts, three by the National Assembly, two by the Senate of the Republic, and two appointed by the President of the Republic. Members of the Constitutional Court serve until age sixty-five. The court may at any time consider cases involving constitutional questions, but the right of parties, deputies, and government or quasi-government bodies to bring annulment actions directly to the court is limited to a period of ninety days after promulgation of the law. (Art. 149)

Judicial autonomy is strongly underscored. Promotion, transfer, or disciplining of judges is handled by an autonomous Supreme Council of Judges, chosen by the judiciary itself.

The Constitution may be amended by two-thirds vote of each chamber of the legislature, acting separately. No amendment of Article 1, declaring the Turkish State to be a Republic, may be moved or considered.

The Challenge of the New Constitution

In some important respects the Constitution for Turkey's Second Republic is superior to its predecessor of 1924. Few will disagree that significant advances have been made in guaranteeing civil liberties, expanding the commitment of the nation to improve the standard of living of the groups most in need of help, and instituting judicial review. In the area of government organization, the bicameral legislature may prove useful in providing more careful consideration of laws, and be one of a number of checks and balances to prevent a renewed despotism by a majority in whose hands all power is concentrated.

Another aspect of the new Constitution, however, poses what may prove to be a far more important question, of interest not only to Turkey but to other rapidly developing nations as well. This is the question of the efficacy of liberal constitutions for achieving rapid social change. The victory of the political over the legalist school of constitution makers means that it is almost entirely up to the political parties to evolve and implement policies for development, and to take responsibility for the results.

It has been asked whether fragmentation resulting from proportional representation and other devices to assure that Menderes-type domination will not happen again is not the feature that potentially may be most disastrous. The answer to this question is probably negative. In the first place, this was never really an issue. Both the military and virtually all segments of political opinion in Turkey had believed well before the May 27 revolution that such changes were necessary if multiparty democracy was to be preserved. Second, it was the deep division into two political camps that was important in causing the crisis of May 27. To have reorganized the structure of government without attempting to modify this bipolar situation would have left untouched what is probably Turkey's most fundamental political problem. The system developed in the election laws of 1954 and 1957 had in effect forced political groups of all shades of opinion to choose one of two sides. If this had resulted in the development of large parties that integrated various interests and compromised issues within their own structures, a two-party system might have been useful to Turkey. This had not happened, however, and interests and issues were submerged under the all-pervading enmity between the Democratic and the Republican People's parties. The first election held under the new Constitution brought these submerged interests prominently to the surface. Whether fragmentation will produce better differentiation of issues and interest cannot, of course, be predicted after so short a period, but if nothing else, the bipolar deadlock has been broken.

The real question is whether the parties—meaning in this case chiefly the RPP—were wise in taking on themselves virtually all initiative in political, social, and economic development. There can be no doubt that the RPP at least implicitly assumed that it would hold the power in the new Assembly, and from this point of view it is understandable that its members desired maximum freedom from interference with innovations for rapid progress. This misreading of the future has resulted in all responsibility as well as initiative being placed on the party in power, however. A more conservative—or legalistic, in this case—constitution might have shifted much responsibility for failure as well as success to extra-parliamentary bodies such as the High Economic Council proposed in some way both in the Onar and Ankara proposals. Preoccupation with the controls such outside groups might acquire over the freedom of initiative of parties, may conceal the positive contributions these groups, whose orientation is only semipolitical, might make to the process of evolving and implementing development policies. It is, of course, possible that the Turkish parties will in fact involve other groups in these tasks, but the tenor of the Constitution, set against the background of the legalist-political debate which went on during its evolution, does little to encourage the development and strengthening of these groups by giving them the authority and responsibility to make their contribution effective.

The 1961 Constitution presents Turkish political parties with a formidable challenge. Having gained almost complete victory over the legalist school of political thought, and by implication over those radical elements in the army who were ready to restrict the freedom of action of political parties for other reasons, the parties must show that the new Constitution can be a basis for effective solution of the nation's problems. Should the parties fail again, there would be only small chance that the army would grant them another opportunity to lay down the basic structure of the machinery of government. The challenge is all the more formidable because it may be the very safeguards against one-party despotism incorporated into the Constitution which return to plague the parties.

The kind of coalition government that is necessary because of the failure of any single party to win control of the legislature in the October 1961 elections is something with which Turkey has had no experience. Yet it may be the very compromises needed for successful operation of a coalition between proponents of relatively fast modernization and those of slower change that will be the most serious hindrance to devising the bold, far-reaching policies that are Turkey's best hope of accelerated development. The new Constitution will not, as many Turkish intellectuals maintained after the overthrow of the Menderes regime, be an answer to all of Turkey's political problems. For capable leaders, however, it does offer opportunities for rapid development under a system of democratic, multiparty government. The coming test period will be as severe as Turkey has ever faced.

5

New Parties and Old Votes

IN OCTOBER 1961 the Turkish army made good on its promise, given during the first hours of the May 27 revolution and repeated countless times thereafter, that they would turn power back to a civilian government based on free elections. As preparation for the elections, the military junta had encouraged the organization of new political parties to fill the gap left when the Democratic party of fallen premier Adnan Menderes was ordered disbanded. The result was a contest among the old and new parties for between 4 million and 5 million "homeless" voters. These, according to the speculation by numerous impartial observers, might well have voted back into office the Menderes government whose attempts at retaining power illegally had led to its overthrow.

Probably the most surprising aspect of the process of returning government to civilian hands is the amount of freedom the army allowed. During the pre-election period it became more and more clear that many politicians were not disposed to stay voluntarily within the limits of controversy that the National Unity Committee had outlined, and the NUC issued repeated warnings. But in the end the hands-off policy was carried to such an extreme that even the most obviously pro-Menderes candidates were permitted to run and win. A number who had been jailed on suspicion of anti-revolutionary activity had to be released when they were elected deputies. It is this very freedom that may come back to haunt those whose belief in democracy is strongest.

Reorganization of the party system received high priority on the NUC agenda soon after May 27. There was the problem of who would contest with the Republican People's party (RPP) so that the election would be more than a pro forma event to hand the nation to the former opposition. The only other survivor of the Menderes period, the Republican Peasants Nation party (RPNP), was small, ineffective, and very conservative. The Democratic party, despite the fact that the NUC had said the revolution was neither for nor against any group, was obviously in no position to reenter the political arena through the election campaign planned for 1961. And while the NUC and the RPP thought alike on many issues, it was well known that many NUC members were far from enamored with the Republicans.

Perhaps even more important was the fact that it was the development of the party system that had been in large part responsible for the breakdown in the political process which led to the revolution of May 27. Actually neither the Democratic nor the Republican party was exclusively pro-reform or anti-reform, statist or liberal, secularizing or nonsecularizing, but the situation developed in a way that made them symbols of the two extremes on all of these issues. Differences of view on specific topics had been submerged under the blanket of political and personal hostility to the point where few public problems could any longer be rationally approached. Thus when by the end of 1960 several groups had arisen which wanted to compete for votes, they received encouragement from the NUC.

The reorganization of the party system proceeded in several steps. First came a tearing down of the old structure. Party activity had, of course, been immediately suspended, or rather the suspension which had been in force during the last month of the DP period was continued. On July 7, 1960, Law No. 8 of the National Unity Committee abolished all party organizations below the county level, i.e. all village, town, and neighborhood branches.[1] The reason given for this move was that the party struggle had reached such a point that the existence of rival organizations at the local level had led to total enmity, mutual hatred, and frequent violence among the factions in numerous villages and towns. A side effect of the NUC action—possibly not unintentional—was to reduce the chances that the RPP would have the field to itself before other parties could be sufficiently organized to contest the election, which was then envisioned as coming in a matter of weeks.

On September 29 an Ankara court ruled that the Democratic party should be closed, avoiding complications by relying on the technical grounds that the DP had violated the Law of Associations which required all organizations to hold periodic membership meetings. Though the party by-laws called for a national congress every four years, it had been five years since the last such convention. Thus ended a political existence calculated by one newspaper as fifteen years, four months, fifteen days, one hour, and thirty-four minutes.[2]

Thereafter the rebuilding phase began. A November attempt by persons close to the NUC to organize a new party was rebuffed because the junta thought it too early and because it resented the new party's move to parlay its supposedly nonpartisan associations with the junta into political advantage.[3] In January, however, official permission to form new parties was given. Almost immediately maneuvering began among various groups of politicians, negotiations which produced mergers one day and splits the next, until mid-February, the deadline for registering parties for the coming general election. Eleven new parties registered. On February 11 there were: (1) The Republican Professional Reform

[1] *Cumhuriyet*, July 7, 1960, for text of law.
[2] *Cumhuriyet*, Sept. 30, 1960.
[3] This incident is described further below in connection with the New Turkey Party.

party, whose primary interest was reported to be the revival of minting gold coins; (2) the Justice party; (3) the Labor party (Ankara); (4) the Nationalist party; (5) the Turkish Workers' and Farmers' party; and (6) the Moderate Liberal party. These were followed on February 13 by (7) the New Turkey party; (8) the Workers' party (Istanbul), formed by Istanbul labor leaders; (9) the Principle party; (10) the Confidence party; and (11) the Service to the Nation party. Most of the parties were nothing more than a few men who had no real intention of entering politics, but registered before the deadline in case they ever wanted to exploit their "charter."

Only two of these parties developed to contest the election, the Justice party and the New Turkey party joining the RPP and the RPNP, survivors of the Menderes period, in the campaign of 1961.[4] These four parties will be discussed separately below. Organizing went on rather quietly at first, but as the government gradually let political activity expand, politics became once again the overriding national preoccupation. In March permission was given for district and province party congresses, in April for national congresses and limited forms of propaganda, in June for most forms of propaganda except outdoor rallies, and in late September all stops were pulled out in the campaign which climaxed in the election of October 15.

The Republican People's Party

The Republican People's party has, in large part as a result of the coup and of the events culminating in the 1961 election, reached a major turning point in its existence. The RPP has a history of much accomplishment as the instrument of many of the Atatürk reforms, and as the main opposition to the Menderes regime, but for these and other reasons it also has developed opponents to the point where it is without doubt a minority party. In the situation that has developed, the RPP is often pitted against all the other parties, even though these parties have little in common and oppose the RPP for widely varying reasons. In the face of these difficulties the RPP is beset by internal ruptures which threaten to split the party down the middle the moment the strong hand of Ismet Inönü is removed. The troubles of the RPP raise important questions about the future of Turkish politics, as well as about some possible dangers which may beset reformist parties in the course of rapid political change such as is taking place in Turkey.

The early history of the RPP has been described in Chapter 1. The long period of single-party rule between 1923 and 1946, broken only by the short-lived ventures with opposition in 1924-25 and 1930, had left the RPP with some major handicaps when the time came in 1946 to

[4] What few details are available about the other parties are in *Cumhuriyet* and other newspapers for Feb. 12 and 14, 1961.

really compete for votes. First, reform had been far from universally popular in Turkey. Conservatives opposed to secularism, anti-étatist businessmen, and anti-authoritarian liberals all had reason to oppose various RPP policies. Second, twenty-three years of rule had made attractive the political slogan that has been effective in almost every country where one party has ruled for an extended period—"it's time for a change." For this reason alone, many who agreed with the RPP's reform program in almost every respect supported the opposition. Third, the opposition had the advantages of a springboard of attack and of a group which was against leadership that had become entrenched, usually unimaginative, and often enchanted with its own power.

Most foreign observers, as well as many Turks, predicted an RPP defeat if the 1950 election were fair.[5] Few, however, were prepared for the magnitude of the defeat.[6] Many explanations were offered, that it was an accident, a temporary reaction to the deprivations of the World War II period and the beginnings of the Cold War, or, as some RPP stalwarts maintained, a show of blatant ingratitude for what the RPP had done for Turkey, an attitude which would be reversed at the next election after the Turkish people had seen the light. When in 1954, however, the Democratic margin increased to almost 2 million out of about 9 million ballots, certain facts could no longer be ignored. One was that the DP far outran the RPP in organizational achievement. Another was that rapid reform still had far from universal appeal among the Turkish voters. If after 1954 the DP had not alienated virtually the entire Turkish urban educated class through its increasingly repressive policies, it is uncertain how long it might have been before the RPP returned to power. In the 1957 election the DP polled about 750,000 fewer votes than it had in 1954, but an impressively large number of these votes went to the small Nation and Freedom parties, not to the RPP.

During the latter half of the 1950-60 decade the Turkish urban middle class gradually drifted back to the RPP. In part the return to the RPP was a reaction to the antidemocratic tendencies of the Menderes government—to the growing number of steps by the regime that could be called

[5] There has been much interesting speculation about why Inönü allowed a really free election in 1950. Some say that he did not really conceive of the possibility of an RPP defeat, although to judge from his often-demonstrated political sagacity, such an explanation is unlikely to be accurate. Tending to support those who contend that Inönü was sincere is the report of several witnesses that in a private interview with an American Senator shortly before the 1950 election, Inönü asserted that "I have been a General, Foreign Minister, Prime Minister and President. All that remains is to be leader of the Opposition."

[6] The RPP polled about 3,195,000 votes, or 40 percent of the ballots compared to the Democrats' 4,275,000 or 53 percent, but the real magnitude of the defeat is seen in the fact that in only 11 of Turkey's 67 provinces was the RPP able to poll a majority, and received only 67 of 487 seats in the Assembly. In 1954 the RPP retained only Kars, Malatya, and Sinop, and added Tunceli—their representation was reduced to 21 seats.

concessions which undermined the revolution, especially in the matter of religion. Many young people rallied back to the RPP because they were the product of the party's education program, which put great emphasis on continuing rapid social reform. Groups that did not particularly like the RPP joined it merely because it was the only alternative to the Democrats, whom they liked even less. The move of many businessmen to the Freedom party in 1957 should have alerted the RPP to the fact of this negative attraction. Probably the most important fact about the 1954-60 period, however, is that the RPP failed to make significant gains among the Turkish peasants. The 1960 revolution was the work of the urban intelligentsia alone, and as mentioned earlier, many impartial observers were of the opinion in the spring of 1960 that had Menderes held an election at that time, his chances of victory on the basis of the peasant vote would have been excellent.

It is against this background that the RPP's actions during the military government period and its performance in the 1961 election should be considered. By virtue of its having borne the brunt of the repression which preceded May 27, the RPP was understandably one of the chief heroes of the day. Though political activity was officially suspended, RPP leaders played a large role in the post-revolution reorganization of public affairs. Inönü was careful to avoid statements which would tarnish the image of the revolution, which the NUC worked to maintain, of "not for anyone, not against anyone, but only to bring back democracy." He was consulted on several occasions by General Gürsel, as the latter sought experienced advice on the many matters that were completely foreign to his experience as a soldier. Other RPP members performed central tasks, for example, Turhan Feyzioğlu chaired the committee which drafted the statute for the Constituent Assembly. Indeed, given the fact that the Menderes regime had driven almost all intellectuals into the opposition, frequent NUC reliance on RPP experts could hardly have been avoided.

There was also a good deal of parallel, intentional or not, between the actions of the NUC and the demands the RPP had made during the Menderes period. The NUC released political prisoners, mainly journalists and students; repealed the laws infringing freedom of the press; opened the state radio to equal use by all political parties; and took many other actions aimed at restoring democracy. It was easy to assume that the RPP would form the civilian government to take over when the army kept its pledge to return to the barracks.

If civilian rule had come fairly quickly, this assumption would in all probability have been correct. The extensive organizational network of the ousted DP still existed below the national level, but it was headless and faced with the hostility of the intellectuals and the army, certainly no longer a match for the RPP. Using the momentum of May 27, therefore, the RPP did all it could to assure elections as soon as possible.

But as the situation developed, the NUC began to have other ideas. First, it became apparent that the pre-election actions, a constitution, election law, the Yassıada trials, would take much longer than had at first been envisioned. Second, civilian elements began to emerge which were not sympathetic to turning power over to the RPP without a murmur. These elements included much of the business community which was hostile to étatism, political rivals of the RPP such as the men involved in the abortive November attempt to form a new party, and conservatives like the Republican Peasants' Nation party. Several members of the NUC seem also to have been less than enamored with the Republicans. Thus the curious appearance in *Cumhuriyet* on July 6, 1960, of two lead stories, each with large headlines: Inönü saying elections should be at the earliest possible moment; General Gürsel asserting that elections would be held in due course when they were appropriate.

As the months passed, the RPP more and more dominated the civilian end of political activity, and their skill and experience in politics began to tell in relation to that of the relatively green soldier-rulers. In consequence, general public feeling increasingly attributed to the RPP responsibility for the actions of the military regime. And as the popularity of that regime declined considerably between its coming and its going, the standing of the RPP also declined.

In some cases, of course, events themselves worked to identify the activities of the NUC with the cause of the RPP. The Yassıada trials, for instance, often focused on actions of the Menderes regime and the Democratic party that had been directed at the RPP (such as the Investigating Committee), its leaders (the attacks on Inönü in the Topkapı and Kayseri incidents), or its sympathizers (as in the Democrat Izmir case). In other instances, however, the RPP itself was mainly responsible for the close identification. The best example of the latter is the Constituent Assembly, created by the NUC in January 1961 to enact a new constitution and an election law, as well as passing the national budget and other laws, and generally assisting in getting popular national understanding (and hopefully approval) of actions of the NUC. Convened with much fanfare and coinciding with the opening of the new Parliament Building (which had finally, to use the phrase of one American diplomat, been "rushed to partial completion" after about twenty-five years of planning and construction), the Assembly quickly became a major focus of public attention.

The Constituent Assembly was corporate in its composition. Its membership included representatives of the judiciary, press, universities, youth, labor, agriculture, and other organizations, as well as provinces and political parties.[7] In the allotments for political parties the RPP received forty-nine and the Nation party twenty-one, all selected by the

[7] For a description of the composition of the Constituent Assembly see Robert Devereux, "Turkey and the Corporative State," *SAIS Review* (Spring 1962), pp. 16-24.

central Executive Committee of each party. The RPP delegation was led by Inönü himself, who had said earlier that he would not enter the Assembly, but had been persuaded to change his mind after the Nation party leader Osman Bölükbaşı had reversed his own stated intent and headed the Nation party contingent in the Assembly. In addition to this contingent, the RPP put up candidates in almost all the province selection committees, and lawyers, teachers, and others who were RPP members stood for election in their respective private organizations. The result was that over 200 of the almost 265 members of the Assembly were members of the RPP, including virtually every important party figure.

The Constituent Assembly completed the Constitution and Election Law on May 27, the anniversary of the revolution.[8] On July 9, the Constitution was submitted to a national referendum, which approved the new charter by a margin of 6,347,588 to 3,934,637. The importance of the referendum had little to do with the Constitution, however. On the contrary, it was widely regarded as an expression of the public attitude toward the NUC and toward the whole idea of May 27. The referendum was preceded by a campaign conducted by the parties and the NUC itself to get out a huge "yes" vote as a sign of confidence in Turkey's Second Republic. The RPP, of course, put its entire organization behind the "yes" drive. The New Turkey party did likewise, and the Republican Peasants Nation party generally went along as well. But a newcomer to the political scene, the Justice party, took a different line. The party, which under retired General Gümüşpala was to go on to become the second-largest party in the new Assembly, told its supporters that while it could not advise a vote "no," it could at the same time not advise a vote "yes." Certain technical flaws in the Constitution were cited as the reason for this position. The Justice party, as will be discussed shortly, was having great success in making itself the heir to the fallen Democrats, and its implied message for the referendum came through loud and clear. The vote on the referendum is shown in the following table.[9]

Total eligible voters	12,473,693
Total votes cast	10,282,225
"Yes" votes	6,347,588
"No" votes	3,934,637
Percentage participation	*82.4*
Percentage "yes" of votes cast	*61.7*
Percentage "no" of votes cast	*38.3*
Percentage "yes" of eligible voters	*50.9*

[8] The evolution of the Constitution is discussed in Chap. 4 above. The Constituent Assembly is considered in more detail in Chap. 6.

[9] From official figures as reported in newspapers. Final verification of results in isolated areas caused slight changes in later figures, but did not significantly affect them.

The results of the referendum were hailed by the NUC, but few either in the junta or the RPP took pains to hide their disappointment and concern. More important than the overall totals was the distribution of the "no" votes. Eleven of sixty-seven provinces rejected the Constitution. Eight of these had been among the provinces that led in supporting the Democratic party in 1957.[10] One analyst concluded the following from the tabulations:

> . . . In other words, [the analysis] indicated a very strong, positive association between "no" voting in the constitutional referendum and DP voting in the 1957 general election. There may be many suggestions of tobacco failures, unpopular forest provisions in the constitution, confusing propaganda, and so on, but the statistical fact remains that most of the vote cast against the constitution can be accounted for simply on the basis of the assumption that DP supporters in 1957 would vote against it.[11]

Despite this clear warning, the RPP still came to the election in October with full confidence that it would win a majority. Instead, as will be detailed below, the election was a significant RPP defeat. The poor showing of the party in the 1961 election can be attributed to several factors. Of relatively immediate origin were the identification with the acts of the military regime, and the fact that even after his overthrow, Menderes retained a great popular following, which would in no circumstances vote for the RPP. There are two factors of a more fundamental nature, however: the difficulties of simultaneous rapid reform and free multiparty government; and the internal situation of the RPP itself. The difficulties of modernization through free elections in Turkey will be discussed in the concluding remarks of this study. Suffice it to say here that the often-voiced claim of Turkish leaders that the people, if only given proper leadership, will understand the situation and make sacrifices voluntarily, has never been borne out in Turkey. The fact is that when given the free ballot, the Turkish nation has not at any time in the past voted for the representatives of rapid reform, and there are convincing reasons for believing that such an eventuality is equally unlikely today.

The RPP is also plagued with serious internal problems. While making

[10] The provinces rejecting the Constitution, in order of size of "no" vote and the rank in supporting DP in 1957, were:

Kütahya	12	Sakarya	4
Samsun	31	Bursa	5
Manisa	6	Çorum	39
Aydın	3	Denizli	19
Bolu	11	Izmir	10
Zonguldak	13		

[11] Frederick W. Frey, "Notes on the Turkish Constitutional Referendum of 9 July 1961," p. 5 (mimeo.) .

reform palatable to the Turkish peasants may require long-range solutions, this is not the case with the internal problem. The core of the problem is rivalry for personal influence fully as much as disagreement over matters of party policy and organization. During its entire history the RPP has been firmly controlled by first, Atatürk, then Inönü, which is to say that in the last analysis the party has remained in the hands of the heroes of the War of Independence and the rapid reformers of the period before World War II. Atatürk, of course, was never challenged as RPP leader, and only one man, Recep Peker, ever came within hailing distance of Inönü. Peker was ousted as Prime Minister in 1947 in his struggle with Inönü, who was then President, over whether to continue giving full scope to activity by opposition parties. He never made a come-back and died in 1950.

The victory over Peker gave Inönü firm control over the party once again. But as the veteran leader advanced in age, and when the 1950 defeat shook the foundations of the RPP, the issue of an eventual successor assumed first importance. In the years since the party went into opposition, the issue gradually crystallized into a split centering on the 1950-59 Secretary-General of the RPP, Kasım Gülek. Gülek became Secretary-General at the eighth RPP Congress in 1950 following the election defeat. He resigned in September 1959, in the midst of controversies over some of his actions. The party has usually managed to keep the dispute from full public view, though few leaders bothered to hide the fact that they were increasingly resentful of the personal following which Gülek was able to win within the party and among voters on the basis of his attractive personality and aggressive campaign activity. It became more and more difficult for the party to present a united front, and in the fifteenth RPP Congress in August 1961 the clash was aired in the most public and bitterly hostile way. Gülek attempted to by-pass Inönü by getting the Congress to name him Secretary-General rather than re-electing Inönü's candidate, incumbent Ismail Rüştü Aksal. It was only with the personal intercession of Inönü that Gülek's bid fell short.

The problem is deeper than personalities, however. Gülek's main criticism of his own party, that it has failed to do what is most important in winning an election, namely to interest itself in something outside of city life, has much validity. Few RPP leaders have either roots in or close relationships to the countryside or town. Even the most promising RPP leaders are vulnerable to charges that they have little knowledge of what the Turkish peasant is like. The observation by villages that it is only at election time that they ever see politicians—of any party—is still frequently heard in Turkey. The chief exception was during 1946-50 when the DP victory came largely on the strength of vigorous work in the rural areas. Many young members of the RPP agree with Gülek, and there are many observers who think that even if Inönü were to name his own successor before retiring,[12] Gülek would soon win the top spot, or pull out of the party and take a large following with him. Almost all agree that the only reason the party has not split before this is that Inönü has held it together, and that the struggle after his departure may be to the death.

Gülek has some good qualifications. A wealthy farmer and economist, he was educated at Robert College in Istanbul, the Ecole de Sciences Politiques in Paris, and at Columbia, Cambridge, London, Berlin, and Hamburg Universities. He entered the Grand National Assembly in 1940, was elected to the RPP Executive Committee in 1942, was a delegate to the International Labour Conference of 1944, Minister of Public Works in 1947 and of Communications in 1948, and a delegate to the Council of Europe in 1949, 1950, and 1951. He was defeated in the election of 1950, but was re-elected to the Assembly in 1957 and 1961. His work as RPP Secretary-General between 1950 and 1959 is considered good. He has also dabbled in journalism, and since 1961 has published his own newspaper, *Tanin,* in Ankara in at least indirect competition with the RPP's official organ *Ulus.*

At least four others are potentially future RPP chairmen, however. High on the list is former professor of international law Nihat Erim. Educated at Istanbul and Paris Universities and at the Institute des Hautes Etudes Internationales in Paris, he entered the Assembly in a 1945 by-election running as an independent, an unusual thing in Turkey. His role in the dispute between Recep Peker and the "35" liberal RPP deputies over allowing multiparty activity after 1946 brought him to the attention of Inönü, and he was at various times Minister of State and Deputy Prime Minister. He was also editor of *Ulus* until its confiscation in 1953. In the early years of the Menderes regime he was outspoken against the government, but alienated many RPP regulars by his independence, as when he competed with Kasim Gülek's new RPP organ *Yeni Ulus* (New Ulus) and published his own daily *Halkçı.* In 1954 he seems to have made peace with Menderes, which led to an unsuccessful RPP attempt to expel him from the party in 1955. In 1959 he was a delegate to the Constitutional Preparatory Commission for Cyprus. Erim is intelligent and enterprising, but may be handicapped because his recent record has led many within the RPP to distrust him.

Turhan Feyzioğlu is also expected to contest strongly for the post of RPP leader. His political star has risen with meteoric rapidity since 1956 when, as Dean of the Ankara University Faculty of Political Sciences, he strongly criticized the Menderes government incursions into academic freedom.[13] Suspended from his position, he went into politics and was elected RPP deputy from Sivas in 1957. His name was frequently

[12] At the age of eighty this is not unlikely, though Inönü likes to point out to doubters of his stamina that his mother lived well past 95.

[13] See Chap. 3 on academic freedom and problems of higher education.

in the news during the rest of the Menderes period. After the revolution he became Rector of the Middle East Technical University, chairman of the commission to draft the statute organizing the Constituent Assembly, and Minister of Education for a brief period in 1961. He received the post of Minister of State in the first coalition government following the 1961 election, and became one of three Deputy Prime Ministers in the second coalition in the spring of 1962. Probably his chief handicaps are the reputation he has acquired as Inönü's "fair-haired boy" and the opinion of many Turks that he is too ambitious. But he is able and intelligent and has acquired much experience in both domestic and foreign affairs.

A fourth person to watch in the RPP leadership race is the recent Secretary-General, Ismail Rüştü Aksal. A close colleague of Inönü, Aksal has administered the party competently through its most difficult crisis, though many people doubt that he has the personal dynamism necessary to fill a post as political as that of party leader and potential prime minister. Among his assets in a leadership contest is the fact that he is older than most other aspirants and would less likely alienate the many politicians who would resent being out-ranked by a young man like Feyzioğlu. Recent ill health which forced Aksal to relinquish the Secretary-General post may eliminate him permanently, however.

Finally, it would be well to keep an eye on a young deputy and journalist named Bülent Ecevit. Only 37 years old, Ecevit is one of the most popular personalities on the entire Turkish political scene. Educated at Robert College and Ankara University, he spent four years in England in the office of the Turkish Press Attache. Since 1950 he has worked for the RPP newspaper *Ulus,* and for its replacement during the period of suspension. He was elected to the Assembly in 1957 and by 1960 had become one of its best-known members, as well as having acquired his own front-page daily column in *Ulus.* In 1961 he was put on the RPP Executive Committee. Following the 1961 election he became Minister of Labor in both the first and second coalition governments, one of the most sensitive cabinet posts, as labor began to emerge as a political force, and as problems of wages and unemployment became severe as a result of the economic upsets surrounding the May 27 revolution. If Ecevit handles the Labor Ministry well—and there is every sign that he will—he is sure to be a key RPP leader for many years to come, though his youth may well keep him from the top job in the immediate future.

That these men, able as they may be, are not really politically exciting, is not necessarily reason to conclude that the RPP has failed to build new leadership. Only rarely has a leader of overwhelming stature groomed his own successor, especially in the context of transferring from first to second generation revolutionary leadership. On at least one previous occasion, the RPP showed that it can produce new leadership—the DP leaders, who did, after all, run the nation for a decade; and though they may have been poor statesmen, nobody can accuse Menderes and his followers of having been poor politicians. What is often forgotten, not least by the RPP itself, is that it is by no means axiomatic that continuation of the revolution requires the guidance of national affairs by the RPP. Indeed it is not inconceivable that the replacement of the RPP by one or more new parties may even enhance the prospects of modernization, for to many peasant voters the very name of the party so closely identified with rapid and drastic reform is anathema. It can also be argued that the gradual division of the nation into two polarized political camps, a polarization which has grown steadily more pronounced since 1946 and which continues today in a less extreme form, is largely responsible for the seeming inability of the Turkish political system to transcend the single issue of reform versus nonreform.

This is not to say that the RPP has not been responsible for, or while in opposition advocated, many programs of public works and social improvements in rural areas. Probably the party's chief failure, however, a failure possibly going back to the very beginning of the Republic, is that it has not adapted larger reform policies to local situations or considered the personal dimension which must be taken into account if modernization for the peasants, the individuals who will in the long run be most affected, is to be something more than a disruptive process. Politics in Turkey is today on a firmly competitive basis. The critics, Gülek prominent among them, point out that the RPP must stop acting as if the voters had a duty to put it in power, but must live up to the name, People's party. The RPP has once before, in 1946, split on this sort of issue, and it may well be that another split would again benefit the cause of modernization. There is a great concern among many RPP members today about these matters. The calibre of leadership built by Atatürk's party in its forty-year history is sure to be tested in the near future when both the need and opportunity for revamping will test the party's entire body.

The Justice Party

Many were dismayed but few were surprised at the strong showing made in the 1961 election by the Justice party. In program, personnel, and appeal, the Justice party is as close a successor to the Democratic party as it is possible to be. From the beginning of its existence the Justice party had difficulties with the NUC, and the latter several times charged that the JP was anti-revolutionary. As mentioned above, several victorious candidates on the JP ticket were in jail when the results were announced and had to be released in order to take up their offices.

The Justice party was formed in February 1961, by retired General Ragıp Gümüşpala. A novice in politics, Gümüşpala was Commander of the 3rd Army in Erzurum prior to May 27, was Chief of the General Staff for a short period after the revolution, but was among the 5,000 officers retired in August as part of the "rejuvenation" of the armed forces by the NUC. He was the highest ranking officer to be so retired. Rumors circulated in Ankara during the period immediately after May 27 that the 3rd Army had been considered by the conspirators as one of the most likely sources of potential resistance, and that only as they became satisfied that Gümüşpala would not actively oppose them did they go ahead with the ouster of Menderes.

Almost immediately the Justice party began to take on the appearance of a successor to the DP.[14] Various statements by Gümüşpala indicated at best a lukewarm attitude toward the military government and a distinctly conservative bent. On March 5 he asserted that there was much good in the DP despite everything (a sentiment with which many impartial observers agreed, but which was easily interpreted in the circumstances as a slap at the NUC), and that use of the words "tail-end" (Kuyruk) and "fallen" (düşük) in describing the former regime was "regrettable."[15] More indicative was the JP's position on the Constitution referendum. Noting many flaws from the administrative viewpoint, the official party position was "Vote Yes," but party officials most of the time said they could not really advise either a yes or no vote. The main objection seemed to be the mention of political parties in a "national document."[16]

The JP's program as issued for the 1961 election is conservative in several important respects and in others ambitious to the point of being completely unrealistic. "It is our aim to tax only earnings and those who receive earnings," says Article 9 of the JP's Election Manifesto. It favors exemption from taxes for those whose income stems from real estate or from assets whose value is fixed. It declares its intention to abolish taxes on agricultural produce, on farm animals, and on wealth, and to revise downward income and profits taxes. The party also favors the compulsory purchase of savings bonds by all employees on the government payroll and in private enterprise which was instituted by the NUC. It deplores what it calls a mentality of making the public purse the most important consideration in public policy.[17]

In administration, the program proposes transfer of as many functions as possible to the control of local authorities and the gradual creation

[14] It should in all fairness be pointed out that many newspapers took special pains to emphasize the connections between the JP and the DP, making it appear more sinister than it was at first. Later the evidence of DP connections was much more reliable and varied. The JP frequently charged that the press was biased against it, a charge which was undoubtedly true.

[15] *Oncü*, March 6, 1961.

[16] *Cumhuriyet*, June 27, 1961.

[17] *Adalet Partisi Seçim Beyannamesi* (Istanbul, 1961), pp. 6-7. Cited hereafter as Manifesto.

of strong local administrative units. This would be accomplished by step-by-step integration of heretofore "independent" village and rural governments into county units, which would then be able to make use of important sources of revenue that the JP would take from the central government and give to local authorities. In this way "the political equilibrium which is necessary for democracy will be assured," the Manifesto (p. 28) states, noting that in Western nations local budgets total several times the national budget.

Many of the state monopolies would be transferred to private industry, an aim which the DP and other parties have long subscribed to, but which the Menderes government failed to carry out. Other areas in which adjustments would be made include reducing taxes and prices on gasoline, kerosene, oil, auto licenses, and traffic imposts, fares on state transportation lines (which include all railroads, shipping lines, and air lines in Turkey), lowering rates of postage, telephone, and telegraph, as well as the prices of goods produced by state monopolies.

Large programs of development are based on great needs which are cited in roads, harbors, airports, irrigation, and housing for the large number of people who have recently moved to cities and live in "overnight shacks."[18] The party also promises "to build indoor and outdoor sports arenas in every part of the nation," and to organize a "Sport Bank" to enable sport clubs to develop. Subscribing, as do all other parties, to the need for rapid industrialization, the JP would put primary emphasis on private industry. "We do not reject the need for using state resources to solve economic problems, but we prefer the principle that the state does not do, but causes to be done. That is, the state shows private enterprise the way, and assigns national duties to private concerns, even to the extent that it is in Germany [with Krupp, Bayer, etc.]."[19] The party favors abolition of import controls and import quotas at the earliest opportunity, and adds that "we do not accept state planning of private enterprise in industrialization, only that the state support it."[20]

Two important social fields in which the party program makes pronouncements are health and education. In health affairs, the party "accepts the idea that, as in other civilized Western nations, our problems can be solved by socialized medicine," though this must be done in such a way that the development of private medical services will not be harmed.[21] Health insurance has not been satisfactory to date, the party

[18] The "gecekondu problem" is similar to that plaguing municipal authorities in most developing nations. Migration to cities is rapid, and the only housing is wood, stone, tar-paper shacks built literally overnight. In Turkey it became a political issue in that the Menderes government wooed these slum dwellers with the promise of ex post facto building permits, and it is now difficult for municipal authorities to do anything other than this, for fear of political repercussions.

[19] Manifesto, p. 11.

[20] *Ibid.*, p. 9.

[21] *Ibid.*, p. 24.

maintains, and health services receive only 4.5 percent of the Turkish budget, as contrasted to 15 percent in "some Western nations" (presumably Great Britain and the Scandinavian countries). The most important principle, however, is the maintenance of the right of patients to choose their own doctors. What is probably Turkey's most pressing problem in the health field—the provision of services to areas outside the cities and rich rural areas—is to be handled by various schemes of financial incentives for doctors and nurses who voluntarily move to such areas. The last-named idea is highly unlikely to work.

Education is to be greatly expanded as well. The distinctive parts of the JP's program in education are the changes in philosophy which are urged. One provision in the Manifesto states that "we will prevent the filling of the heads of Turkish children with all sorts of useless and needless knowledge." The present examination and grading system "which causes the loss of many capable students" will be revised, and increased powers given to school authorities to correct such inequities. Changes must be made to discourage the continued implantation in young minds of "the chief system and clique and single-party mentality." The possibility of education according to individual aptitudes is to be provided "already at age 12," apparently meaning a lowering of the period of compulsory general education. The party also urges the opening of new university-level schools in various parts of the nation to serve local needs.[22]

In operation, both before and after the 1961 election, probably the most outstanding characteristic of the Justice party was the lack of coordination among its own speakers and candidates. At the center, Gümüşpala seems to have spent more time in personal feuds with leaders of other parties—chiefly the Nation party's Osman Bölükbaşı—than in discussing his own program. One gets the impression that he thought the program was not particularly important. On lower levels the party took on a definite tinge of successors to the DP. A typical case was that of JP vice-chairman Mehmet Yorgancioğlu, who was arrested in Izmir in March for asserting that the JP is in fact a "continuation" of the DP.[23]

General Gürsel spoke out several times against the way the JP was waging its election campaign, and in July he sent a letter to Gümüşpala in the strongest possible terms. He noted that there could be no other conclusion about the JP's stand on the Constitution referendum than that they had urged a "no" vote, saying "If you say 'yes' to the Constitution, they will hang Menderes." "In effect it is impossible for a party organized in the way yours is to take any other position," Gürsel asserted, "because all its executive committees and those acting on the party's orders are made up of former Democratic Party elements." Gürsel pointed out that in several statements, and in two private talks with

[22] *Ibid.*, pp. 22-23.
[23] *Vatan,* March 16, 1961.

Gümüşpala, he had "tried to awaken" the JP leader, but had apparently not succeeded. "If there is no basic cleaning-out of your party, if it does not turn back from the road which the whole nation recognizes as evil, and turn to honorable ends which the democratic system demands, it will not even be possible for me to recognize you as a legitimate political party."[24]

What clean-up there was was apparently just enough to keep out of the direct way of the NUC, for the JP's representatives in the Grand National Assembly include some individuals about whose attachment to the DP there can be little doubt. The three most outstanding of this character are Burhan Apaydın (deputy from Ankara), who was defense lawyer for Menderes at Yassıada; Melahat Gedik (deputy from Aydın), widow of long-time DP Interior Minister Namik Gedik, one of the most fanatic and hated Democrats, who committed suicide shortly after he was arrested following the May 27 coup; and Neriman Ağaoğlu (deputy from Manisa), wife of Samet Ağaoğlu, formerly a leading DP deputy against whom numerous political and corruption charges were aired at Yassıada while others were pending before regular courts. The connection with the DP is also clear from the presence on the JP Executive Committee of men like Fethi Tevetoğlu (Senator from Samsun), former Samsun Province DP Chairman. At the outset, Gümüşpala also had the strong support of the 5,000 retired officers who looked to him to get their jobs back, but the officers became less important an element as other groups consolidated within the JP.

Few people were surprised when the JP became the second-largest party in the Assembly and the largest in the Senate. When it was the Justice party that formed a coalition government with the RPP, however, there were none who believed that anything other than irresistible pressure from the armed forces had brought the two most bitter opponents together. The coalition had two important results for the JP. The positive advantage was that it was able to have a considerable voice in public policy, and keep a closer check on the RPP. The negative effect was probably more important in terms of the party's future, however, for it did not take long to expose the flimsy basis on which the party was built.

As soon as other matters than continuation of the RPP-DP feud arose, the party literally broke into numerous pieces. When it became necessary to consider social and economic problems, the party was never able to arrive at a unified position. Even the crucial issue of amnesty for the Yassıada defendants, an issue which overshadowed everything else for the first several months after the election, soon became a disruptive rather than a unifying factor for the JP. Amnesty had in effect been made into a *sine qua non* by the JP for cooperation on all other issues. The armed forces, however, refused to let the subject be considered. A part of the JP parliamentary group recognized the impossible position they were

[24] Text *Ulus,* July 26, 1961.

in, but the extremists, who make up a large part of that group, remained adamant. By the end of the first six months after the election the JP had several times been swept by a wave of resignations among its deputies and senators, who together with moderates from the NTP and the RPNP formed an independent group. When the JP Executive Committee accepted in May several conditions put forward by the government to attempt to reach a compromise on the amnesty issue, a meeting of province JP leaders and JP Assembly members was called at which extremists succeeded in ousting the moderates from party leadership.

On this basis, the JP did not participate in the second coalition government formed in June 1962 from among the RPP, NTP, RPNP, and the independent group. The JP in the Assembly has become little more than a conglomerate of individuals, without effective party discipline. The agreement between the parties—and tacitly with the armed forces—to effect a phased amnesty in October has taken away the JP's chief issue. The party is built on local organizations of considerable size and experience, most of which it inherited from the DP, but it is uncertain how effective this base can be in the absence of united leadership in Ankara. Whether a party built on such a flimsy ideological basis can long exist will be shown before many more months have passed.

The New Turkey Party

The New Turkey party (NTP) finished last in the popular vote in the 1961 election, but third in terms of number of deputies and senators. It is a combination of economic liberals, some former Democrats, and opponents of the RPP for a variety of political and ideological reasons. In many ways it is the outgrowth of the Freedom party of 1957, which had failed to cut into the support of either large party in the election of that year, seating only four deputies on less than 4 percent of the votes. In the election campaign of 1961, the chief aim of the New Turkey party seems to have been to counter the idea current at least among the urban educated class, that the RPP was the only progressive party.

The leaders of the New Turkey party were not for the most part professional politicians. The most outstanding figure is its leader, Ekrem Alican. Alican has had considerable political experience, in the Democratic party as deputy from Kocaeli from 1954 until he was expelled in 1955, then as an unsuccessful candidate of the Freedom party. He served as Finance Minister in the nonparty civilian cabinet of the NUC until December 1960. Thereafter he devoted himself entirely to preparing to launch into party politics.

What in February 1961 became the New Turkey party was first heard from three months before that time when, although party activity was still banned, a trial balloon was sent up by a group composed chiefly of several former members of the Freedom party. They sought to take advantage of the close personal association some of them had with several members of the NUC and the civilian nonpartisan cabinet. The chief members of the group were Ekrem Alican, then Finance Minister; Hikmet Belbez, Ankara lawyer and professor; and Aydın Yalçın, former professor of economics on the Political Science Faculty of Ankara University. Yalçın was also the editor of the newspaper, *Oncü,* which had been founded soon after the May 27 revolution and was the chief counter-voice to the RPP's *Ulus.*

There is no doubt Yalçın and his colleagues had the ear of the NUC at the time. Many members of the junta were more or less openly looking for somebody to undertake to contest what was beginning to look more and more like an RPP landslide by default in any forthcoming election. Those who sent up the trial balloon, on the other hand, felt that the NUC would throw its support to them because of the junta's confidence in the fact that the new party would plainly support the ideas of May 27. The potential party leaders' misreading of the situation quickly became apparent, however. It was the first in a series of political blunders that cost them dearly in the respect and confidence of the NUC, the armed forces, and much of the urban educated class.

The newspapers of November 27 carried stories of the formation of a new party by a group of Ankara journalists, professors, businessmen, and former deputies, and broad hints that ministers and NUC members were also involved. But after a series of party meetings attended by at least six cabinet ministers, the NUC made it clear that when it said party activity was suspended, it meant just that. The potential third party was not nearly as close to the NUC as many people had imagined. This was seen shortly afterwards, when *Oncü* was closed for printing an article about some leaflets disapproving of the NUC, which were distributed in Ankara. The article expressly violated an NUC order that such news was not to be printed. The suspension was followed by other brushes with the committee, and a second suspension of the newspaper occurred in March over the misinterpretation in an allegedly harmful way of what General Gürsel had told to a group of visiting foreign journalists.

The NTP program reflects the party's primary interest, economic development through liberalist means. Alican in fact characterized his party's position as "not advanced étatism, but advanced liberalism."[25] More than anything else the NTP is opposed to the étatism of the RPP, although it has no difficulty in carrying over its opposition from economics to RPP personalities and political doctrines. The party states in its program that all wealth and income differences except those based on differences in individuals' work and service are injurious to social harmony and equilibrium, and demolish the moral confidence of citizens in each other. Modernization and westernization, it goes on to say, are

[25] *Oncü,* Jan. 27, 1961.

not only matters of form, "but will become possible only with basic changes in spirit and content." The party's understanding of étatism is that: "The state assures to individual initiative and enterprise whatever aid and support will enable it to work more productively toward economic development." State planning, according to the NTP, should coordinate economic activity, but must not become a means for tight control of all enterprise by the central administration. The NTP also advocates maximum use of foreign capital, and, as rapidly as possible, removal of obstacles to free trade. In order to prevent the development of monopolies, it urges that measures be taken to assure that state and private enterprise, when they work in the same field, be subjected to the same standards.

In other fields the NTP generally parallels the lines of the basic political doctrines of the Atatürk revolution and of the political forms evolved in the military government period. Secularism is strongly subscribed to, and there is support for a two-house legislature, for proportional representation in national elections, advocacy of the right to strike, etc. The two proposals which are original in these areas are that labor committees including workers' representatives be formed for each state economic enterprise, and that compulsory education be extended to include both primary and middle school (through about the ninth grade).

The campaign which the NTP waged was primarily directed against the RPP, as Alican often emphasized. Opposing the RPP on economic grounds while supporting the political aims of May 27 was potentially a potent combination, in the sense that it might pick up former DP votes, while at the same time getting the sympathy of many members of the urban middle class who were having at least two "progressive" parties in the running. The party did succeed in picking up over a million votes from new voters and former DP partisans. But for a number of reasons the New Turkey party has largely forfeited the possibility of picking up support from elements of the RPP which were attached to the latter only because it was long believed to hold greatest promise for forward-looking political groups.

An important reason for both these developments was the rather extraordinary antipathy of some members of the NTP to the person of Ismet Inönü. This had been demonstrated several years earlier when some former Freedom party members chose to withdraw from politics rather than join the RPP in a solid opposition front to the DP. After the 1961 election had produced the need for a coalition government, this hostility was again demonstrated in the absolute refusal of the NTP to join in a government in which the RPP participated unless it received assurances that Inönü would never head it. The fact that the NTP joined the second coalition in June 1962 even with Inönü at its head is a sign that a more rational evaluation of the party's interests has prevailed, at least for the time being.

A second important reason for the NTP's failure to take better advantage of its situation was the political ineptness of much of the party's work in the pre-election period. Three specific incidents can be cited as illustration. The first occurred on August 30, when the new Ankara daily, *Oncü,* the organ of the NTP, printed large headlines to the effect that General Gürsel would be the NTP's candidate for President. What had been meant, of course, was that the party would support Gürsel when the Assembly chose a President after the election. Putting it the way *Oncü* did, however, harmed the image which General Gürsel had tried to create of himself as being above parties and willing to run as a nonparty candidate in case he felt this to be in the national interest. The following day Gürsel strongly denied that he was identifying himself with the NTP or any other party and was clear in showing his displeasure.

A second incident was more potentially explosive. Coming, like the first incident, on August 30, a press conference was called to announce the adherence to the NTP of Yüksel Menderes, oldest son of the former Prime Minister. Recruiting former members of the DP was a regular practice of almost all the parties, but in the last days of the Yassıada trials, this NTP move was too much. The Menderes name might have picked up some votes, although in the face of the great Justice party strength in the Aegean region, it is doubtful that the attractiveness of the New Turkey party on this ground would have been sufficiently increased to outweigh negative factors in linking the former Premier's son with the NTP. In any case, young Menderes withdrew from candidacy shortly after his father had been hanged, stating that his father, in a last letter, had asked him to stay out of politics.

The third incident which attracted much public attention was the arrest and conviction for anti-NUC propaganda of the young professor-politician-journalist Aydın Yalçın. An ardent opponent of both the DP and the RPP, Yalçın had joined the Freedom party in 1957 following a clash with the Menderes government over the latter's refusal to promote Yalçın to the rank of professor. After the rout of the 1957 elections Yalçın went to the United States and spent two years teaching economics at Columbia University, returning to Turkey shortly after May 27. Soon after his return he became lead columnist of *Oncü,* of which his wife later became owner. Yalçın returned to his Ankara university post, with his promotion, and also became active in politics.

During the period between the autumn of 1960 and the election of 1961 *Oncü* increasingly clashed with the NUC. The most surprising aspect of these clashes was that during the early part of this period the members of the future NTP, and Yalçın himself in particular, had the ear of General Gürsel in the most complete fashion. One must conclude that it was chiefly ineptness on the part of the NTP which brought about the eventual alienation from the members of the junta.

The first clash, mentioned above, was the abortive November attempt to establish a new party, which was brusquely halted by the NUC. Shortly afterward there were two more incidents: in December *Oncü* printed a scathing indictment of the "backward" ceremony of whirling Mevlana Dervishes in Konya, the same day that a large group of NUC and cabinet members occupied front row seats for the performance. This took place only one day after martial law authorities had lifted the suspension of *Oncü* for printing the leaflets disapproving of the NUC, a subject specifically banned from discussion by the government. In March came a further incident, when an *Oncü* report of a statement by General Gürsel to foreign journalists about the retirement of army officers and the dismissal of the 147 professors made it appear that the NUC leader looked on these actions as "purifications," rather than the "rejuvenation" that had always been the official version, at least in the case of the officers. Gürsel's anger brought *Oncü* another suspension.

The climax of the clashes, however, came shortly before the 1961 election. On September 1, Yalçın spoke at a rally of the NTP in Izmir, in which he said that: "Despite all the mistakes and all the shortcomings, in the Izmir district the DP period was a Golden Age."[26] Yalçın was arrested almost immediately for anti-revolutionary statements, and brought to trial about two weeks later after intensive questioning and much publicity about the case. He was convicted and given a six-month suspended sentence.

The New Turkey party probably has the potential to become a constructive, progressive force in Turkey, especially because it contains some capable economists like Alican. Its leaders—though not always its rank and file members—are honest and for the most part forward-looking. It is handicapped in part because of the lack of political experience of many of its leaders, but this can presumably be overcome with time. Probably the most serious obstacle the party faces in its efforts to grow is the fact that it includes diverse elements which frequently split over the issues of the May 27 revolution, which continue to dominate Turkish political life. One reason for this conglomerate state is that in the race for former DP votes there was comparatively little differentiation of issues prior to the 1961 election other than between pro- or anti-RPP sentiments. If in the period before the next election differences among the four parties on important issues other than this one occur, it should enhance the position of the NTP in that progressive political groups will have a constructive alternative to the RPP, which many have long sought.

The Republican Peasants Nation Party

Although the leaders of the Republican Peasants Nation Party (RPNP) have had their own party since 1948, their experience was apparently

[26] *Oncü*, Sept. 1, 1961.

not enough to prevent them from finishing last in the 1961 election. The party represents the most conservative and clericalist sector of the Turkish political spectrum. It was opposed to both the DP and RPP.

What later became the RPNP was organized in 1948 as the Nation party from among dissidents in the DP. Despite the presence of several well-known personalities such as Marshal Fevzi Çakmak, Chief of Staff of the armed forces for many years under Atatürk, and Turkey's only Marshal other than Atatürk himself, the party could not match the skill and appeal of the Democrats and won only a single seat in the 1950 election. After 1950 the party became increasingly right-wing, and there was little disagreement among informed observers with the government's determination that the party was anti-Kemalist, and that its dissolution by the government in 1953 was justified. Osman Bölükbaşı, a more able politician than the party's earlier leaders, reconstituted it as the Republican Nation party the following year (later merging with the small Peasants party), and succeeded in winning about 425,000 votes in 1954 (compared to 265,000 in 1950). This total rose to 660,000 in 1957, about 7 percent of the total votes cast, but only in the province of Kırşehir did the party get a plurality which gave it four seats in the Assembly.

The RPNP took on new and somewhat inflated importance after May 27 in that it was the only party other than the RPP which survived the Menderes regime. In the Constituent Assembly it was allotted twenty-one seats. Bölükbaşı had declared his intention to help keep the Assembly nonpartisan by staying out himself, but at the last minute he reversed his position and led the RPNP group, impelling RPP leader Inönü to follow suit. In the 1961 election the RPNP joined in the race for the former DP votes, and succeeded in winning 14 percent of the votes cast, approximately doubling its 1957 total. The party's strength is localized, however, in the heavily conservative provinces just east of Ankara in the center of the Anatolian plateau. Thirty-eight of the party's fifty-four deputies were elected in thirteen provinces roughly in a circle around Ankara.

The RPNP's appeal is based almost entirely on its social conservatism, and on several attractive personalities. The fact that it was able to win eight of Ankara's deputies was undoubtedly due to the presence on the Ankara RPNP ticket of both Bölükbaşı himself and Muhlis Ete, a well-known economist who was instrumental in evolving much of the economic program of the DP, but who quit the DP when it began to be politically unsavory. Bölükbaşı has no real rivals for leadership of the party except possibly Ahmet Tahtakılıç, a DP deputy in 1946-50 and later an independent democrat, who during the latter part of the NUC period made himself unpopular among educated groups by his actions as Minister of Education. The fifth RPNP Congress at the end of August was little more than a series of mutual insults between these two and their followers. Bölükbaşı was re-elected party chairman by a wide margin.

The election campaign waged by the RPNP consisted mostly of attacks on the RPP. The other parties were not spared either, though, and hardly a day passed when Bölükbaşı was not in a personal dispute with Alican, Gümüşpala, or any handy RPP target. Bölükbaşı was warned by General Gürsel several times shortly before the election that his campaign was not meeting the standards expected by the NUC. The most significant incident was connected with Bölükbaşı's refusal to sign the National Declaration setting conditions for conduct of the election campaign. At first he had explained his absence from the signing meeting because of health, fatigue, and other duties, but he later said in a radio speech that "I saw in the text some important points which did not conform to my beliefs or to my understanding of law."[27]

This statement moved Gürsel to comment that Bölükbaşı had been misusing the radio.

> ...We gave the radio to the parties in order that they could expound their beliefs, but he [Bölükbaşı] has used it for personal defense. Unfortunately the radio authorities were not able to silence him and remove him from the broadcasting station. I telephoned, but could not get through. . . . It is strange that a man as well-educated as Bölükbaşı would fall to such a low level. But it is not education which makes a man, it is character and good morals. I listened regretfully to Bölükbaşı's speech. It happened once, but will not happen again.[28]

That the NUC did not take stronger action against Bölükbaşı, who undoubtedly gained some votes by his defiant answer in Konya that "no legitimate force can take us by the arm and expel us from the radio. . . . We are not obligated to any individual or any authority . . .",[29] was probably due only to the closeness of the end of the campaign.

When after the 1961 election, combinations were being sought with which to form the coalition government, the RPNP was more opposed than the Justice party to working with the RPP. There was some talk of the RPNP combining with the JP and the NTP, but the armed forces were unwilling to allow formation of a conservative government. It should be noted, however, that even when such a solution was being talked of in the press, the RPNP indicated it was unwilling to work with *any* of the other parties. So adamant were many RPNP leaders in their conservative positions that amnesty and other issues caused moderates in the party to break completely with Bölükbaşı, with the result that a second Nation party was formed in the spring of 1962, one of which led by Hasan Dinçer and Muhlis Ete, joined the second coalition cabinet. The future of the RPNP is probably not bright.

[27] *Cumhuriyet,* Oct. 4, 1961.
[28] *Ibid.*
[29] *Oncü,* Oct. 5, 1961.

The Campaign

The election campaign opened formally late in September, having been delayed to allow the Yassıada verdicts to be pronounced before electioneering started. It lasted until October 12, the election law providing that most campaign activities stop three days before the balloting. It was only the formal rally holding and radio propaganda which began as late as September, however. The efforts of all the parties in the previous months had been spent on the coming election. So eager were the parties to have the election, in fact, that countless times some newspaper, usually the organ of one of the parties, would interpret a vague statement by General Gürsel as a promise of elections on a certain early date, and hopes soared and plunged frequently.

There was a more important question in the air than the date of the election, however. This was whether the election would be held at all. The NUC had publicly committed itself to elections on numerous occasions, but during the months after political activity was gradually permitted to resume, there had been frequent intimations that the armed forces were dissatisfied with the state of the nation. The most serious of these signs was the growth of the Justice party, and as was mentioned earlier, the NUC several times had warned the Gümüşpala forces that they were on the wrong road. The results of the Constitution Referendum in July, with almost 4 million negative votes, also gave the NUC pause.

The most difficult problem was how to handle the record of the ten years of the Menderes regime. Such matters as Menderes' suppression of freedom of the press were hardly arguable, but other aspects, economic policy for example, were areas where differing opinions were quite plausible. (Even here, however, there were difficulties, for after the revolution the public learned that Menderes had left Turkey heavily in debt and had badly mismanaged national finances. To praise his economic and financial policy, therefore, could easily be construed as anti-May 27.) In the circumstances, though, any reference to the fallen regime was potentially sensitive, especially with the Yassıada verdicts pronounced only a month before the election. On August 22, the NUC had banned publication of anything concerning the trials or which might influence the coming verdicts. In the first week of September the NUC moved to make the ban on the past general. At a ceremony in Ankara, the leaders of the four major political parties signed a National Declaration outlining the limits within which the election campaign was to be waged.[30]

The round table meeting of party leaders with representatives of the NUC on September 6 had been preceded by several meetings of party

[30] Though RPNP leader Bölükbaşı refused to sign the declaration personally, an RPNP representative signed.

general secretaries in which the text of a declaration had been worked out. Though no parts were made public until after it had been signed, it is clear from reports of the discussions that not all of the points in the declaration were accepted happily by the parties. And even the round table meetings were made the scene of party strife when the JP and NTP accused the RPP of seeing the revolution as setting one class against another, the RPP replying that the other parties were sowing seeds of discord.[31]

The National Declaration was published in two parts. The first, made public immediately after the signing on September 6, concentrated on pledges by the parties on how they would conduct themselves. The parties promised not to revive the "DP mentality"; to preserve the Atatürk revolution as a whole (though not necessarily any specific policies) ; not to engage in divisive or exploitative political activity; not to make any statements influencing the coming Yassıada verdicts, or disputing them; to make no claims or statements casting doubt on the fact that the forthcoming election would be anything but completely free; whichever party came to power would maintain public services in a nonpartisan way; all parties would work against extreme political views, i.e., communism and racism; the matter of deciding whether local branch organizations of political parties could be reestablished would be left for the new Grand National Assembly; no propaganda would be made which is harmful to Turkish forests,[32] or to Turkish foreign policy; and both pre- and post-election conduct of all parties, whether the government or the opposition, would be democratic in spirit.[33]

The more striking part of the declaration came after the Yassıada verdicts had been handed down on September 15. Since it dealt with the record of the Menderes regime, even the existence of the second part of the declaration had been kept secret. It was published on September 17, following another meeting of party leaders with General Gürsel, to which, significantly, RPNP leader Bölükbaşı was not invited. One can only speculate about how much pressure was needed to get all the parties to accept all the points of what was the most damning possible condemnation of the Menderes regime and all its policies, as well as a justification of the revolution of May 27. The former regime was condemned for

[31] *Oncü*, Sept. 2, 1961.

[32] The inclusion of this somewhat unusual item in a document of this importance is due to the special place which the forest problem occupies in Turkey. The Anatolian plateau was reportedly covered by many forests in the past, but today is largely bare. This situation has long been considered serious enough to justify such measures as providing a possible death penalty for starting a forest fire, and severe penalties for unauthorized cutting of trees. Forests are often virtually the only source peasants have for fuel and building materials, however, making the problem potentially a political football, and leading to the insertion of a forest protection clause into the Constitution of 1961.

[33] Text of Part I in *Cumhuriyet*, Sept. 6, 1961.

"step by step departing from democratic practices and freedom," "exploiting religious feelings for political ends," "opening the road to the repudiation of the reforms which are the basis of our civilized existence." In addition, mention was made of many of the charges of which the DP had just been convicted, such as using the state radio for partisan purposes. Probably the point most open to legitimate controversy was the condemnation of Menderes for "especially after 1955, having ruined the economic and social order of the nation by unplanned, wasteful and inflationary policies and various irregularities, and having caused our foreign economic and financial relations to be shaken." Finally, the declaration stated that the Turkish nation had insisted that the armed forces exercise in its name the right to demand the cessation of these activities, to restore freedom and democracy and the functioning of the Assembly. It repeated the assertion that the revolution of May 27 had been neither for nor against any group, and that the coming elections would be free and would not bring a return to the "DP mentality."[34]

The campaign was lively, and included use of every available means of propaganda. At the beginning the NUC issued a statement reminding the parties of the National Declaration. The Minister of Justice said that the campaign would be watched carefully. During the campaign the NUC several times warned some party spokesmen, especially the Justice and Nation parties, that they were exceeding the prescribed limits. A number of Justice party speakers were arrested and held for investigation in the Izmir area, and had to be released when some were elected to the Assembly. And in one case the NUC charged all the parties with exceeding the boundaries of the National Declaration, when on October 4 it issued a statement that leaders of not only one, but of every party, had petitioned to have the Yassıada sentences lightened. It is conceivable that the declaration could have been interpreted to cover the Yassıada verdicts but not the sentences, although it is more probable that campaign considerations rather than shadings of meaning or pity for the convicted deputies carried most weight in the petition of several of the parties. The NUC statement on the matter asserted that "this is not our idea of political morality."[35]

The contents of the campaign consisted chiefly of promises of increased prosperity, development, and freedom. The programs of the parties are discussed above. There was also a considerable amount of personal attack of leaders of one party against leaders of others, mainly involving the JP and RPNP, and to a lesser extent the New NTP and the RPP. The JP, RPNP, and NTP also devised various ways of singling out the RPP for special attack, often referring back to the single-party era before 1946.

Despite the National Declaration and the efforts of the NUC, the chief

[34] Text of Part 2 in *Cumhuriyet*, Sept. 17, 1961.
[35] Text of statement in *Cumhuriyet*, Oct. 4, 1961.

issue in the campaign was the record of the Menderes regime. In the circumstances it could hardly have been anything else. What is perhaps more surprising is that the limitations put on the campaign and election were so few. The results of the election revealed how overriding the issue is in Turkey.

The Election Law

The election was conducted under a completely new election law designed to eliminate all the abuses alleged to have occurred under the Menderes regime.[36] The election was in the charge of a High Elective Council composed of seven members selected by the members of the Supreme Court of Appeals and the Council of State (the highest tribunal trying cases between the government and private persons) from among themselves. The election council of each province was similarly composed of the highest members of the judiciary. On the district level the election councils were chaired by the senior member of the district judiciary, and included a representative of each political party in the district. If necessary the membership of seven would be completed by persons selected by a vote of all schoolteachers (from primary to higher education level) in schools in the district capital. These councils were responsible for carrying out all functions laid down by the law before, during, and after the election. There was elaborate provision for appeal of any actions of the councils through the judiciary, and political parties were given the right to inspect voting registers, question decisions, or offer opinions and suggestions at any point in the proceedings.

Two elections were conducted simultaneously, one for the Senate and one for the National Assembly. One of the ways devised to prevent one party from winning disproportionate strength in both houses was to elect senators by majority vote, deputies by proportional representation. This device did in fact yield some important differences in party representation in the two chambers. The elections for the Senate and the Assembly had some complicating features for the voter, however. In the former, the ballot showed the candidates by name along with their party affiliation, followed by independent candidates. Since many provinces were to elect more than one senator, this form of ballot presumably was designed to facilitate voting for the man rather than the party. It is significant that such split voting did not occur. Not a single province returned senators of more than one party (except Ankara and Istanbul, which had been divided into senatorial districts. In these provinces also, however, each

[36] In many technical aspects the new law was similar to its predecessors. The law under which the 1957 election was conducted is discussed in Kemal Karpat, "The Turkish Elections of 1957," *Western Political Quarterly*, Vol. 14 (June 1961), pp. 436-59.

electoral district elected all its senators from the same party.) That voting for senators was in fact party rather than individual voting is also reflected in the fact that the official results of the Senate election break the vote down by party, not individual candidate.

In the election for deputies, a separate ballot was provided for each party, and for each individual independent candidate. A voter was required to select only one ballot, thus eliminating split tickets within the limits of the election for deputies. He did have the opportunity, however, to alter the order of candidates on the ticket of the party of his choice, simply by indicating numbered preferences opposite various names. It is impossible to determine without further data whether there were any changes which resulted in displacements of some candidates, but the provisions for invalidating preference ballots indicate that such a thing was unlikely. Ballots marked preferentially would be considered nonpreferential if preferences were written outside of the correct box, and more importantly, if either more or less than half of the candidates on the ballot were assigned preference numbers. In counting, the procedure called for using a system of proportional representation (dividing the number of votes by the number of seats, declaring elected any candidate exceeding the required number, and redistributing the lowest party or independent as many times as necessary), to divide the seats among the parties or independents, and then examining the ballots to see whether the names to be elected on a party ticket should be rearranged. It is doubtful that the complicated nature of the preference provisions deprived the voters of much freedom, because the very nature of preferential voting necessitates considerable knowledge among the voters about individual candidates, a condition not fulfilled by most of the Turkish electorate.

The Election Results[37]

The table on page 110 shows that almost 82 percent of the eligible voters, over 10 million people, cast ballots in the election. This percentage is higher than in 1957, but lower than in either 1950 or 1954.

[37] The source of election figures used in the following tables is the officially published data printed in the *Proceedings of the Turkish National Assembly*, 1st Session, 1st Meeting, Vol. 1, Jan. 5, 1962, pp. 514-76. Official results in terms of Senate and Assembly seats were published in the newspapers. Percentages and other calculations were made by the author, unless otherwise stated. The source for data on the 1950, 1954, and 1957 elections, the results of the 1957 election never having been published officially, is the RPP Research Bureau publication *Seçim Neticeleri Uzerinde Bir Inceleme* (Ankara, 1959). For the purpose of this analysis the 1961 returns are those of the Assembly election. The differences in results of the Senate election, held separately but simultaneously, do not appear to be significant.

Election Year	*Eligible Voters*	*Votes Cast*	*Percentage*
1950	8,908,824	7,934,449	*89.06*
1954	10,250,338	9,097,451	*88.75*
1957	12,111,183	9,334,246	*77.15*
1961	12,864,299	10,522,446[38]	*81.80*

The results of the election in popular votes and seats are given in the table that follows.

Popular Vote and Seats Won by Parties in 1961 Election

Party	Popular Vote (in thousands)	*Percentage*	Assembly Seats	*Percentage*	Senate Seats	*Percentage*
Justice Party	3,527	*34.8*	158	*35.1*	70	*46.7*
Republican Peoples Party	3,726	*36.7*	173	*38.4*	36	*24.0*
Republican Peasants Nation Party	1,415	*14.0*	54	*12.0*	16	*16.7*
New Turkey Party	1,392	*13.7*	65	*14.5*	28	*18.6*
Independents and others	82	*.8*	—	—	—	—
Total	10,142	*100.0*	450	*100.0*	150	*100.0*

There are no important variations by province or region. Of 67 provinces, participation was between 85 and 89 percent in 17, 80-84 percent in 37, 75-79 percent in 10, and 70-74 percent in three. The increase of almost a million in the vote over 1957 warrants some comment. The most obvious explanation for this increase is heightened interest in the election. It is significant to note that a similar increase occurred in 1954 over 1950, 1954 being the first election after the Democratic victory of 1950, which had shown that it was possible to turn out the regime. In regard to the 1957 election, the lower percentage of participation may have been due to the fact that the voters believed it was unlikely the Democratic party would have trouble staying in power.

Analysis of the election results of 1961 sheds light on two important points: the disappointing showing of the RPP, and the distribution of the former DP votes. The broader reasons the RPP must fight an up-hill battle both organizationally and ideologically have been discussed earlier. The election results demonstrate how difficult this battle will be. Despite the fact that there were a million more votes cast than in 1957, the RPP polled fewer in 1961 than four years earlier. Analysis by regions shows that a pattern of decline is general for most of the nation.

[38] After subtracting invalid ballots, the total vote is 10,142,243. Sources, CHP Arastırma Bürosu, *Seçim Neticeleri* for 1950, 1954, 1957; official government statistics for 1961.

Change in Total Votes and RPP Votes, 1957 to 1961

(Thousands of votes)

Region	Increase in Votes 1957 to 1961	Change in RPP Votes 1957 to 1961
Marmara	+212	+55
Aegean	+ 84	+ 3
Black Sea	+123	−27
Southeast Anatolia	+ 48	− 5
East Anatolia	+150	−33
Central Anatolia	+221	−24
West Anatolia	+ 59	+12
South Anatolia	+ 82	−18
Total	+979	−37

The one significant exception to the pattern, the Marmara region, is largely accounted for by Istanbul, although even there the RPP received only 22,000 out of 104,000 added votes, and Balıkesir, where the presence of large air force installations and the votes of officers who received the franchise for the first time probably accounted for much of the RPP increase. The three regions with the greatest decline are: the Black Sea provinces, which are prosperous and little inclined to return to étatist policies; Central Anatolia, where the decline reflects the failure of the RPP to increase its total in rapidly growing Ankara; and East Anatolia, where the drop indicates that the RPP has added little to its support since the 1930's when those provinces profited from the government's reaction to armed resistance to reform by taking drastic measures to break the hold of many feudal leaders. What should have been one of the bastions of RPP support would have been even more disastrous except for a gain of 11,000 out of 14,000 new votes in Inönü's home province of Malatya.

It is also significant, as shown in the table that follows, that the RPP did no better in urban than in rural areas. The RPP's share of the vote in these ten cities declined from 41.3 percent in 1957 to 37.1 percent in 1961, compared to a decline in the country as a whole from 40.9 percent to 36.7 percent. Probably the most surprising result was Ankara, the center of the May 27 revolution and the location of much of Turkey's rapidly growing urban educated class. The fact that the Republican Peasants Nation party gained most of the homeless DP votes is probably largely due to the personal candidacy of Osman Bölübaşı on the RPNP Ankara ticket. It may also be possible to explain the Nation party's capture of the bulk of the 79,000 new votes in Ankara by the presence on the ticket of the highly respected and popular economist Muhlis Ete. Nevertheless,

Change in Total Votes and RPP Votes in Ten Large Cities, 1957 to 1961

(Thousands of votes)

City	Increase in Votes 1957 to 1961	Change in RPP Votes 1957 to 1961
Istanbul	+104	+22
Ankara	+ 79	+ 2
Izmir	+ 36	+ 7
Adana	+ 19	−17
Bursa	+ 29	+ 9
Konya	+ 39	− 5
Samsun	+ 31	− 6
Eskisehir	+ 15	+ 3
Erzurum	+ 27	+ 1
Kayseri	+ 14	+ 3
Total	+393	+18

it must be pointed out that the RPP had attractive candidates of its own, who might have been expected to do better. The large decline in Adana should also be noted with urgency by the RPP, for Adana is the home province of Kasim Gülek, who is conceded by most impartial observers to be the party's best individual vote-getter after Inönü himself.

It is impossible without further detailed data to determine the character of the new voters, whether they were predominantly young people newly of voting age, or older persons who had not previously exercised their franchise. There was probably a combination of both. Of the new voters 40 percent were in the ten large urban areas listed in the table. It is likely that most of these came from the lower income groups that are continuing to move to the cities in large numbers. Their support went to the Justice and Nation parties in Bursa, Izmir, Samsun, Istanbul, Ankara, Konya, Adana, and Eskişehir, and only in two cases, Konya and Erzurum, in any significant numbers to the New Turkey party, the only party other than the RPP that could be in any way labeled progressive. The conservative trend can probably be explained in part by the record of the Democrats in catering actively to these low-income groups. A part of the explanation might also be found in the inability of most Turkish cities to keep up with the provision of housing, jobs, schools, and other services needed to integrate the mushrooming urban population into the fabric of their new environment. This is, of course, a problem which will not be solved overnight. While the situation continues, it is likely that the unintegrated newcomers will be more influenced by both conservative and opportunistic appeals than by the representatives of the Atatürk reforms.

It may also be speculated that at least part of the persons newly of voting age supported the RPP. The students were constantly in the forefront of the revolution, and certainly in the cities it is hardly plausible that they would have voted against the RPP. The extent to which this spirit carried over into young voters in towns and villages is difficult to determine, but from the strong support given to the revolution by teachers, it is reasonable to assume at least some diffusion of pro-RPP spirit to young people in outlying districts. If this hypothesis is correct, of course, it means that the RPP probably lost voters from among those who had supported it in 1957.

The other important question which throws light on the meaning of the election results is what happened to the former DP votes. On an overall basis, the results reveal a more even division between the parties than in 1957, as indicated in the table below.

Turkish Election Results, 1950–1961

(Numbers in thousands)

	1950	*Percent*	1954	*Percent*	1957	*Percent*	1961	*Percent*
Republican People's Party	3,196	*40.0*	3,215	*35.3*	3,764	*40.9*	3,726	*36.7*
Democratic Party	4,275	*53.5*	5,151	*56.6*	4,395	*47.7*	—	—
Justice Party	—	—	—	—	—	—	3,527	*34.8*
Republican Peasants Nation Party	266	*3.3*	425	*4.9*	660	*7.2*	1,415	*14.0*
Freedom Party	—	—	—	—	347	*3.8*	—	—
New Turkey Party	—	—	—	—	—	—	1,392	*13.7*
Other	259	*3.2*	306	*3.2*	40	*.4*	82	*.8*
Total	7,995	*100.0*	9,097	*100.0*	9,205	*100.0*	10,142	*100.0*

This pattern is not unexpected. The Justice party, the most open contender for succession to the Democrats, inherited much of their organization and mantle, but it would have been too much to expect it to equal the record of the Menderes regime at its height. In trying to determine whether the redistribution of former DP votes indicates a regional or other pattern, however, the results are far more revealing.

In this connection it is possible to attempt to separate the former DP votes from the new votes. If it is hypothesized that, had other things remained equal, the Justice party would have inherited the DP votes, the New Turkey party received the Freedom party ballots, and the Republican Peasants Nation and Republican People's parties held their own, a table of increases and decreases by region can be compared.

When analyzed in this way, the figures tend to corroborate the rumors which circulated in the period before the election, namely that the Justice, Nation, and the New Turkey parties had at least informally

Net Election Gains and Losses, 1957–1961, by Regions

(Thousands of votes)

Region	DP-JP	RPP	RPNP	FP-NTP	Others	Net Change
Marmara	−123	+ 55	+117	+131	+ 32	+212
Aegean	+ 79	+ 3	+ 27	− 27	+ 2	+ 84
Black Sea	− 69	− 27	+ 80	+134	+ 5	+123
Central Anatolia	−234	− 24	+292	+177	+ 9	+220
Western Anatolia	− 54	+ 12	+116	− 16	+ 1	+ 59
Southern Anatolia	+ 26	− 18	+ 17	+ 50	+ 7	+ 82
Eastern Anatolia	−271	− 33	+ 51	+383	+ 6	+136
Southeastern Anatolia	−235	− 5	+ 65	+216	+ 7	+ 48
Total	−881	− 37	+765	+1048	+ 69	+964

agreed to refrain from campaigning against each other, and instead concentrated on defeating the RPP. The division of the former DP votes in at least three regions are lopsided enough so that it is improbable that personality factors or better campaigning can account for the phenomenon. Nor does the fact that not all parties ran in every province account for much of the pattern. In Eastern Anatolia, for instance, the four provinces where either the JP or the RPNP did not run account for only 101,000 of the 383,000 votes which the NTP garnered from among new and former DP voters. In Western Anatolia where the RPNP gained 116,000 while the RPP gained 12,000 over its 1957 vote and the NTP fell 16,000 behind the 1957 Freedom party total, 107,000 of the RPNP increase came in provinces where candidates were entered by all four parties.

When increase and decrease figures are broken down by provinces, the pattern becomes even more pronounced: In 11 provinces the Nation party increased its total over 1957 by 10,000 votes or more, no other party doing the same. In 21 provinces the NTP received 10,000 or more votes in 1957 than in 1961 in provinces where the Freedom party both had and had not run in 1957, and neither the JP nor RPNP made substantial gains. In 15 provinces, the JP topped the DP 1957 performance by 10,000 votes or more, and neither the NTP nor RPNP polled over 10,000 new votes. In 12 provinces, increases of 10,000 or more were recorded by two of the three anti-RPP parties (but in no case did all 3 add such an increment), but in 5 of these the ratio of one increase to the other was more than 2 to 1.

Closer analysis may, of course, reveal that there were indeed natural reasons for the peculiar character of the redistribution of former Democratic votes. There were many important changes in the political environment in Turkey between 1957 and 1961. But the character of the campaign and the pattern of the election results show clearly the legacy left to Turkey by the Democratic party. Almost any way in which the election returns are analyzed yields a picture of a nation split on the surface into four segments, but basically into only two.

The provinces in which the most striking changes occurred are given in the table below.

Changes in Voting 1957–1961: Selected Provinces

(Thousands of votes)

	DP-JP	FP-NTP	RPNP	RPP	Net Change
Ankara	−53	+115	+11	+ 2	+ 79
Sivas	−76	+101	+ 7	−27	+ 15
Erzurum	−67	+ 79	+13	+ 1	+ 27
Tokat	−40	+ 64	+ 3	− 9	+ 18
Istanbul	−19	+ 8	+62	+22	+104
Tekirdag	−44	+ 54	+ 1	− 2	+ 9
Giresun	−52	+ 49	+19	− 6	+ 10
Hatay	−28	+ 43	+ 2	− 8	+ 14
Afyon	−25	+ 2	+43	− 3	+ 17
Ordu	−23	+ 41	+ 5	−10	+ 13

There are some factors which may lead to modification of this extreme polarization. One is the eventual disappearance of some important personalities—or their memories—from the political spotlight. Another is the increased differentiation of the interests of the various parties, as issues other than the DP-RPP rivalry begin to come to the fore once again. Such a shift of attention may be slow in coming about. Probably the chief reason the issues were partly transcended in the compromise on amnesty, which led to the formation of the second coalition government in June 1962, was that strong outside pressure was applied by the armed forces. As soon as it became necessary to take positions on more specific matters of social and economic policy, however, the Justice and Republican Peasants Nation parties went through major internal crises, showing on what flimsy programmatic bases they are presently built. The RPP is also in trouble. If what may be roughly described as the reform anti-reform gulf is indeed bridged or at least pushed into the background as parties and other groups realign themselves on the basis of more specific problems, progressive and moderate elements may well be a more formidable challenge to the RPP—especially among the urban educated classes—than even the Democrats were. The NUC set out to reorganize the party system. It is doubtful that they were aware of all the implications of a two-party versus a multiparty system, but in creating the latter they may have been instrumental in alleviating the polarization that has been characteristic of Turkish politics almost from the beginning of the multiparty system.

6

The Soldiers as Rulers

ON JUNE 24, 1960, in the main hall of the Turkish Parliament, the thirty-eight members of the National Unity Committee stepped up to the rostrum after General Gürsel, and over a nationwide radio hook-up, in turn, took the following oath:

> I pledge myself to the service of the Turkish nation, without expecting any reward, and without any other motivations than the principles of morality, justice, law, human rights, and the dictates of my own conscience. I will work for nothing else than the welfare of the nation and for its sovereignty. I will not depart from the goal of rooting the Republic in the new Constitution, and transferring power to the new Parliament. To this I pledge my honor and all that is sacred.

Unlike many other military juntas that have taken similar oaths, the NUC kept its pledge, although the reestablishment of constitutional government required eighteen months rather than the two or three originally envisioned. During those eighteen months the NUC steadily moved—or was moved—in a direction which would have made it more and more difficult for the armed forces to reverse this basic course or to postpone for any considerable time the holding of elections, even if they had wanted to do so. Such events as the purging of fourteen "radical" NUC members in November, the convening of a Constituent Assembly in January, and the holding of a national referendum on the new constitution in July were all milestones on a road from which there would be turning back only at the cost of clashing with virtually all of the urban educated class which is the center of Turkish politics. The reasons power was turned back to elected officials, however, are far more complicated than just the action of the NUC. The NUC had, in fact, lost most of its control over both the rest of the armed forces and the political parties by the time it went out of office. This chapter will try to assess how and why the NUC lost control; why its goal of getting the armed forces out of government was adhered to; what the NUC's positive and negative contributions to Turkish political life were; and what may be the future consequences of these matters.

Several aspects of the specific Turkish situation must be taken into account both in evaluating the results of the NUC period and in comparing the NUC with military regimes in other underdeveloped countries.[1] In the first place, the army that took over power in Turkey in 1960 was not a defeated army and was not characterized by the many frustrations which motivated a military regime like, say, that of Nasser in Egypt. The Turkish army was not primarily driven by a sense of loss of national or personal honor to attempt to remake the nation in its own image. Second, the army in Turkey was neither the vanguard of a new middle class nor its chief component in numbers or in operational abilities. On the contrary, one of the striking things is that there were so many officers who continued even after the revolution to maintain the opinion that the army's proper role was in the barracks. Third, the revolution did not come about, as in Pakistan, because virtually the entire civilian political complex was discredited. The survival of a substantial body of Turkish politicians in good standing meant that these men could and did legitimately demand a voice in public affairs. Fourth, there existed in Turkey a tradition of a nonpolitical army, and while it may be argued that that tradition has now been negated—a question which will be considered below—it is generally agreed that this tradition figured in the thinking of the majority of the Turkish army forces in 1960-61.[2]

It is in this context that the NUC's performance must be considered in its relations with (1) the rest of the armed forces, (2) the political parties, (3) the peasants, and (4) economic and financial problems. First, however, it will be well to look at the committee members themselves.

[1] An important contribution on the political role of the military is the recent volume edited by John J. Johnson, *The Role of the Military in Underdeveloped Countries* (Princeton University Press, 1962), which includes regional and general studies by a number of experts in the field.

[2] The history of the Turkish army's disengagement from politics goes back to the strong measures taken by Atatürk to separate the two institutions. That it was Atatürk who inaugurated this separation, and that separation is the pattern in modern, Western nations, are two factors which have combined to instill it in the thinking of present-day Turkish officers. The deliberate dissociation by Atatürk of the army from politics, and the continued development of this separation into a tradition, are discussed in Dankwart A. Rustow, "The Army and the Founding of the Turkish Republic," *World Politics* (July 1959); Frederick W. Frey, "Arms and the Man in Turkish Politics," *Land Reborn* (August 1960). (See also Dankwart A. Rustow, "The Military in Middle Eastern Society and Politics," *The Military in the Middle East: Problems in Society and Government*, Sydney Nettleton Fisher, ed., Ohio State University Press, 1963.) The strength of the Atatürk example is also noted by Manfred Halpern: "In Turkey, the example created by Atatürk in transforming army rule into civilian rule carried enough weight to persuade General Gürsel to do the same by November, 1961. . . ." "Middle Eastern Armies and the New Middle Class," in Johnson, ed., *op. cit.*, p. 308. The opposite view is taken by Daniel Lerner and Richard Robinson, who imply, quite wrongly in this writer's view, that many Turkish officers have never accepted the legitimacy of their separation from politics. "Swords and Ploughshares: The Turkish Army as a Modernizing Force," *World Politics* (October 1960), especially pp. 39-44.

The Character of the NUC

Data on rank, place and date of birth, and years since graduation from the Military Academy of members of the NUC do not reveal anything which might indicate that they are different from the rest of the armed forces.[3] They come from all parts of the nation. Only eleven come from the three large urban areas of Istanbul, Ankara, and Izmir. Diagrams plotting birth dates and military academy graduations against rank show only a small number of cases in which a man was noticeably ahead or behind his rank-group either in age or seniority. All except one graduated from the military academy between the ages of 18 and 22. The occupations of their fathers reflect the traditional channels of entry into the Turkish officer corps: Of 27 for whom we have data, 12 are the sons of army officers, 4 of civilian government employees, 4 of businessmen, and 7 miscellaneous; 22 have been abroad for schooling, service, or travel (only seven have never been outside Turkey, and there are no data on nine), and at least five served in the Turkish brigade in Korea; twenty speak a foreign language to some extent.[4]

It is not yet clear how these particular thirty-eight came to make up the committee. At least eight, Ataklı, Celebi, Erkanlı, Karavelioğlu, Soyuyüce, Türkeș, Yildiz and Yurdakuler, were, according to their own accounts in *Cumhuriyet,* active in planning the revolution, and it may safely be assumed that others were also involved, although this information will come to light only with analysis of the individual stories beginning to appear in various publications. Most of the committee were apparently recruited from among those already in key positions in Ankara and Istanbul, whose cooperation was needed to assure success of the coup. Fahri Ozdilek was Martial Law Commander for Istanbul. His support of the revolution was vital to its bloodless success there. Sitki Ulay was commander of the Military Academy that had staged the cadets' march shortly before May 27, the last warning to the Menderes government to change its policies. Osman Köksal held the key post of Commander of the Presidential Guard Regiment. Erkanlı, Karan, and Ozkaya commanded important armored forces in Istanbul and Ankara. At least seven NUC members had held important General Staff posts on May 27, including posts in the personnel section, which had enabled them to assign several sympathetic colleagues to strategic jobs.

Among other things the NUC members discussed in the interviews what they thought were the main problems of Turkey. Education was mentioned by all, usually first, though the specific emphasis varied, some

[3] The source for much of the data cited below is a series of interviews with 29 of the 38 NUC members by the newspaper *Cumhuriyet* published between July 16 and August 23, 1960. See table p. 119.

[4] Seventeen list English, 7 French, 3 German, 1 Russian, 1 Spanish, 1 Arabic, 2 list no language and there are no data on 16.

The Character of the NUC

Name	Rank	Year of Birth	Place of Birth	Year Graduated Military Academy
Gürsel, Cemal	General	1895	Erzurum	
Özdilek, Fahri	General	1898	Bursa	1916
Madanoğlu, Cemal	Maj. Gen.[1]	1907	Esme (Uşak)	1926
Bastuğ, Irfan	Brig. Gen.[2]	1908	Van	1929
Ulay, Sitki	Brig. Gen.[2]	1907	Izmir	1930
Acuner, Ekrem	Colonel	1916	Tokat	1935
Ataklı, Mucip	Col. (Air)[3]	1919	Erzurum	1940
Köksal, Osman	Colonel	1916	Salonica	1938
Kuytak, Fikret	Colonel	1915	Ankara	1936
Küçük, Sami	Colonel	1916	Drama (Macedonia)	1938
Tunçkanat, Haydar	Col. (Air)	1921	Bandirma	1941
Türkeş, Alparslan[4]	Colonel	1917	Cyprus	1938
Yurdakuler, Muzaffer	Colonel	1915	Istanbul	1936
Akkoyunlu, Fazıl[4]	Lt. Col.	1914	Yozgat	1936
Aksoyoğlu, Refet	Lt. Col.[5]	1921	Istanbul	
Kabibay, Orhan[4]	Lt. Col.[6]	1918	Istanbul	1937
Kaplan, Mustafa[4]	Lt. Col.	1923	Drama (Macedonia)	1942
Karaman, Suphi	Lt. Col.[5]	1922	Bayburt (Gümüsane)	1941
Okan, Sezai	Lt. Col.[6]	1917	Istanbul	.
Yildiz, Ahmet	Lt. Col.[5]	1921	Sürmene (Rize)	1941
Celebi, Emanullah	Major (Air)[7]	1926	Yalova	1947
Erkanlı, Orhan[4]	Major	1924	Kırşehir	1944
Ersü, Vehbi	Major[8] [5]	1918	Erzincan	1939
Gürsoytrak, Suphi	Major[6]	1925	Ankara	1945
Kaplan, Kadri	Major	1922	Istanbul	1940
Karan, Muzaffer[4]	Major	1917	Istanbul	1938
Köseoğlu, Münir[4]	Lt. Cmdr.	1923	Sakarya	1943
Özgüneş, Mehmet	Major[7]	1921	Kayseri	1943
Özgür, Selahattin	Lt. Cmdr.[9]	1925	Istanbul	1944
Özkaya, Şükran	Major	1925	Antalya	1943
Soyuyüce, Şefik[4]	Major[7]	1924	Sivas	1943
Taser, Dündar[4]	Major	1925	Gaziantep	1944
Baykal, Rifat[4]	Captain	1926	Izmir	
Er, Ahmet[4]	Captain	1927	Akhisar (Manisa)	1949
Esin, Numan[4]	Captain	1929	Biga (Çanakkale)	1949
Karavelioğlu, Kamil	Captain[10]	1927	Antalya	1949
Özdağ, Muzaffer[4]	Captain	1933	Kayseri	1950
Solmazer, Irfan[4]	Captain	1925	Gönen (Balıkesir)	

[1] Promoted to Lt. Gen., August 1960.
[2] Promoted to Major Gen., August 1960.
[3] Promoted to Brig. Gen., August 1961.
[4] Dismissed with "radical" group, November 1960.
[5] Promoted to Colonel, August 1961.
[6] Promoted to Colonel, August 1960.
[7] Promoted to Lt. Col., August 1961.
[8] Promoted to Lt. Col., August 1960.
[9] Promoted to Cmdr., August 1961.
[10] Promoted to Major, August 1961.

stressing literacy, others practical education, or the universities. Most urged that the Village Institutes be reopened as soon as possible.[5] The next most frequently mentioned problems were land reform and economic development. These were followed by tax reform, "village development," forest problems, health problems, "moral" and "cultural" deficiencies, agricultural modernization, and revamping of political parties. Only four NUC members included religious reform among Turkey's most urgent needs.

Interesting also were the NUC members' reports of when they first became concerned with the political state of the nation. Of those who discussed this subject, the largest number put the turning point at 1954, another sizable group said that they had become gradually more disturbed starting as far back as 1950.[6] Only one observed that he had not thought about possible military action prior to 1960. The most definite statement was by Muzaffer Karan, who asserted that he had been ready for revolution since 1954 and had been meeting secretly with friends about it since then.

There was great variation in assessments by NUC members of their tasks as rulers. Most noted that the 1960 revolution was a continuation of the Atatürk revolution, and its main job would be to set the nation back on the Atatürk road. Many expressed dissatisfaction with the work of the civilian political leaders who, they believed, had failed to explain the Atatürk revolution to the Turkish peasantry and gain its support. One theme that appeared several times was that of setting basic goals and directions for the nation in such fields as education and economic development, on which the parties could then build methods and action policies. Although most were moderate in their specific goals for their tenure in power, several voiced ambitious objectives. Ahmet Yildiz asserted that the NUC would do what vote-seeking political parties could not; for example, handle forest problems, reform the tax structure, reform party organization, and education. Muzaffer Ozdağ expressed the most disillusionment with civilians, and vowed that from now on "the army

[5] The Village Institutes were teacher-training institutions which operated in many parts of Turkey between about 1938 and 1950. The idea behind them was to take promising students from village schools and give them extensive training not too far from their homes, to prepare them to go back to their own villages and become teachers. Primarily the result of efforts by then Education Minister Hasan Ali Yücel, the Village Institutes achieved notable successes, and countless Institute graduates continue to serve well the cause of Turkish education. The Institutes were closed under the Democratic party government for allegedly having become infiltrated with leftists, but many observers think that partisan political considerations had more to do with the decision to close the schools. There is considerable sentiment today for reopening the Village Institutes.

[6] They did not cite any specific events in 1954 which started them thinking of revolution. As will be recalled, however, 1954 was the beginning of the Menderes regime's tendencies toward abridgement of freedoms of the press, the universities, the opposition, etc. See Chap. 1 above.

will be the strongest guarantor of the nation and the Republic." As a whole, however, the newspaper interviews were too early and too public to contain much material useful for an assessment of each of the men. Certainly the important differences both as to ends and means between the fourteen radicals and the rest of the committee, and which led to the purging of the former in November, were not apparent.

Among the thirty-eight there are at least three who were of pivotal importance in many of the events of the NUC's tenure in power, and who will continue to be heard from. They are Cemal Gürsel, Cemal Madanoğlu, and Alparslan Türkeş.

General Cemal Gürsel

General Cemal Gürsel was flown to Ankara from his home in Izmir on the morning of May 27 to become chairman of the NUC. His position within the army and his record of opposition to the Menderes government made him a natural choice. He was born in Erzurum in Eastern Anatolia in 1895. Son of an army officer, he entered the Military Academy after finishing elementary and secondary education in civilian schools near his home. In World War I he fought in the Dardanelles and in the Palestine campaign. In the latter he was captured by the British, and, as he somewhat regretfully recalls,[7] he was so angry at this that he resolved to resist learning English while a prisoner. He fought on the western front in the War of Independence, winning several decorations for gallantry. He graduated from the General Staff College in 1929. His service since then has included the posts of chief of intelligence and commander of various troop units, leading to his promotion to brigadier general in 1946. From 1954 to 1956 he was Commander of the Second Military Zone based in Izmir. In 1957, as a full general, he was appointed Commander of Turkish Land Forces, a post which he held until May 3, 1960.

Until that date the name of Cemal Gürsel was virtually unknown outside the army and a few civilians. On May 3 he sent a letter to the government through Defense Minister Ethem Menderes (no relation to the Prime Minister), protesting the treatment of students by the police and the use of the army for political purposes, and listed a number of steps which he thought the government must take if the political situation was to be righted. These steps included calling off the Investigating Committee looking into the activities of the press and the opposition, replacing the governors of Ankara and Istanbul, releasing journalists and students arrested in connection with the university incidents, and such longer-range matters as repealing antidemocratic laws, ending the exploitation of religion for political purposes, and solving problems of concern

[7] In an interview with this writer and Professor Manfred Halpern of Princeton University.

to the army. At the head of the list was the demand that President Bayar must resign, because "the general conviction in the nation is that he is responsible for all the present difficulties."[8] The letter was not published until after May 27, but when, as a result of it, Gürsel was given "forced leave," his farewell message to his troops received wide publicity. Urging them to keep the honor and integrity of the Army high despite everything, he recommended that his comrades-in-arms "keep out of politics at any cost." He then lived in retirement at his home in Izmir, though undoubtedly he maintained some contact with the active planners of the revolution in Ankara and Istanbul. On May 27 he was hurriedly requested to come to the capital to assume leadership of the NUC.

Cemal Gürsel is a man of medium height, a bit on the heavy side, with a shock of white hair. Every feature of his face radiates alertness, interest, and deep feeling. He shares with his fellow countrymen a tendency toward strong emotions in approving as well as disapproving ideas or policies. When the occasion warrants, he can be as sharply critical, ironic, or sarcastic as many experienced politicians. While the stroke, which he suffered in December 1960, has slowed his pace of work, his activities since his recovery have shown no diminution in his critical faculties. He is widely read, especially in history and the social sciences, though he is the first to admit that his grasp of many technical problems is limited. His greatest regret, as expressed in a November 1960 interview, was that the press of work left him only two hours each night for reading. As testimony of the effects of his broad interests, this unusual soldier responded knowingly to a wide variety of questions from the meaning of Kemalism to the problems of industrial workers in Turkey as compared to the United States or Europe.

Gürsel has played a somewhat dual role in his position as NUC Chairman, and since November 1961 as fourth President of the Turkish Republic. In important respects he is a sort of father-protector of Turkish politics. He played important conciliatory roles in the moderate-radical schism of the first months within the NUC, and in the rebellion in the summer of 1961 by senior military officers against NUC attempts to make certain command changes. Since the formation of a civilian government he has been working to ease the interparty strife which has threatened political stability and national development. He has not, however, hesitated to range himself squarely on the side of political, social, and economic reform although he is critical of certain policies that were followed during Atatürk's time. In addition, he is committed to democratic, secular methods of political action. Though he has usually tried conciliation first, he has taken strong stands when necessary, as he did in the case of the fourteen radicals in the NUC, and in regard to the more extreme opportunistic elements among the civilian politicians.

Probably the most important question in regard to General Gürsel

[8] Text of letter in *Cumhuriyet,* June 14, 1960.

will be whether he can successfully make the transition from military to civilian leadership. In the NUC period he had two major sources of strength which may not be readily transferable. One is the control provided by the institutions of martial law and government by military junta. These included the Revolutionary Courts (discussed below), which were authorized and never used, but nevertheless available as a potential weapon. There was also the existence of the NUC itself as the formal representative of the armed forces, a nonpartisan body but one which had the power to oversee and criticize the political process. Through the NUC the armed forces had a veto in case they felt it necessary to interfere drastically. In the post-NUC period President Gürsel will have to make use of less summary political practices.

The second major strength which may be lost to Gürsel is his personal influence in the armed forces. As chairman of the NUC he was also commander-in-chief of the armed forces. Although the NUC as a whole several times came into conflict with other senior officers on matters of military policy, Gürsel himself was senior to all members of the armed forces, in addition to representing the spirit of May 27. His personal relationship to the rest of the army was also a great strength, for his popularity among his comrades included both great respect and affection.[9]

In the future, however, he will be in a more equivocal position halfway between the army and the civilian political establishment. It is true that the Turkish soldier's memory is a long one,[10] but if the armed forces again become dissatisfied with political action of government, they would no longer be rebelling against their own commanding general. There is still a difference between a revolution and a mutiny.

Lieutenant General Cemal Madanoğlu

A second personality of some interest is that of Lt. General Cemal Madanoğlu. A soldier's soldier, apparently without personal political ambitions, he led the "moderate" faction in the NUC which ousted the

[9] Several times this writer was told by Turkish officers that Gürsel had been known as a staunch defender of the army's honor, of keeping the armed forces out of politics, yet also a firm opponent of the dictatorial methods of the Menderes regime. In a sense this is, of course, paradoxical. It was impossible in pre-May 27 Turkey, however, for any thinking Turk not to have opinions about the political issues which so greatly dominated public affairs. Menderes apparently mistook the lack of overt indications for a lack of political opinion in the armed forces, and as a sign that the armed forces would put higher value on retaining a legitimately elected government than on political democracy. One thing which amazed many officers was that Menderes and Chief-of-Staff General Erdelhun (also tried at Yassıada) retained Gürsel, whose opinions were apparently known to almost all insiders, as long as they did in the key position of Commander of Land Forces.

[10] The army's affection for former General Inönü, for instance, is still strong, and it was often said that one of the reasons many officers opposed Bayar is that he was the first President who was not a former officer. Both President Atatürk (1923-38) and President Inönü (1938-50) had been important military commanders during the War of Independence.

fourteen radicals. Sticking to his principle that the army should completely detach itself from politics, he refused to take the ex officio seat given to each member of the NUC in the Senate of the Grand National Assembly when power was turned back to elected leaders. His future is uncertain, but he is sure to be heard from when the role of the army in politics comes up again, as it is likely to do before long.

Madanoğlu was born in 1907 near Uşak in southwest Turkey, the son of a local merchant. Most of his youth was spent in Istanbul where his family moved soon after he was born. He at first wanted to be an engineer, but changed his mind and went through the Kuleli Military Lycée and the Military Academy, graduating from the latter in 1926. He served in many parts of Turkey, attended the General Staff College, and during the Korean War was Commander of the Turkish Brigade so noted for gallantry in action. At the time of the May 27 coup he was head of the Logistics Branch of the General Staff in Ankara.

Madanoğlu has often said that his chief interest is in maintaining a modern Turkish army, detached from politics. His dissatisfaction with traditional military habits is illustrated by a story told about how he became aware of some of the differences between Turkish and American military practice. Early in his career as an officer, when he needed several additional helmets for his troops, he had to go all the way to Marshall Fevzi Çakmak, then chief of the general staff. In Korea on the other hand, when he wanted to shift his forces to a better defensive position, the move was authorized by an American major who happened to be duty officer on the front at the time, and who did not even bother to wake his superiors for what was obviously a logical movement.

Madanoğlu strongly resisted efforts by the press to give him personal publicity, as when he refused to be interviewed for the *Cumhuriyet* series. He was one of the two NUC members who kept troop commands. He served as Ankara garrison commander simultaneously with his NUC duties.[11] It was not until the ousting of the radicals that he gave his first press conference, and even then he insisted that it be a "background briefing," and that the fact that it had even been held should not appear in the press.[12] There is little doubt that it was Madanoğlu who led the movement to oust the fourteen.

He came prominently into the public eye only in June 1961, when the

[11] The other NUC member keeping a troop command was Colonel Osman Köksal, who retained his pre-May 27 post of Commander of the Presidential Guards Regiment. Both Madanoğlu and Köksal relinquished their troop commands in June 1961 in connection with the dispute between NUC and Air Force leaders over command changes ordered by the NUC in the latter.

[12] The fact that such a press conference had been held was revealed when the Istanbul daily *Akşam* failed to keep the agreement and published some of Madanoğlu's statements. Once the secret was out, some details about the conference were published in the weeklies *Kim* and *Akis,* but most of the details of what Madanoğlu said about the radicals were excluded from the reports.

NUC clashed directly with the active senior armed forces leadership. The details of this dispute and its implications will be discussed below. The upshot for Madanoğlu was that he who was the staunchest supporter of keeping the military out of politics, and who on that account had been allowed to keep a foot in the NUC and one in active troop command, was forced to resign from both. While serving as the bridge he had also become the symbol of NUC and junior-officer control over the armed forces, control which was resented by the generals in the active services. Several efforts of the NUC to get Madanoğlu to reconsider his resignation (after the quarrel with the generals had been patched up) did not succeed. General Gürsel revealed that it was Madanoğlu's fifth resignation. He was retired from the army along with the rest of the NUC in October.

Madanoğlu's future is uncertain. He still has great respect in the army because of his record as a fighter and as upholder of the tradition of military aloofness from politics. Whether he will have a chance to carry out his ideas in reforming the Turkish army will depend largely on the future complexion of military-political relationships.

Colonel Alparslan Türkeş

The third NUC personality who deserves special attention is much-publicized and highly controversial Colonel Alparslan Türkeş. The leader of the radicals is generally thought to have considerable personal political ambition, and until the fourteen were removed from the NUC, Türkeş was everywhere considered as the "Eminence Grise" behind General Gürsel. Born in Cyprus in 1917, he lived there until, as he put it, he persuaded his family to move to Turkey in 1932. He declared to *Cumhuriyet* that his two loves were "soldiering and literature." He noted that before May 27 he read four to five hours per night, mainly poetry, novels, philosophy, and especially Turkish and Ottoman history. He graduated from the military academy in 1938. In 1944, while still a young, eager, fiery officer easily affected by the tides of German and Russian influences current at the height of World War II, he had a brush with politics when he was arrested for publishing some poems deemed by the authorities to be Turanist.[13] He was acquitted, but the incident has haunted him ever since, and it was one of the first things brought up when he became controversial during the NUC period. Some knowledgeable observers think that his interest in Turanism remains considerable. He served in the office of the Turkish Military Attaché in Washington in 1957-58, and speaks excellent English. Just prior to May 27 he was attached to the NATO Land Forces Command in Ankara.

Few people had heard of Alparslan Türkeş before May 27. His tend-

[13] The doctrine advocating the unity of all Turkish-speaking peoples, more of whom reside in the Soviet Union than in any other single country.

ency to remain in the background caused most people who made his acquaintance to attribute little importance to him, though when he spoke, his words carried the authority of wide reading, and a keen ability to generate ideas. He was active in various phases of prerevolution planning, but his exact role will become clear only when the rapidly multiplying accounts of those days are analyzed.[14] At 4 a.m. on May 27, however, it was his voice which intoned the "Attention! Attention!" which first apprised the Turkish nation of the fact that a revolution had taken place. From then on his star rose rapidly. When the NUC organized itself, Türkeş became counselor to the chairman of the NUC, and through extraordinary perseverance, application, and energy guided a large proportion of the work the NUC turned out.

But he went too fast. It was not long before others on the committee, chiefly the seven other colonels, began to resent the drift of power into Türkeş's hands. When his power became so obvious that the issue could no longer be avoided—as when during General Gürsel's press conferences Türkeş would sit beside him and seem almost to whisper what should be the answers to reporters' questions—the "Colonels Group" forced him to resign as counselor on September 22. On November 13 he and the other radicals were removed entirely from the committee and sent abroad.

Türkeş represents what is probably the most ardent Kemalism among an intelligentsia whose Kemalism is its prime common characteristic. In his speeches he constantly repeated his opinion that the chief task for Turkey is to return to the rapid and drastic reform policies of secularism, populism, and revolutionism which were the hallmarks of the period when Atatürk guided the nation.[15] As to means, it would be doing Türkeş an injustice to say that he opposed democracy, but he felt that the NUC's steady movement to early elections would significantly retard the prospects for reform.[16] The long period of one-party rule under Atatürk, and Atatürk's return to a single party on two occasions after unsatisfactory experiences with opposition parties, do of course, provide Türkeş with respectable precedents. At the same time, however, Türkeş seems to have held a rather over-optimistic view of the problems of putting into effect many of the reforms he envisioned. It was widely reported that he believed that short cuts could be found so that socialized medi-

[14] One account of Türkeş's prerevolutionary activities traces planning by him and other officers back at least as far as 1956, even though Türkeş spent much of the time between 1956 and 1960 abroad. See *Akis*, Feb. 19, 1962.

[15] The fact that Türkeş was a Cypriote may have had a bearing on his almost super-patriotism. It is not unusual for Turks born outside of the present frontiers—nor indeed for individuals marginal to their societies in any number of ways—to feel they must go to unusual lengths to show that they deserve full social acceptance.

[16] It should be mentioned that he was not alone in this view. Many in the Ankara civilian intelligentsia, while not directly opposing early elections, at least felt that major modifications were necessary, such as introducing an education qualification for voters.

cine, land reform, as well as the national culture union which finally brought his demise could be fully implemented in a matter of months. How much harm these views will do him when he returns to active politics, as he undoubtedly will, remains to be seen. His past record of loyalty to his friends, as well as the popular quality of his reform goals, can provide him with political colleagues whose advice could help him at least to avoid repeating his past tactical errors.

The NUC and the Rest of the Armed Forces

Relations between the NUC and the rest of the armed forces were generally hidden from public view during the NUC period. But on three occasions they resulted in crises which spilled prominently into the headlines: in August when several thousand officers were retired as a "rejuvenation" of the armed forces, in November when the radicals were purged from the NUC, and in June 1961 when there was an open clash between the NUC and top active armed forces leaders over personnel changes. Because of the nonpublic nature of these relations, few outsiders realized how bitter the struggle was. The details are still not known, but few dissent from the view that the crisis of June 1961 marked the end of NUC supremacy,[17] though for reasons to be considered shortly it did not mark either the end of the formal existence of the NUC or a significant reversal of the political direction which the NUC had set.

The differences involved a changing combination of ideological and personal factors. The crux of the problem was that a relatively junior group of officers, not necessarily representing all segments of the armed forces or having their full confidence, inherited formal power both over those armed forces and over the political system which the armed forces as a whole had just set out to reform. Ideological issues were not, of course, clear-cut either between the NUC and the armed forces, or within either one. Nor did they necessarily coincide with personality issues. The attempt of Colonel Türkeş to retain controlling power in the NUC in the fall of 1960, and a similar move by some of the active leaders of

[17] Probably the most vivid statement of this view was made by the Ankara correspondent of the *Economist:* "For some months it has been clear that the real rulers in Turkey have not been the junta, who are powerless and partly discredited, but a secret cabal of some two hundred officers in the armed forces known as the *Ordu Şurası* (The Council of the Army). This powerful body is said to include the chiefs of the air and naval staffs, and to have the patronage, though not the actual membership, of the elderly chief of the general staff, General Cevdet Sunay. Four or five extremist members of the junta are also in it, and it is said to have high-placed civilian members in the ministries." *Economist,* Oct. 21, 1961, p. 233.

Dana Adams Schmidt of the *New York Times* reported that a senior army officer told him, "So far as I am concerned there is no Committee. There is only the army. After all it was the army that carried out the Revolution. The Committee depends on us, not we on the Committee." *New York Times,* June 16, 1961.

the armed forces in the summer of 1961, for instance, were motivated by quite different complexes of personal-ideological factors.

The NUC and the armed forces each had several strengths which weighed in the ups and downs of their relations. One NUC strength was that it represented at least the stated aims of the armed forces, to turn power back to elected leaders as soon as possible, an aim which most members of the armed forces shared to one degree or another. Another lay in the fact that the NUC actually held power, an advantage which, barring an internal upset, could be overcome only gradually, the NUC in the meantime being able to evolve and put into operation some basic policies. A third strength was the personal esteem enjoyed in the armed forces by General Gürsel. It is also important to point out that as the NUC gradually brought civilians back into politics, it knowingly or unknowingly strengthened its own position vis-a-vis any dissident tendencies in the armed forces, thus creating a situation in which a reversal or long delay of the movement toward elections might have meant opposing virtually the entire civilian body politic. It is unlikely that the majority of the armed forces would have been willing to engage in such an action.

Probably the chief strength of the armed forces was their control of troops and weapons. That this was no small asset was demonstrated in the effectiveness with which the air force buzzed Ankara and won its point in the clash over new command appointments in June 1961. It was also significant that one of the results of that clash was that Cemal Madanoğlu and Osman Köksal, the only two NUC members still holding troop command positions, gave these up. An additional strength later came from the growing dissatisfaction in the armed forces as well as among some members of the NUC with the progress of public affairs. Both the NUC and the armed forces generally wanted to avoid an open clash with the civilian politicians, and as the leaders of the armed forces found—or said they found—more and more difficulty in keeping their own more zealous officers in line, the NUC was forced to yield further.

The Retirement of the 5,000

Each of the three NUC-armed forces crises was important in relation to the final outcome of the struggle, and almost certainly in relation to the future of Turkish politics. Each crisis created forces that may well bring members or former members of the armed forces into the political arena again in the future. The first crisis came less than three months after the revolution, when in August the NUC tackled the problem of army reform. Turkish and foreign military experts alike were almost unanimous in recognizing that some sort of reform of the Turkish army was necessary. The chief problem was top-heaviness in the officer corps. This had come about largely as a result of policies of the Menderes government to use increases in the number of officers and administration of promotions partly to win the officers' political support, partly to strengthen Turkey's international prestige, much of which came from the size of its contingent put at the disposal of NATO. General Gürsel outlined the general lines of action in a speech to the graduates of the General Staff College in Istanbul on August 2:

> ...Unfortunately the Turkish army has for years been used as the tool of politics, and the structure of the army has become diseased. There is no way to restore it to health except surgery. This operation will be performed, but with extraordinary justice, honesty, and respect for right and law. The army will be made into a dynamic body....[18]

What he meant became apparent the following day, when the "rejuvenation" operation was begun by retiring 235 generals and admirals.[19] The following day the second phase was the retirement of 5,000 additional officers of the rank of colonel, lieutenant colonel, and major. Simultaneously new appointments were made to most of the key posts which many of the retired officers had occupied.[20] In addition, the time

[18] *Cumhuriyet,* Aug. 3, 1960.

[19] The retired list included from the army 5 Generals, 13 Lieutenant Generals, 54 Major Generals, and 118 Brigadier Generals. From the navy 1 Admiral, 2 Vice-Admirals, 3 Rear Admirals, and 9 One-Star Admirals. From the Air Forces, 4 Lieutenant Generals, 7 Major Generals, 14 Brigadier Generals. From the Gendarmerie, 5 Brigadier Generals. Among the most prominent was General Ragıp Gümüşpala, commander of the 3rd Army in Erzurum on May 27, then brought to the post of Chief of the General Staff, who after his retirement entered politics as head of the Justice party. It was not completely clear why Gümüşpala was brought to the highest active military post one day and retired the next, but it was widely rumored that the 3rd Army was one of the doubtful groups whose support was badly needed to assure the revolution's initial success. It may be that once the NUC felt that this support was assured, it was also felt that the retirement of Gümüşpala could be risked.

The retired list also included Fahri Ozdilek, second-ranking member of the NUC and former Istanbul Martial Law Commander, who put himself on the list "as an example of the movement toward a more youthful army of which this is a part." Explaining the action in a speech a few days later, Gürsel stressed the top-heaviness of the army in noting that though the army table of organization provided for only 50 general officers there were 240, and that 2,600 colonels were on the books for 1,200 jobs at that rank. "If we had not undertaken this rejuvenation, it would soon have gotten to the point where each naval vessel was commanded by an admiral, each regiment by a general, and each battalion by a colonel." Gürsel never specifically mentioned the reports which were frequent in Ankara that the retired list included many officers who had been cool to the plans for May 27.

[20] The total of 5,000 was denied by the NUC after it had been printed in the newspapers. The actual number retired, plus those higher officers who took advantage of the NUC offer to retire voluntarily and receive certain extra emoluments, was probably around 3,000. The retired officers were given pensions, and severance pay equal to two years' pay at their last rank. They also retained their eligibility for new officers' housing which was to be constructed in Ankara, Istanbul, and Izmir. Many also were given civilian government jobs, including many who were assigned to various departments, and some private, tax-exempt institutions, as "civil defense" directors. Others

period in rank for eligibility for promotion was reduced for all officers from lieutenant colonel down.

How the retirement list was compiled is difficult to determine. The one identifiable category of those removed was virtually the entire group of older general officers who had received all or part of their training prior to the advent of the full influence of Atatürk in military circles. It has been variously speculated that the list of colonels, lieutenant colonels, and majors was made up with an eye to removing those who were pro-Menderes, politically conservative, or who favored the ideas of Madanoğlu rather than Türkeş. Which, if any, of these considerations was most relevant cannot be accurately assessed with the available data. Scattered reports and conversations with a few people familiar with the officer corps tend to lead to the conclusion that ability or the lack of it was not generally a large factor. It is also not known precisely who made up the list, but it seems a safe assumption that most of those retired were personally known to at least some members of the NUC or those assisting it.

The rejuvenation created two new forces in Turkish politics. Of lesser importance is the group of those retired, many of whom have been absorbed in the bureaucracy or in business. Some, like Gümüşpala, have entered politics, but there does not seem to be any mass movement of the retired officers to support any particular party. Except for pressure to increase their pensions, and so far completely unsuccessful attempts to get back into the army,[21] the "5,000" do not seem to be a significant political force.

Of greater importance is what the rejuvenation did to the younger officers. In removing the old generation of officers, many of whom had risen in rank on bases other than merit, the NUC released energies which had been pent up through most of the Menderes era. Coupled with the momentum already generated by the May 27 revolution, the unexpected and sudden promotion of younger officers to top command positions created a heady feeling which no doubt played a large role in later developments. This is not to say, however, that it made the army into a hotbed of radicalism. The Atatürk legacy, besides urging rapid reform, also included the separation of the military from politics, and both of these elements were strong.

---

have done well in private industry and business. Many wanted to get back into the armed forces. They formed the Association of Retired Officers of the Revolution (EMINSU), issuing statements as in the incident of the 147 professors (see p. 52 above) and attempting in other ways to put pressure on the government. When the new political parties were formed, the retired officers generally tended to support the Justice party formed by retired General Gümüşpala.

[21] As in the matter of the 147 fired professors, where the retired officers threatened that "if one professor is restored to his post, we will put on our uniforms again." See Chap. 3 above.

The Purge of the Fourteen Radicals

The second crisis, the purging of the radical members of the NUC in November, was not entirely unexpected, for it was widely accepted that Colonel Türkeş and others had been primarily responsible for one of the NUC's worst political blunders, the firing of the 147 professors late in October.[22] Needless to say, the purge was greeted with a great sigh of relief by civilian political figures who, no matter what their opinion of Türkeş's political ideas, had begun to fear that their own return to power might be delayed indefinitely. It is unclear what importance the radicals may yet have in Turkish politics, but for the immediate future, the purge set the NUC once and for all on the road toward early elections.

The purge was handled in typically military fashion. Messages were sent out in the predawn hours of November 13 telling fourteen members of the NUC that they were dismissed and that they were to remain in their homes until further notice. Special bulletins on the Turkish radio starting at 7:30 a.m. announced that the NUC had been dissolved and that a "new" NUC had been formed consisting of the remaining twenty-three members of the original junta.[23] Within a few days, all fourteen had been retired from the armed forces, assigned as counsellors to Turkish embassies abroad, and sent out of the country with their families.

In his announcement to the nation, broadcast in his own voice, General Gürsel said he had taken the action "on the petitions of the Turkish Armed Forces and the members of the National Unity Committee, because the activities of the NUC had fallen to a point which endangered the high interests of the nation."[24] He elaborated on this in a press conference the same evening. All thirty-eight members of the original NUC were patriotic, hard-working, and sincere, he said, "but gradually such different ideas, such disagreements have emerged that committee discussions have become battlefields more than means to solve problems." He asserted that contradictory public statements and speeches had understandably driven the nation to ask what was going on, with especially serious consequences for the nation's economic activity. The decision could no longer be postponed, "because there remained no possibility

[22] It is generally agreed that the firing of the 147 university professors was primarily the work of the 14 radicals. Though the action was approved by almost the entire committee, many reliable hints have been dropped that it was some of the 14 who took the initiative in instigating the move, preparing the list of professors to be fired, etc. It is also notable that when the University Senates asked for the files on the professors as a basis for the re-evaluation which the NUC at one point sought from the universities, the NUC replied that the files were not to be found, having presumably disappeared along with the other "private" papers of the 14 after they were dismissed. See Chap. 3 for more details.

[23] The 38th member, General Irfan Baştuğ, had been killed in an automobile accident in September.

[24] *Cumhuriyet*, Nov. 14, 1960.

of agreement, nor could remedies be found to return to the right direction." Although not referring directly to any particular person or group, he concluded by saying that "it is the opinion of my colleagues and myself that the Turkish nation must develop its future in the clean and true atmosphere of the democratic spirit. And we are resolved to attain this end and to remove all obstacles which may arise before us on this road."[25]

Who were the fourteen, what were the differences General Gürsel referred to, and what led to the purge? Probably the most outstanding common characteristic of the radicals is their youth, as compared with other NUC members. They included no generals, one out of eight colonels, three of seven lieutenant colonels, five of twelve majors, and five of the six captains. Few other objective measures differentiate them from their colleagues. There are no significant differences in rate of promotion or place of origin. As a group they were articulate, intelligent, and energetic. At least three, Erkanlı, Esin, and Ozdağ, had advanced education in law and public administration. Between May 27 and November 13, most had become well-known public figures.

That the NUC was not internally a unified body began to become clear soon after May 27. Comparatively uncomplicated decisions were announced only after meetings that often lasted many hours. The committee by-laws permitted no public discussion of the proceedings of NUC meetings, but did not bar any other kind of statement of individual opinion by NUC members. And committee members made frequent public statements on various aspects of public affairs that revealed a whole range of different attitudes and emphases. The main issues, in a general sense, were philosophical. What was the optimum relationship of the army to Turkish politics, and the army's proper role in furthering Turkish democracy and development? To determine the views of most of the individual members of both the old and the new NUC will require detailed research, but it can be generally stated that the fourteen radicals favored more firmly controlled and centralized implementation of the Atatürk reforms and a longer period of military tutelage of the nation than was favored by the remainder of the NUC. It should be pointed out, however, that there is no conclusive evidence that the fourteen were operating as a bloc.

Psychological considerations no doubt played a part in widening the gap between the fourteen radicals and the other twenty-three members. What was most galling to the twenty-three—and especially to the "Colonels Group"—was the behavior of the young Captains Esin, Ozdağ, and Solmazer. What did these juniors think they were doing, going around the country like victorious generals, scattering statements on every conceivable subject? Though the operating rules of the NUC allowed individual members to speak freely as long as they did not claim to speak for

[25] *Ibid.*

the whole NUC or reveal the content of NUC discussions, they were, after all, still soldiers, and the disappearance of all semblance of discipline or respect for rank could hardly be tolerated. Worst of all, some of the young officers had begun to take on a habit identified with the old regime, namely the frequenting of Ankara night clubs. Highly unsoldierly.[26]

The 147 incident, both the content and the summary military way in which it was handled, had brought about the first serious and concerted criticism of the NUC by civilian political groups.[27] It was at this time that the interminable NUC meetings began to be the rule rather than the exception. But the incident that directly precipitated the dismissal of the fourteen was the proposal for a Turkish Ideal and Culture Union *(Türkiye Ulkü ve Kültür Birliği)*. A sort of superministry, the Culture Union would replace the Ministry of Education, and the Directorates of Physical Education, Pious Foundations *(Vakif)*, Religious Affairs, and Press and Radio.[28] Among the aims of the proposed new institution were the following:

> To mobilize the nation's intelligentsia to work with its entire energies on recognized problems in order to strengthen the progressive and civilized Turkish nation in the national consciousness, and to advance the nation toward these goals. . . .
>
> To take all necessary measures, *free of political pressure and interference*, to save the nation from the schism, backwardness, laziness and darkness in which it now finds itself. . . .[29]

The Culture Union was to have eleven divisions: People and Workers; Universities and Schools; Army; Press, Publications and Radio; Arts, Culture and Social Organizations; Women's and Family Affairs; Turks

[26] Most of the other members of the NUC eventually began to appear on the "cocktail circuit," though not for some time after the firing of the fourteen radicals. Actually the most ardent drinker and carouser in the Turkish Republic was probably Atatürk himself, who did a great deal of his consultation with others on political problems over all-night dinner parties. One of the significant things which distinguished Menderes from Atatürk is that whereas this behavior was largely tolerated in the latter, it became the symbol of corruption and decadence when Menderes engaged in it.

[27] Nadir Nadi, for example, wrote: "Mistakes have been made, and the magnitude of the mistakes is very great," and added that since it was impossible to believe that the NUC had been equipped to review the case of each fired professor personally, it must be that the junta was under the influence of individuals with personal interests in the affair. *(Cumhuriyet,* Oct. 30, 1960.) Even Aydın Yalçin, up to that time one of the staunchest supporters of NUC, was forced to join the critics. Though upholding the need for university reform, he asserted that it could not be accomplished summarily and overnight, and that "our basic opinion is that this dismissal law will bring more harm than good to Turkish intellectual life and academic institutions. *(Oncü,* Oct. 29, 1960.) The strength of critical feeling on the part of university students was shown when they boycotted Republic Day ceremonies.

[28] Details of the aims and proposed organization of the Culture Union are given in *Cumhuriyet,* Nov. 7, 1960, and *Vatan,* Nov. 11, 1960.

[29] *Vatan,* Nov. 11, 1960. Italics added.

Living Abroad; Minorities; Discoveries and Inventions; Harmful Ideologies; and Communication Abroad. The director of the Culture Union would be appointed by the President of the Republic on the recommendation of delegates from the Judiciary, the General Staff and Military Courts, and University rectors, for a six-year term, removable only for moral turpitude or malfeasance of duty. He would have an ex-officio seat in the Cabinet, but not be responsible to any Ministry (presumably including the Prime Ministry). The director would be authorized to establish any and all subsections which he felt necessary and would maintain "continuing liaison" in villages, cities, schools, universities, factories, the army to bring to light basic problems and to submit plans prepared for the solution of these problems for review by the Culture Union's Scientific Consultative Council.

The outcry about the Culture Union was not equal to that over the firing of the professors, but among the political leaders and intellectuals in Ankara and Istanbul the protest was sharp and immediate. Though only in the form of a draft proposal which the NUC would discuss, few discerning observers failed to see the seeds of dictatorship in the Culture Union proposal. Ankara talked of nothing else, and even the statement by NUC member General Sitki Ulay that he thought the Culture Union unnecessary—noting that it was his belief that national unity already existed in Turkey—failed to calm the tidal wave of anxiety that engulfed the capital.

Journalist Ahmet Emin Yalman spoke for most of the political community when he wrote that such a proposal was not only a betrayal of many of the basic freedoms of a democracy and of the principle of representative government, but was also highly illusory if its authors thought that merely through such an institution there would come the immediate unity and maturity which the impatience of the young and fiery members apparently demanded. "Their known goal is to gather the Turkish nation to the same ideas and beliefs down to the tiniest detail. . . ." But unity gained in ways other than opening the road to free and tolerant discussion would be nothing but sterile discipline.[30] In his press conference following the dismissal of the fourteen, General Gürsel took pains to state that "there is no such thing as a Culture Union. Let me put it this way: You raise the Turkish nation 100 meters, but what is this? What does it achieve? We are determined to develop the democratic spirit in the nation. No decision whatever which would throw a shadow over this spirit will ever emerge from the NUC."[31]

The exiling of the fourteen was probably the turning point in the NUC's affairs in many ways. As will be discussed shortly, it greatly accelerated the rate at which the political parties reentered the arena. In regard to the armed forces there were two important effects. In the eyes

[30] *Vatan,* Nov. 12, 1960.
[31] *Cumhuriyet,* Nov. 14, 1960.

of some officers the fourteen received a sort of martyrdom, and far from losing their influence, there has since grown up almost a mystic concept of them. The second effect was that even the more moderate reformists in the officer corps began to wonder what reforms the NUC would accomplish before capitulating to the resurgent civilian influence.

Both the continuing strength of the fourteen, and the growing skepticism in the armed forces could be seen in the NUC's clumsy, but probably unavoidable change of attitude toward the exiles. Not many weeks passed before NUC members were taking pains to state that the fourteen were not really traitors, that the remaining members of the NUC considered them brothers in ideals. It is not unlikely that most of the NUC members soon developed doubts about the wisdom of what they had done. The NUC's main point in their conciliatory moves was that the differences between them and their former colleagues were only on means, not on ends. One of the NUC's final statements before relinquishing power read:

> ...In proceeding toward a democratic and lawful state, which 38 comrades in revolution affirmed to be their common belief in the oath they took before the nation, and whose patriotism is left to the unchanging judgment of history, the difficult nature of the revolution led to some differences of method. Our 14 comrades, who as a result of these differences were given duties outside the nation through Law 127—and it was only a personnel action—have performed their duties with great conscientiousness. We wish to inform our beloved nation that the result of the revolution which we have today attained, and in whose preparation, execution and responsibility before history they shared, has been a goal in which they also believed.[32]

When asked about the possibility of the fourteen returning to Turkey shortly, several NUC members noted that there was no law saying they could not return, and that all they had to do was to resign from their posts as political counsellors. "In my opinion May 27 owes a debt to these 14 heroic comrades," added Colonel Sami Küçük,[33] and General Gürsel, in his press conference on October 19, admitted the possibility that he would include some of the fourteen in the group of senators he would have the right to appoint should he be elected President.[34]

Since their dismissal, the fourteen have not been idle and have maintained close contact with each other and with many of their friends in Turkey, both military and civilian. To emphasize publicly that they were still in existence, six of them gathered in Paris on October 30, 1961, coming from as far away as Ottawa and New Delhi, and held a press conference. Commenting on the failure of any party to win a majority in the recent Turkish election, they said (speaking as a group but refusing to give individual statements), "We said a year ago that it would be

[32] *Cumhuriyet,* Oct. 17, 1961.
[33] *Oncü,* Oct. 18, 1961.
[34] *Cumhuriyet,* Oct. 20, 1961. None of the 14 was thus appointed.

this way. Because our predictions have come true, it will be only normal that we make new proposals to our friends in the political parties." They added that until their return to Turkey they would work through friends there, noting that they had many friends among the Turkish intellectuals, the army, youth organizations, and the people at large. In answer to the question whether new elections were necessary, their joint comment was "We do not believe that the important problems existing in our nation can be solved by a parliament which is established at this time . . . The result of the election proves the rightness of the view that it was wrong to have elections so soon after May 27."[35] At a meeting of the fourteen in Brussels in July 1962, following visits of two of their number to Turkey, there was talk of forming their own political party, but in the end it was decided to refrain from any formal organization and leave each individual free to act as he chooses. Few people believe this is any more than a tactic. The fourteen and their ideas are by no means to be counted out.

The "Personnel Crisis" of June 1961

The months after the purge of the fourteen must have been frustrating for both the NUC and the active officer corps. The NUC, because of its decisions to refrain from interference in the Yassıada trials even though they began to drag interminably, and to allow new political parties, a Constituent Assembly, and a national referendum on the Constitution, was badly overshadowed and often outmaneuvered by other political groups. In the campaigns before the referendum and before the October election its belated efforts to curb political aspirants who hardly bothered to camouflage their appeals to pro-Menderes followers had practically no effect whatever. The frustration among the active officers at these troubles of the NUC must have been even greater. The retirement of the 5,000 had at last given many of the younger officers a chance to use their energies and abilities for the good of the nation. The purging of the radicals had strengthened those active officers who, while still ardently reformist, also maintained their adherence to the tradition of a nonpolitical army. It is not hard to understand why the officers' patience with the NUC ended as soon as even a peripheral crisis provided an opportunity to wrest control from the junta and try to salvage what was left of May 27.

The crisis came when in June 1961, the NUC appointed Air Force Commander Lieutenant General Irfan Tansel to the post of adviser to the Turkish Military Mission in Washington. A 1930 graduate of the Military Academy, Tansel had a brilliant record including duty as Air

[35] *Cumhuriyet*, Oct. 31, 1961.

Attaché in Paris, and had been made Air Force Commander after the retirement of the 5,000 in 1960. Very popular among his Air Force colleagues, he was generally regarded as a strong supporter of getting the armed forces out of politics, in a sense almost the Air Force's counterpart of Army General Madanoğlu. The reasons the NUC appointed him to Washington are unclear, but the repercussions were plain. The Air Force sent a squadron of jets over Ankara, and the NUC announced that the Tansel appointment had been "reconsidered."

The repercussions continued, however. The armed forces had long been unhappy about the NUC keeping control of certain troop units, and the June 9 announcement of Tansel's reinstatement as Air Force Commander was accompanied by word that NUC member Colonel Osman Köksal had relinquished his post as Commander of the Presidential Guard Regiment, and General Madanoğlu had stepped down from his position as Commander of the Ankara Garrison. The following day Madanoğlu resigned from the NUC altogether. The next few days saw the replacement of Colonel Ağası Şen, General Gürsel's Aide-de-Camp who had at various times been identified with Türkeş; replacement of the Defense Minister, Ground Forces Commander, and several high naval officers; and the retirement of several other high army and navy officers. On June 15 the Chief of the General Staff, General Cevdet Sunay, for the first time sat in on a meeting of the NUC, a practice which he continued frequently thereafter. Meetings between the NUC and the armed forces commanders also became frequent, justified in the press by the possible dangers to public order during the tense period of the end of the Yassıada trials and the election campaign. Though the active officers apparently prevailed over the NUC from then on, and did their best to curb the reactionary civilian political groups more effectively than the NUC had managed to, it was too late to effect a basic reversal of direction.

The events of the NUC period tend to support the inference that the Turkish army's tradition of staying out of politics remains strong. One of the notable things about the NUC-armed forces dispute was that neither group questioned the plans to turn power back to elected leaders. One of the chief points made in the protocol announcing settlement of the "personnel crisis" was that there was complete agreement on this point. It is possible, of course, that this position was taken partly in the face of the growing difficulty of deviating from the road to elections, but the general attitudes of military leaders throughout the NUC period would indicate that the desire to get out of politics as soon as possible was also sincere and genuine.

It is only if political parties fail to solve Turkey's social and economic problems that there would arise the possibility of that tradition being broken. The attempted coup d'état on February 22, 1962, led by Colonel Talat Aydemir and a group of young officers around the Military Academy, showed that some elements in the armed forces, at least, were already becoming impatient. These elements have also hinted at indirect ties to the radicals. The remainder of the officer corps failed to support Aydemir. Even after four months of activity the newly elected Assembly had produced nothing but wrangling about a possible amnesty for those convicted at Yassıada. This may, of course, mean only that the majority of officers have more patience than Aydemir. There are clearly a number of different attitudes within the officer corps, with a line of demarcation which is probably not a fixed one. If the armed forces do feel that they must again interfere in order to put the nation once more on the road to progress, it is unlikely that they would get out of power again without achieving political, social, and economic reforms which the NUC period should have stimulated the civilians into achieving. But during the NUC period the armed forces clearly showed that they are part of that new middle class which values progress, but values political democracy as well.

The NUC and the Political Parties

From the very beginning the NUC gave a large role to the political parties with the exception, of course, of the DP. A cabinet made up largely of nonpartisan civilians was formed on May 28, 1960, but it was not long before members of both the RPP and RPNP had found their way into cabinet office. Political party activity was formally suspended, but this did not prevent leaders of existing parties or aspirants to the leadership of new parties from meeting, planning, and using various means to get publicity while not directly violating the ban against political activity. The NUC tacitly encouraged this activity by frequently succumbing to the obsession of the parties and the press and speculating on the date for general elections. The parties, controlling the press, had little trouble in holding the limelight of public attention when in January the NUC convened a Constituent Assembly which not only wrote a new constitution and election law, but also passed on the budget, debated proposed laws, and entertained questions about government actions which the ministers were obliged to answer on the Assembly platform. When during the spring and summer of 1961 danger signals began to arise in the form of parties racing to become successors to Menderes, the NUC was virtually powerless to do more than attempt to curb the most extreme elements, to say nothing of altering the course of events in any important way.

Probably the basic shortcoming of the NUC in this regard was its failure to realize how deeply the struggle of the 1950's between the Democratic and Republican parties had become imbedded in the political structure of Turkey. The ouster of the Menderes regime and arrest and conviction of its national leaders did not at the same time eliminate either the remainder of the vast Democratic organization, or the issues that had caused the fundamental division in the nation which was the direct cause of the interparty enmity leading to the May 27 revolution. It is not too much to say, in fact, that by allowing individuals closely identified with the RPP to play a large role in the preparations for a return of power to elected leaders—granted that a large proportion of the qualified political and technical leaders were by 1960 identified with the RPP—the NUC probably sharpened the bipolarization even further.

The NUC, as will be recalled, included in their proclamation of May 27 the intention of having early elections based on a revised constitution and election law, and generally let it be known that it envisioned a timetable of about one month for the constitution, two months for trials of the fallen regime, and elections within three months. This hurried timetable led to selection of a group of constitution-writers who were highly controversial, and not representative of much of Turkish legal and intellectual opinion. Chapter 4 on the making of the constitution has shown how the underestimate by both the Onar Commission and the NUC of the time required for the job, coupled with the controversy which characterized every step of the writing process, stretched the period of evolution of the constitution into a full year instead of a month.

With almost equal speed a seventeen-man cabinet was appointed on May 28.[36] It included three professors, two generals, and the rest career civil servants, businessmen, and technicians. Only two, Foreign Minister Selim Sarper, a highly respected career diplomat, and Minister of Customs and Monopolies Fethi Aşkın, up to 1960 Director-General of Customs, lasted throughout the NUC period. What is known as the Second Revolutionary Cabinet was installed late in August after ten of the original ministers had been dismissed, the NUC discovering that professorial, business, or technical skills are not necessarily convertible to ministerial ones. Among those dismissed were physician Dr. Nusret Karasu as Minister of Health, Professor of Political Science Cahit Talas as Minister of Labor, former President of the Demir (Iron) Bank Orhan Kubat as Minister of Construction and Housing.[37]

The second cabinet was on the whole much better qualified than the

[36] Prime Minister and Defense Minister, Cemal Gürsel; Ministers of State, Amil Artus and Şefik Inan; Justice, Abdullah Gözübüyuk; Interior, Muharrem Ihsan Kızıloğlu; Foreign Affairs, Selim Sarper; Finance, Ekrem Alican; Education, Fehmi Yavuz; Public Works, Danış Koper; Commerce, Cihat Iren; Health, Nusret Karasu; Customs and Monopolies, Fethi Aşkın; Communications, Sitki Ulay; Labor, Cahit Talas; Industry, Muhtar Uluer; Press, Radio and Tourism, Zühtü Tarhan; Construction & Housing, Orhan Kubat; Agriculture, Feridun Ustün.

[37] New cabinet members appointed August 25, 1960 were: Ministers of State, Hayri Mumcuoğlu and Nasır Zeytinoğlu; Defense, Fahri Ozdilek; Justice, Amil Artus; Finance, Kemal Kurdaş; Education, Bedrettin Tuncel; Public Works, Mukbil Gökdoğan; Commerce, Mehmet Baydur; Health, Ragib Oner; Labor, Mehmet Raşıt Beşerler; Industry, Sahap Kocatopcuoğlu; Construction and Housing, Fehmi Yavuz; Agriculture, Osman Tosun. Later replacements were as follows: Deputy Prime Minister, Fahri Ozdilek (Oct. 22, 1960) and Sitki Ulay (June 28, 1961); Minister of State, M. I. Kızıloğlu (Feb. 4,

first. Especially effective later appointees were Minister of State Nasir Zeytinoğlu, later Interior Minister; Kemal Kurdaş, who became Finance Minister in December when Ekrem Alican resigned to head the New Turkey party; and Minister of Commerce Mehmet Baydur. Among the more controversial ministers were Muharrem Ihsan Kiziloğlu, a Major General who was Interior Minister until February 1961, when his own lack of tact and his inability to adapt his operating methods from military to civilian activities led to his dismissal (he was appointed Ambassador to the Vatican); and Ahmet Tahtakılıç, Education Minister during the last part of the NUC period, whose membership in the conservative Nation party and his intransigence on the issue of the 147 fired professors made him anathema to many other political leaders in Ankara.

Other cabinet changes came when Fehmi Yavuz, Professor of City Planning, and Turhan Feyzioğlu, former Dean of the Ankara Political Science Faculty, resigned over the failure to solve the 147 problem. The posts of Deputy Prime Minister and Minister of Defense remained in the hands of active or retired generals during the entire period.

Along with continual speculation about the date of the election, the press and the political circles in Ankara began measuring every act of the NUC in relation to themselves. The NUC continued to insist that it was impartial, and in many ways it seriously worked to demonstrate this. One example was the July 30, 1960, arrest of some seventy-one students who were demonstrating in protest against the activities of Istanbul University Law Professor Ali Fuat Başgil. The fact that Başgil had been prominently identified with Bayar and Menderes did not deter the authorities from enforcing the decrees of martial law which forbade demonstrations. Yet the very nature of the situation, the policy of noninterference in the Yassıada trials which became more and more pro-Republican in content, the RPP's virtual monopoly of experienced political advice which the NUC needed so badly—all these combined to identify the committee more and more with the RPP.

Because of cross-pressures on the NUC and civilian political interests, both seemed to vacillate frequently in their attitudes toward each other. The 147 incident brought bitter criticism of the NUC from almost all political quarters. The firing of the radical NUC members again raised the stature of the NUC in civilian eyes. The protracted failure to solve the 147 problem, ending with its summary removal from the NUC agenda in January, gave rise to renewed fears that the NUC would not really

---

1961) and Sitki Ulay (Feb. 3, 1961); Defense, Huseyn Ataman (Oct. 22, 1960), Muzaffer Alankuş (Jan. 5, 1961) and Fahri Ozdilek (July 28, 1961); Justice, Ekrem Tüzemen (Jan. 5, 1961) and Kemal Türkoğlu (Aug. 16, 1961); Interior, Nasır Zeytinoğlu (Feb. 4, 1961); Education, Turhan Feyzioğlu (Jan. 5, 1961) and Ahmet Tahtakılıç (Mar. 2, 1961); Communications, Orhan Mersinli (Jan. 5, 1961); Labor, Ahmet Tahtakılıç (Jan. 5, 1961) and Cahit Talas (Mar. 2, 1961); Press, Radio and Tourism, Cihat Baban (Jan. 5, 1961); Construction and Housing, Rüştü Ozal (Feb. 6, 1961).

honor its pledge to turn power back to elected leaders. The convening of the Constituent Assembly, the NUC displeasure with the actions of the Justice and Nation parties in the campaigns for the July referendum and the October election, and the imposition of the national agreement on the political parties all resulted in renewed sweeps of the optimism-pessimism pendulum.

The increasing inroads of conservative groups into political affairs posed dilemmas for both the NUC and for a growing number of progressive-minded civilians. For the NUC the question was whether the problem of new parties using pro-Menderes arguments to appeal to voters was serious enough to warrant modifying the goal of early, free elections. For many intellectuals the difficulty of radical social and political reform through multiparty politics began to loom large as the prospect of a sizable conservative representation in the Assembly increased. Many agreed that a period of renewed "political education" was necessary among the peasants, and while few among the urban educated class favored the ideas of the radical former NUC members, many wished that the NUC moderates had not been quite so moderate in shaping the new parliamentary system. Among both the NUC and the civilians, however, the drive to return speedily to civilian government turned out to be the stronger, and once the entire complex of political parties got behind it, the NUC's decisions were in effect made for it.

The amount of authority which the NUC relinquished to the Constituent Assembly can only be noted with amazement. According to the Assembly's charter, written by a committee of five professors headed by former RPP deputy Feyzioğlu and including Muammer Aksoy, Bahri Savcı, Suat Derbil and Ilhan Arsel, a shrewd and generally RPP-oriented group, a bicameral institution was created with the NUC as the upper house. How the Assembly despite its composition turned out to be a near-monopoly of the RPP, has already been described.[38] It is not likely that the NUC anticipated such a turn of events. On the contrary, one report stated that while the cabinet wanted to reduce the number of direct political party representatives proposed by the Feyzioğlu Committee, the NUC wanted to increase it.[39]

The Constituent Assembly received broad powers. Besides making the new Constitution and Election Law, the original purpose for which it was to have been convened, it was empowered, as one newspaper quoted the Assembly Charter, "to make all other laws, amend, interpret or repeal them, discuss and pass the budget and appropriations, declare war and peace, ratify treaties and agreements, pass on martial law if proclaimed by the cabinet, and proclaim a general amnesty;"[40] all the powers of a regular legislature, in other words. Proposed laws had to be signed

[38] Chap. 5.
[39] *Vatan,* Nov. 28, 1960.
[40] *Cumhuriyet,* Nov. 26, 1960.

by at least one member of the Constituent Assembly, and one member of the NUC. Proposals were to be debated first in the Assembly, then sent to the NUC whether they were passed or rejected. If the NUC passed a bill which the Assembly had rejected, it went to a conference committee. Approval of both the Assembly and the NUC were required for enactment. One western correspondent pointed out rightly that the NUC thus kept a veto on the decision of the Assembly.[41] He failed to add, however, that by the same token the Assembly was given at least in theory an equal veto over the NUC.

The Assembly and the NUC clashed several times, though not on the fundamental issue of moving toward free elections, which both groups supported strongly. It should also be noted that the NUC still had at its disposal the instruments of martial law, and the Assembly had no role in the administrative actions the authorities took against antirevolutionary activities. Nor were there significant protests from the Assembly against the military's interpretation of what activities were antirevolutionary. The outcry among New Turkey party adherents even in the Aydın Yalçın case was relatively mild.

The NUC used its veto most prominently in the 147 matter, no NUC member agreeing at any time to sign a proposal regarding the professors who were discharged. Most of the other clashes were on economic and financial matters. In at least one instance, a tax revision bill in June 1961, the NUC showed that if it really wanted to, it could pressure its version through the Assembly. But in the public eye the NUC clearly played second fiddle. Questions to ministers by members of the Assembly, even if on insignificant topics, usually got far more play in the press than did the work of the NUC.

The final phase of the process by which the NUC lost power to the political parties began with the organization of new parties, and culminated in the referendum and election campaigns. These subjects have been discussed in Chapter 5. The significant point is that as the campaigns progressed, various parties and individuals publicly criticized not only many of the NUC's policies, but sometimes the premise of May 27 itself. The more extreme of these critics were arrested for investigation, and at least one was tried by a military court and sentenced to death (though the sentence was never carried out). The more clever critics were seldom deterred, however, merely making sure that the statements likely to be picked up by the press were vague. There is no doubt that the volume of criticism of May 27 made in less public ways, especially in villages, was large. The result of the Constitution referendum, almost 40 percent of the votes cast "no," can be interpreted in no other way than as a vote against May 27. And by the time the election came in October, only the most idealistic or self-deluding seriously predicted anything other than a substantial showing by right-wing and pro-Menderes elements.

[41] "Turkey's Search for Democracy," *Economist* (Jan. 14, 1961), p. 150.

The NUC and the Peasants

The relations of the NUC to the peasants, who make up an estimated 75 percent of the population of Turkey, required: (1) that it be made clear that the army meant to enforce its decrees; (2) that the peasants accept the idea of May 27; and (3) that they understand May 27. The problems were considerable, for though it is true that Turkish peasants traditionally have a healthy respect for armed power, it is also true that they can be extremely shrewd in withdrawing and withholding their opinions at the opportune time. In addition, it must be remembered that it was the image of Menderes versus Inönü, not the niceties of freedom of the press, economic policy, or multiparty government, which most immediately shaped Turkish peasant attitudes toward the revolution. And the image of Menderes that most peasants had was a highly favorable one.

To help overcome these handicaps the army had several advantages. One was that its ranks were made up largely of peasant soldiers, who were susceptible to the influence of their officers, which they could then carry back to the villages. Another was that many of the officers themselves had family connections among the peasants. A third advantage was that the cause of May 27 was espoused by the vast majority of village teachers, many of whom had been trained in the Village Institutes or elsewhere where the Atatürk influence was strong. It is doubtful, however, that many peasants had much understanding of the meaning of May 27.

One of the first acts of the NUC in relation to the peasants was the abolition of local and county branches of all political parties.[42] Commenting on this action, General Gürsel asserted that he had not found village party branches serving as channels for bringing democracy, as Inönü had maintained. On the contrary, he claimed

> ...Because of local and district party branches, villages and districts have been split in two in a bloody way, the rival factions have refused to use the same mosque, coffee-house, even to let their daughters have contact with people of the other side....When our parties will have developed to the extent that parties have in the West, when political education will have reached such a level, perhaps these organizations can be profitable instead of harmful....[43]

But the negative action of prohibiting party organizations to function on the local level could hardly be counted as more than a first step. As a minimum, it was necessary to add some positive measures to emphasize the fact that illegal political activity would be swiftly punished. On June

[42] Law No. 8, amendment to Law No. 3512, the Law of Associations, July 4, 1960.
[43] *Cumhuriyet*, July 10, 1960.

28, 1960, the NUC gave the police and gendarmerie new and wide authority. On August 12, the period for which offenders could be held for investigation without being charged was extended to thirty days. And on August 18, the NUC passed a law setting up "Revolutionary Courts." Roughly akin to the Independence Tribunals of the 1920's in Turkey, the courts could be set up whenever and wherever needed, their members being appointed directly by the NUC. The courts would try those who either committed crimes "against the National Revolution Movement and its principles," or who made propaganda against it. Sentences of from five to fifteen years imprisonment, and in extreme cases, the death penalty, could be passed. Actually Revolutionary Courts were never set up, but the NUC frequently reminded the public that they could be, one NUC member at one time adding: "There are many more Yassıadas which we can use if it is necessary." Martial law authorities also frequently arrested persons for anti-revolutionary activities and brought them before regular military courts.

Along with these measures the NUC took steps to meet the second requirement, the acceptance of the idea of May 27, and hopefully the third, getting the peasants to understand May 27 as well. Acceptance was sought chiefly through massive efforts in the press and through the radio to publicize the crimes of the former regime. Some of these efforts have been described in Chapter 2 above. The NUC took no steps to halt the flood of reports of physical, political, and financial misdeeds of the Menderes regime. For days after May 27 the newspapers were filled with hundreds of details, individual accounts of suffering, and pictures of blood and brutality. Revelations about the state of the Turkish economy were designed to show how everyone, the peasants included, had been hurt. Special campaigns were opened to get more newspapers sent to villages, including the placing of boxes on city street corners urging people to contribute newspapers they had finished reading. The effectiveness of this campaign was probably only moderate, for the attitudes of peasants were deep-seated, and it should not be forgotten that much of what went to the villages in printed form had first to go through those few in each village who knew how to read, and who could screen out what they wished.

One action which potentially could have had great effect, at least in many areas of eastern Turkey, was the removal of fifty-five *ağas* to compulsory residence in western Turkey, and the confiscation for future distribution of their lands. Breaking the power of these owners of large lands and often of many villages, who exercised virtually feudal rule over large numbers of peasants, had been one of Atatürk's chief efforts in eastern Turkey, but much of the old order still remained in 1960—and does today. This NUC action was also less than fully effective, chiefly because the *ağas* were able to resort to legal delaying tactics and to enlist the help of others to soften the terms of the exile and expropriation, and because the distribution of their land to the peasants never really was done on a large scale. The effectiveness of the *ağas'* political power became clear when the coalition government which followed the NUC in office let them return and restored all their land and property that had not yet been distributed.

The NUC twice toured the country making speeches, and several times sent teachers and students out to explain May 27 in the villages. The first tour was in September 1960, when sixteen teams of one or two members spent a week in cities, towns, and villages throughout the country. They discussed a wide variety of subjects, often in response to questions from the crowds which met them everywhere. Mostly they attempted to explain the reasons for May 27, to outline some of the things they planned to do or see done, and to emphasize that they were not interested in staying in power. The latter sentiment probably was largely incomprehensible to unsophisticated peasants, and made peasants less inclined to take the NUC seriously.

Religion and economics were most emphasized. Ozgür said in Antalya that "religious subjects will be left to intelligent hands"; Yildiz in Bayburt asserted that "we will give no quarter to reaction or religious exploitation." On economics, some members talked about current and future problems, others entered more controversial areas. Erkanlı said in Kayseri, for example, "We are not enemies of the rich, merely of thieves," but added that "Some capitalists do not support us . . . but their resistance will be broken." Later he asserted that over the last ten years "Turkey has become a colony of the United States." Ahmet Er in Diyarbakir condemned the Menderes regime on moral grounds, charging that it had gone so far as to "open houses of prostitution and make gifts of Turkish women to foreigners."[44]

Some speakers took care to emphasize the seriousness of the army, as when Erkanlı declared that "many people thought the DP couldn't be toppled, did they?" Numan Esin in a town near Balıkesir promised that "if you vote for immoral candidates, we will collar you!" At least some attempt was also made to win the sympathy of the peasants, as when Münir Köseoğlu promised in Adapazarı that one of the policies for the future would be to enable peasants to pay off the debts in easy installments. The overall picture left by the September tour was that though certain very general lines of policy and opinion were agreed on, the NUC had nothing like a unified ideology or specific program. The results of the tour were more revealing about what each individual NUC member believed than about the committee as a whole. It is doubtful that the tour had much of an effect in shaping further relations between the NUC and the peasants.

The NUC did not go to the country again until the following July, when it undertook a "Yes Campaign" for the Constitution referendum.

[44] *Ulus*, Sept. 22, 1960.

Other parts of the "Yes Campaign" attracted more attention, however, the role of political parties (discussed earlier) and a variety of other attempts to obtain a resounding vote of approval. One of the more interesting of the NUC efforts here was the distribution of a pamphlet entitled "Our Constitution Viewed from a Religious Standpoint," prepared by the Directorate of Religious Affairs and published a week before the voting. Taking a position midway between the two extremes of Turkey's continuing debate over the application and interpretation of secularism, it said:

> ...To refrain from relying even partly on religious grounds for determining the social, economic, political and legal foundation of the state is useful to those who wish to exploit it for political or personal ends. Conditions today no longer permit application of Koranic laws as they were applied by our forefathers who understood matters according to conditions of their own day. But to create a current provoking the pure and clean religious feelings of the majority of the people is harmful to the tranquility, soundness and advancement of our nation. Preventing in advance the use of the Constitution by those who want to use religion in government activities for such purposes is a service to the freedom and dignity of religion....[45]

The action of the NUC that may have the deepest and most permanent effect on the peasants is the Reserve Officer Teacher program. As a model for possible future enterprises in accelerating Turkish education, the changing of the two-year obligation of lycée graduates from service as reserve officers to service as teachers in village elementary schools could be of first importance. In 1960-61 several thousand young men were sent to villages all over Turkey, and many performed their duties conscientiously and ably. The difficulties of such imaginative programs are clear, however, from the volume of protests, complaints, and demands for extra pay, uniforms, and weapons. The NUC could be relatively deaf to the cries of the young men suddenly faced with village life instead of the prestige of officers' status. Whether elected leaders can resist such pressure in the same way remains to be seen.

In the end it is likely that the Turkish peasants did not take the NUC seriously. The NUC really brought only little change in the relation of the peasants to political affairs. The Revolutionary Courts were never set up, parties that hardly hid their pro-Menderes positions were virtually unrestricted, and no major political or economic reforms affecting the peasantry were put through during the NUC period. In contrast to the infrequency of NUC visits to villages, and to the tendency of the military personnel stationed nearby to stay out of political controversy, the parties campaigned vigorously everywhere. Even had the NUC made greater or more successful efforts to reach the peasants, however, it is unlikely that the legacy of a decade would have been easily overcome.

[45] *Cumhuriyet*, July 2, 1961.

The NUC and Economics and Finance

Economic policy during the NUC period was evolved chiefly by the Cabinet rather than the NUC itself, no member of the NUC having had much training in economics. The general economic policy of the NUC and its Cabinet was understandably heavily deflationary. This policy, combined with the uncertain political atmosphere, brought both Turkish and foreign private investment almost to a halt. On balance a substantial amount of stabilization was achieved during the NUC period, but it will remain for future governments to solve many other problems, as well as some new problems created because of the stabilization itself.

Probably one of the most serious of the new problems was unemployment. The NUC suspended work on most of the 448 unfinished major investment projects, pending a review of their soundness. It was not until late 1961 that there were indications that some were to be completed.[46] The substantial number of workers laid off were added to an estimated 3.5 million unemployed and underemployed in the agricultural sector due to poor weather. The government attempted to alleviate the situation by increasing the investment sector of the 1961-62 budget. While this was helpful, it was insufficient in the absence of private investment and consumer spending. Available bank credit in 1961 was higher than even under Menderes, but it was used mostly in the agricultural sector, as industry proved wary in taking advantage of the new facilities. A noteworthy factor was the increase in currency in circulation despite a lack of increase in business activity. The difficulty was that the increased volume was being hoarded, not spent, and was, therefore, on the books as in public hands but not actually in the economy. The Minister of Finance estimated hoarding of money at a level of about 800 million lira. Although this showed increased public confidence in the lira, it was a damper on effective demand.[47]

An important achievement of the NUC period was price stability. During the Menderes period the cost of living had risen from 100 in 1953 to 231 in the second quarter of 1960. The only significant rise in the NUC period was an increase of 3.1 percent in the first four months of 1961, which compared favorably with a 9 percent rise during the same period in 1960.

The NUC was also able to gain sufficient confidence of foreign governments to maintain the flow of foreign aid. Credits and grants between May 1960 and August 1961 were approximately $400 million, including $126.9 million from the Development Loan Fund for the Eregli Steel and Iron Works, various International Cooperation Administration credits totaling $93 million, $87.5 million from the International Monetary Fund and Organization for European Economic Co-

[46] *Three-Monthly Economic Review, Turkey*, No. 40 (November 1961).

[47] *Ibid.*, No. 41 (February 1962).

operation to cover the 1960 foreign exchange deficit, $20 million from the International Bank for Reconstruction and Development and $50 million from the government of West Germany.

The trade gap in 1960-61 was narrowed by almost 29 million lira. Although exports dropped from 313.8 million lira in 1959-60 to 299.2 million in 1961, due largely to poor crops, imports under the government's austerity policy dropped from 495 million to 452 million. A tightening of import regulations, including virtually a total cessation in the import of luxury goods, was an important contribution. By August 1960 the NUC had announced budget savings of 824 million lira, and in 1961 Turkey's budget was balanced for the first time in many years.

While industrial development can presumably revive when political conditions become settled and government credit and investment policies become firm—in 1962 there were already noticeable signs that foreign private capital was interested in Turkey—agricultural development is a much more serious problem. The Menderes regime used manipulation of the price paid for wheat by the government's Soil Products Office as a political lever. One of the first actions of the NUC was to announce that there would be no such increase in 1960. But in 1961 a combination of a poor harvest and the late arrival of shipments of surplus United States wheat raised the price on the open market as much as 60 percent over the government-paid price, leaving no choice but for the Soil Products Office to follow. A combination of economic and political factors produced another rise in 1962. A report by the United Nations Food and Agriculture Organization in 1959 pointed up the long-range and fundamental nature of the problem: "The programme [proposed in the FAO Report] amounts practically to a complete reconstruction of the structure of Turkey's economy, especially of its agricultural basis."[48]

In addition to the general lines of policy worked out by the cabinet, however, the NUC undertook some specific projects for economic reform, which illustrate its approach to such problems. Outstanding were the wedding ring drive, the establishment of a State Planning Organization, forced savings, the declarations of wealth, and tax revision. As a whole these actions were abrupt and often seemingly arbitrary in tone. Usually they were motivated by psychological and political considerations as well as by economic ones. Most distinctive about them was that the NUC undertook actions which the political parties had either been unwilling or unable to take in the past. These, of course, were met with an outcry from the parties, although those who realized the need for some unpopular measures were privately relieved to have them taken by those who did not have to face the voters later. In the end, however, most of the actions were superficial, and few are likely to have substantial impact on Turkish economic development.

[48] FAO Mediterranean Development Project, *Country Report, Turkey,* (Rome, Italy, 1959), p. VI-1.

Typical of all these considerations was the wedding ring drive of the summer of 1960. All Turks were urged to turn in their gold and silver wedding rings to bolster the nation's hard currency reserve. The origins of the drive are unclear, but it seems to have started among army officers. First mentioned in the newspapers on June 9, it quickly spread to many parts of the country, and "ersatz" jewelry soon graced many Turkish fingers. How much was collected is unknown, but it is doubtful that there was more than a token increase in Turkish gold stocks. Psychologically it was useful in dramatizing the seriousness of the financial crisis Menderes left behind him, but here too the impact was probably not great. The drive did not spread beyond the cities and larger towns, areas where the need to dramatize things was least. General Gürsel realized the limited economic effectiveness of such gifts to the Treasury when he thanked the donors, but suggested purchase of governments bonds would be more effective.[49]

The establishment of the State Planning Organization will hopefully have positive consequences for many years to come. Turkey had for some years been one of the only rapidly developing nations without a planning body as such, although during the Menderes period there had been a Ministry of Coordination. It was popularly said that Menderes had a phobia about the word "plan." For the soldiers, of course, planning was a cardinal principle of operation, and they were supported by the great bulk of Turkish intellectuals who had long criticized Menderes on this score. First enacted by Law No. 91 on September 30, 1960, the Planning Organization was incorporated into the 1961 Constitution.[50] The organization is midway between being political and nonpolitical, in that its executive organ, the High Planning Council, is composed of the Prime Minister or his deputy, three ministers elected by the cabinet, the head of the Planning Organization (Under-Secretary for Planning), and the heads of its three departments, Economic Planning, Social Planning, and Coordination.[51] The organization is staffed by a group of able young

[49] An interesting footnote to the affair was the bulletin issued on June 15 by Treasury officials asking citizens to refrain from purchasing new gold or silver wedding rings to replace the ones they had donated to the nation. The bulletin explained how the increased demand was bidding gold prices up to a dangerous level, and added that it would be better to make cash gifts directly to the Treasury than to donate gold and then put more money in circulation by seeking to replace donated jewelry on the open market.

[50] Article 129 of the Constitution, which reads: "Economic, social and cultural development is based on a plan. Development is carried out according to this plan. The organization and functions of the State Planning Organization, the principles to be observed in the preparation and execution, and application and revision of the plan, and the measures designed to prevent changes tending to impair the unity of the plan, shall be regulated by special legislation."

[51] Article 4, Law No. 91, Sept. 30, 1960. The text of the law has been published in English, *Introducing Turkey's State Planning Organization,* Devlet Planlama Teskilatı Yayınları No. 3 (Ankara, 1961).

economists, political scientists, and sociologists, mostly Western trained. It is highly regarded by Western economists, and in 1962 it published a Five-Year Plan which was received favorably by the government. How much attention is paid to the plan or to the Planning Organization's other activities in research and policy recommendation, remains to be seen, but there is sure to be pressure from many quarters for continued planned development.

In January 1961 the NUC adopted a plan under which all persons earning over 500 lira per month would be required to invest 3 percent of their earnings in government savings bonds. The bonds would be issued directly by employers as part of wages, and self-employed persons or those receiving income from sources other than wages would buy them directly from the Treasury. Ten-year bonds, they would become transferable and redeemable after a shorter period. Interest between 4 and 7 percent was to be fixed each year by the Finance Minister. The Finance Minister was also given authority to reduce the percentage of required investment to either 2 or 1 percent if he felt it necessary.[52] The interest rate for the first year starting March 1, 1961, was fixed at 6 percent. It was estimated that the bonds would produce 450 million lira of investment funds yearly. For at least the first year, proceeds were to go toward financing Turkey's second steel mill, to be built with both Turkish and foreign capital at the Black Sea town of Eregli.

There were arguments both for and against this measure. On the positive side were the comparatively low rate of private savings, the serious price inflation which had occurred in Turkey and which could easily continue, and the habitual tendency of Turks to invest in land and real estate rather than industry. Negative considerations were the extremely low level of wages of government employees and the fact that the low-income groups would be hit the hardest. All in all the bond plan was accepted by the public without a great outcry.

One of the most controversial of all the actions of the NUC on the economic-financial front was the inauguration of the Declaration of Wealth. The idea was originally to guard against corruption by requiring all appointed public officials, including the cabinet and the NUC itself, to file Declarations of Wealth both at the beginning and end of their tenure in office. This principle was soon extended to the members of the Constituent Assembly, and to the higher ranks of the civil service. Then, according to Article 116 of the revised Income Tax Law published early in January 1961, the requirement of filing a list of assets was extended to all taxpayers. Drafted carefully to avoid leaving loopholes, the declarations were to include assets held abroad, separate listings for assets held by other members of the taxpayer's family, etc.[53]

[52] Summaries of Law No. 233, the Savings Bond Law, are found in *Vatan* and *Cumhuriyet*, Jan. 19, 1960, and *Ulus*, Feb. 28, 1960.

[53] The first report appeared in *Vatan*, Jan. 8, 1961.

The outcry was, of course, immediate. Few people believed the statement by Istanbul Municipal Treasurer Metin Kızılkaya that the declarations had no relationship whatever to a wealth tax or other such levy, but were only being asked to enable more objective determination of levels of income taxes.[54] The implications of the declaration were too obvious, not less for the fact that corruption cases at Yassıada were prominent in the press at the time. The NUC apparently did not press the issue, and to date the conditions under which the declarations will be filed, and the details of items to be included, are still being worked out.

Finally, the NUC undertook to thoroughly overhaul Turkey's tax laws. The two most outstanding features were the inclusion of agricultural income as a taxable category, and major changes in rates of land and building taxes. One of the chief deficiencies of the Turkish tax system has for many years been the exemption of income from agricultural activity. Atatürk first exempted agriculture by removing both the tithe, the traditional 10 percent levy for support of religious establishments, and the heavy levies imposed by the Ottoman government. For political reasons he never reimposed taxes on agricultural income, and for the same reasons his successors have maintained this exemption. For Turkey's large and middle-sized farm operators, though, this was a windfall. That the NUC included them in the revised tax law therefore was not surprising.[55] As with so many other actions with politically controversial overtones, specific provisions became the subject of haggling and negotiation, and though the law now provides for taxation of agricultural income, little if any has yet been collected.

In revising land and building tax rates, the NUC quickly became involved in a great numbers game. There was much sympathy with the idea of revision, for it was estimated by Finance Minister Kurdaş that low-income groups had been paying 66 percent of all taxes collected in Turkey.[56] On November 4, it was announced that taxes on land and buildings would be increased to between five and fifteen times the rate which had been in effect since 1942. It was estimated that revenue from these sources would increase from 80 to 400 million lira annually.[57] In January more details were given out that land taxes would be ten times

[54] *Cumhuriyet,* Jan. 17, 1961.

[55] The provisions were relatively liberal. Taxes would be levied only on farmers who owned over 100 head of small animals or 25 head of large ones, 400 citrus trees or 800 other fruit trees, 30 dönüms in vegetables or rice, or 150 dönüms in wheat. Above these levels the regular scale of income taxes would be applied: 10 percent of the first 2,500 lira of taxable income; 20 percent of the next 7,500; 30 percent of the next 15,000; 40 percent of the next 30,000; 50 percent of the next 70,000; 60 percent of the next 157,000; 70 percent of the next 217,500; and a straight 60 percent for incomes of over 500,000 lira. For a summary of the provisions as proposed by the NUC see *Cumhuriyet,* Jan. 4, 1961.

[56] *Cumhuriyet,* Feb. 17, 1961.

[57] *Cumhuriyet,* Nov. 4, 1960.

the 1942 level, buildings taxes five times if the buildings were used as homes, six times for other uses. Some tax relief was given to spur new construction, and it was stipulated that 30 percent of revenues from these sources could be retained by province and local governments.[58] More bargaining produced other refinements, a division of Turkey into three zones and smaller districts based on political subdivisions, and increasing land taxes six times in 245 districts, eight times in 81, and ten times in all others. Rate revisions were also differently calculated according to various methods of value assessment which had been used in the past. Proposed rates of building tax increases were cut from five, four, and two times to three, two, and one and one-half times respectively.[59] Tax revision became probably the chief subject of bargaining between the NUC and the Constituent Assembly, with each side winning some points.

All in all, the NUC's record on economic matters was not bad, although it was not impressive. The NUC period was too short to bring about basic changes in the structure of the Turkish economy, but the NUC did succeed in inaugurating some important economic reforms which may prove easier for the political parties to accept than if they had introduced them themselves. Future economic progress depends chiefly, of course, on the actions of the civilian government both on economic and political matters.

Conclusion

What sort of political rulers, then, did the NUC turn out to be? In relation to what they asserted was their primary goal, holding free elections and turning power back to elected leaders, they did very well. Too well, perhaps, for it is doubtful that the NUC experience resulted in important changes which might work to prevent a recurrence of the situation that preceded the NUC.

Although the NUC interested itself in many basic reforms, it never evolved a definite reform program as such. The "must" work prior to holding elections included only measures such as the trials and writing a new constitution and election law. All of these might be termed "technical." More fundamental and long-range items, education, industrial and agricultural modernization and expansion, and land reform were dealt with less urgently, and consequently with less effectiveness. That the members of the NUC recognized the great importance of these problems is beyond doubt, for in the *Cumhuriyet* interviews shortly after May 27 all laid great stress on social-economic difficulties. A large part of the cause of the NUC's failure to achieve more in relation to these problems lay in its failure to exploit its political position.

[58] *Cumhuriyet,* Jan. 10, 1961.
[59] *Cumhuriyet,* April 2, 1961.

At the outset the NUC had the strong support of most of the urban middle class. The discredited Democratic party organization needed about nine months to recover from the shock of May 27 and to begin to re-emerge in the new parties. During this period the NUC ruled alone and began work on important social and economic matters. To have carried them further at this time would in all likelihood have elicited virtually unanimous support from public opinion, for forward-looking groups, at least, would have been more than happy to have the NUC do needed things which the parties themselves could do only with great difficulty. But by the time the Justice party and others swung into action, the NUC had not yet implemented the laws for which it had urban support and as yet little rural resistance. It was not difficult for the fifty-five *ağas,* for instance, to regain most of their lands after the NUC left office, because only a small part of those lands had yet been redistributed. Similarly, there was much talk of a great education drive, but very little was done during the NUC period in terms of investment, construction, or opening of new teacher training institutions.

To say there were no important achievements in these areas would be giving the NUC less than its due amount of credit. Tax reform, for one thing, was a problem of first importance which was handled by the NUC. Other things, such as fundamental changes in the organization of the state economic enterprises, or the modernization of agriculture, could hardly have been fully accomplished in the short period during which the NUC was in power, but much more could have been done at least to start work on these problems.

In acting more like orthodox politicians—and politicians with only minority support—than like nonpolitical, problem-solving soldiers, the NUC may have missed what was a unique opportunity for Turkey to return to the road of rapid development. The 1960 revolution showed that the Turkish armed forces will not stay aloof indefinitely in the face of a national crisis. This demonstration may be a positive gain if it results in the dampening of partisan strife and more concentration on solving national problems. But by becoming not much more than another contending force in the maze of Turkish partisan political life, by retreating in almost every sphere where significant political opposition developed or could have been anticipated instead of pressing forward in the areas where its position was clearly good, by failing to take at least some initial steps in reform which would be reversible by a successor government only with great difficulty, the NUC has left many young Turkish officers far from pleased. If another crisis leads the armed forces to consider intervention once more, what reason have they to believe that dedication to democracy is in the best interest of themselves or their country?

7

A Broader View

FOR FORTY YEARS many Turkish political leaders have worked to make their country into a modern, democratic, prosperous, western state. Yet at the end of this period, which included fifteen years of multiparty politics, the armed forces, which were a product of Atatürk education, believed they had no alternative but to interfere in the political process in order to prevent civil war and preserve the parliamentary system. During at least the first weeks after the armed forces ousted the Menderes regime, they had the support of the overwhelming majority of the urban educated class. Civilian government operates today under the watchful eye of armed forces, which have frequently given signs of impatience with the maneuverings of politicians and the slow pace of economic and social reform.

Despite these setbacks, it would be too much to say that Atatürk's bold program has failed. What has happened is that several important points about the process of political change in a democratic, progressive direction in Turkey have become more clear. One of these points is the persistence of the issue of secularism, at least in part because of the extreme character of this issue in Turkey in the past forty years. Certainly it must be agreed that many of the Atatürk reforms of the 1920's and 1930's were *sine qua non* for much of the achievement in social and economic betterment of the Turkish people that has taken place under the Republic. Whether it was wise to have insisted on as drastic and at the same time as rapid reform in spheres intimately affecting the personal lives of many of the Turkish people, is a question yet to be answered.

What is clear is that once the secularism issue was raised, it became by far the most potent one in the competition for votes. That the polarization reached the extent it did in 1960 is partly due, of course, to some specific aspects of Turkish politics: the personalities of Menderes, Bayar, Inönü, and others, the considerably larger role which personal factors play in Turkish political life than in that of Western countries; the prominence of differences over economic doctrines, combined with the temptations of power increased by sizable doses of foreign aid; the fact that many Turkish politicians have not really grasped the meaning of the concept of loyal opposition, either when they are in power or when they are not; the emergence of only one important opposition party at the beginning of the multiparty period; and the steady growth of that party, together with an electoral system, which discouraged additional parties.

The National Unity Committee and Turkish Political Development

An important result of the National Unity Committee period is that for the first time since the beginning of multiparty government in 1946 there is the strong possibility that the situation might change in a relatively permanent way. The sudden disappearance of one of the two focal points of the largely two-sided political and doctrinal struggle, the Democratic party, which had encompassed opposition to the Republicans for a variety of both reformist and other reasons, opened the way for interests that had previously been submerged under the mushrooming importance of the secularization issue. Proportional representation and the weakening of the Republican People's party were helpful in creating a four-party Assembly in 1961. The necessity of coalition government and the achievement of a compromise on the issue of amnesty for the defendants in the Yassıada trials, an issue which threatened to reestablish the bipolarization until the armed forces insisted that political leaders turn their attention to other problems, these events have begun a process in which each of the parties is defining its interests and views on positive issues related to the future more than to the past. But even with such institutional bases for modifying the extreme nature of Turkish bipolarization, this particular legacy of both Atatürk and Menderes is not likely to disappear easily from the Turkish political scene.

Recent Turkish experience also indicates again the great importance of concrete achievement for winning political popularity. Under Atatürk, the Republican reformers began to reach the people only when in the 1930's great emphasis was put on economic progress and improvement in health, education, and communication facilities. Similarly, a large portion of the popularity of the Menderes regime came from visible things, roads, factories, mosques, and relative prosperity among the peasants. That many of these were supplied at serious cost to Turkey's overall economic health was of little concern to the peasants, even if they could see this usually well-hidden aspect of many such projects. An important reason the NUC period may come to be looked on as relatively unimpressive in terms of long-range Turkish progress is that few of the specific reforms, such as land reform or improved education, got far off the drawing boards. Less concrete matters should, of course, not be forgotten, but it should be apparent to all Turkish political leaders that without concrete achievement even the most high-minded doctrines of progress are not necessarily strong competitors in multiparty politics.

The NUC experience also raises some basic questions about the compatibility of rapid political reform and multiparty politics. The irony of the NUC period is that it was the strong attachment of the Turkish armed forces to democratic forms that gave conservative leaders a chance to organize, and that led to the triumph of a not unexpectedly shortsighted public opinion. Three times the choice of liberal or conservative alternatives has been put up to the Turkish people in a free election: in the local election of 1930 when, although the Free party of that year was ostensibly liberal, its local adherents made it the rallying ground of conservative and reactionary groups; in 1950, when despite the Democrat's economic liberalization and support of less authoritarian government, their differences with the Republicans on secularism were already clear, though not nearly as clear as they were in 1954 and 1957; and in 1961 when at least two of the four parties almost openly opposed not only the reformist Republican party but also the idea of reform itself. In all three instances conservatives received strong support. In this aspect of Turkey, at least, there was little change between 1930 and 1961.

It must be pointed out, however, that the fault cannot be entirely laid to the peasants. When multiparty activity leading to elections began anew in early 1961, a substantial part of the urban educated class which makes up most Turkish political leadership, did not shrink from accepting conservative or reactionary support, even if it meant jeopardizing the prospects for the fundamental social change that would assure continued progress. It may well be that some sort of compromise will emerge in Turkey. It is conceivable, for instance, that the armed forces—now definitely part of the political picture, but still largely interested in government through democratic political institutions as well as in rapid and continuing social and economic advance—will work to retain the principle of popular choice among political parties, but eliminate the more extreme from the running. If, however, the revamped political structure of Turkey's Second Republic proves unworkable as the basis for economic and social progress, neither the military nor the civilian moderates may be able to avoid another period of "tutelage," nor indeed may they want to avoid this. The non-coercive road to democracy, at least in Turkey, is long and hard.

The Turkish Revolution and Other Military Revolutions

Military governments have played a variety of roles since World War II in guiding the political evolution of developing nations. They include short transitional regimes such as in Burma and Turkey, regimes performing more thorough but still limited building or rebuilding operations such as in Pakistan or the Sudan, and those for which an indefinite dura-tion and a revolution from the ground up is envisaged, as in Egypt. There are, however, limitations of two kinds on what a military regime can do in a specific country. There are some general limitations shown by experience to be related to the character of military rule and military thinking in almost all developing countries. In addition there are the specific limitations of any particular case, such as the country's social and political structure, level of economic development, quality of the bureaucracy, political parties and interest groups, as well as the size, character, quality, and ideology of the armed forces themselves.

Many of these factors were illustrated in the Turkish revolution of 1960-61, though it must be added that despite limitations the Turkish junta fell short of accomplishing much that might have been possible. Edward Shils has pointed to four characteristics found in almost all military regimes which act to dampen the effectiveness of efforts to build democratic institutions: (1) "Their program is order and progress, but usually with more stress on order than on progress." (2) They usually have little knowledge of problems of economic growth, nor do they have positive programs other than those they take over from the old regime, for which they have no respect. (3) "Like military hierarchy, military oligarchies allow no place for opposition." (4) They demand consensus when the machinery for its creation usually is inadequate.[1]

The Turkish junta maintained order, but remained dependent on others for virtually all policies of social and economic progress. This dependence extended not only to the definition but also to the implementation of these policies. Few workable ideas came from the members of the NUC itself. The NUC recognized the need and function of an opposition, but was apparently unable to accept it, and proved unable to handle it effectively when it arose. Almost as soon as the armed forces relinquished the formal reins of power, the consensus among Turkish political groups, which was announced at various stages of the NUC period, was shown to be weak and transitory.

These general factors were further shaped by specific Turkish conditions into a constricting framework in which the NUC had to operate. The Turkish armed forces' tradition of staying out of politics, the ideology of staying out of politics inculcated in the officer corps by the Atatürk revolution, and the ideological and class kinship of the armed forces with much of the civilian urban educated class were instrumental in eliminating from consideration the idea of a long-term tutelary military regime.

[1] Edward Shils, "The Military in the Political Development of the New States," in John J. Johnson, ed., *The Role of the Military in Underdeveloped Countries* (Princeton University Press, 1962), pp. 54-59. He summarizes: "The military oligarchy is not a complete regime. It has neither a comprehensive program nor a perspective into the future. Like all non-hereditary oligarchies, it has no provision for succession. It is what some of the military oligarchs call a 'caretaker regime.' But its ideas about what it takes care of are rather scant, and, even where well-intentioned, unimaginative."

The fact that not all political parties were discredited—on the contrary the largest surviving party was in many ways, initially at least, almost as celebrated as the armed forces themselves in ridding Turkey of the oppressive Democratic party regime—dampened many prospects that the armed forces may have had in mind for keeping development on a non-partisan basis. The complicated and technical nature of many economic, social, and political reforms, reforms that often involved continuation, elaboration, or reorientation of long-range programs already under way rather than drastic, summary, uprooting operations for which the armed forces might be better equipped, further lessened the possibilities that the NUC could avoid being drawn into the muddy waters of Turkish politics. Among some important self-imposed handicaps on the NUC were the statement immediately after the revolution of an unrealistic time schedule of three months for a new constitution, trials of the former leaders, and holding elections; the continual succumbing by NUC leaders to the demands of the press for predictions and promises of a definite date when they would step out of power; and the failure of the armed forces to match the political parties in reaching the Turkish peasants.

What the NUC tried to do can be summarized in three points: (1) To remove the oppressive regime of the Democratic party, and deal with the individual offenders. This the NUC did efficiently and on the whole justly. One of the major accomplishments of the NUC period was the overall legality and fairness of the trials and of the hanging of Menderes. Although the political wisdom of some aspects of the trials can be questioned, the handling of the proceedings did much to raise the stature of the NUC in the eyes of both the Turkish and Western publics. It was seen by many as the most important single phenomenon of the NUC period. (2) To reshape the institutions of government which were deemed to have been most instrumental in enabling the Democrats to engage in undemocratic practices: the Constitution, election law, and the party system. This the NUC accomplished in the formal sense, but there are considerable doubts about the wisdom of some provisions of the new Constitution in encouraging maximum development as well as maximum political democracy, and regarding the directions in which the new alignment of parties will lead. (3) To effect some reforms which would be the beginning of an attack on important social and economic problems that Turkey faces. In this area, because of various general and specific limitations and obstacles discussed in earlier chapters, the NUC did not accomplish what it had hoped to. Certain institutions, like the State Planning Organization, are important contributions to future Turkish development, but for the most part the NUC period did not produce ideas and the beginnings of new policies. Spotty though the total record is, however, it must be seen in relation to what the alternative would have been—continuation of the Menderes regime, which was on the brink of the political abyss of violence, repression, and political and economic bankruptcy.

The Turkish Revolution and the United States

The political difficulties in Turkey illustrate several dilemmas of American foreign policy in relation to developing countries. One is the idea, which seems to have prevailed in some quarters at various periods in the recent past, that any internal difficulties encountered by allies of the United States will necessarily benefit the Russians. Reports in the American press in April and May 1960, while noting that foreign policy was not at issue in the Turkish troubles, nevertheless made it clear that the question whether Turkey might become a weaker ally was very much an American concern.[2] Reports appeared, though all were denied by the United States government, that both American Ambassador Fletcher Warren and Secretary of State Christian Herter, the latter in Istanbul for the NATO Foreign Ministers' meeting, had appealed to Menderes to take steps to improve the internal political atmosphere in Turkey.

Fortunately, the fallacy of these concerns was demonstrated in the first hours of the May 27 revolution, when the armed forces made it fully clear that Turkish commitments to NATO and CENTO were in no way affected, and in the months following Menderes' ouster, all civilian political elements also demonstrated that they had no intention of doing anything that might weaken Turkish firmness against the colossus of the North. On the contrary, it was the military regime that became the first to undertake such projects as building radio stations in Eastern Turkey to counter Russian propaganda that for many years had had a virtual monopoly of radio access to the most undeveloped Turkish provinces.

[2] The *New York Times,* for example, opened its "News of the Week in Review" story on Turkey on May 1, 1960 with emphasis on Turkey's military importance for the West, and though duly discussing the internal reasons for the unrest added in the next column, "The upheaval in Korea and the crisis in Turkey raised the question of what the West could do to stave off possible ruptures in its Asian defense structure." (*New York Times,* May 1, 1960, p. 1.) The London *Economist* likewise noted the possible effect of the troubles on Turkey as an ally: "It would be wrong to exaggerate this, since one thing upon which all Turks agree is their determination to repel any Soviet infiltration or attack. Yet if Turkey is either going to go through a period of internal storm and stress, or be battened down under a tight dictatorship, it can hardly remain as satisfactory and effective a member of the alliance as has hitherto been reckoned; and the United States government and Congress may not consider it quite such a suitable base for American rockets or quite such a worthy recipient of aid." ("Nato's Frayed End," *Economist,* May 7, 1960, p. 503.)

An indication of how it was Menderes who might be most guilty of flirting with the Russians was his projected trip to Moscow, which received virtually no mention in the American press. As the *Economist* pointed out; "Mr. Menderes may reckon that a flirtation with the Russians—he is due to visit Moscow in July—will restore his value in the eyes of his allies as well as providing him with some substantial material benefits. He should rather reflect that it is those on the top of their form who tend to get the most out of their visits to Moscow; if by July he is obviously getting into deep waters at home, the Russians may well feel it is more to their interest to push him farther in than to give him a helping hand." *Ibid.*

Another dilemma of American policy is the problem of contact with political opposition groups. The Menderes government, especially in the later part of its decade of rule, discouraged official relationships between foreign diplomats and leaders of the Republican People's party. It is, of course, true that diplomats are accredited to the government of the host country, and might be abusing their privileges by defying express or strongly implied wishes of that government about the behavior of diplomats. It is precisely in a bipolar situation like that of Turkey before 1960, however, that acquaintance with opposition thinking is most important.

Informal channels of information about the opposition are usually plentiful and tend to increase as tension between government and opposition heightens. Where diplomats have no access, there are usually journalists, businessmen, and others who are informed and qualified to assist the embassy staff in evaluating political trends. In Ankara in 1959 and early 1960 Turks and foreigners alike frequently expressed amazement that certain important figures in the American Embassy seemed to persist in the belief that Menderes would surely continue to win as he had done in frequent other crises. The American State Department told reporters on May 27, 1960 that the overthrow of the Menderes regime came as a complete surprise to Washington.[3]

A part of the failure to see Menderes in an objective light is also related to the problem of the optimum use of American foreign aid. In many senses Turkey is high on the list of countries in which American assistance can achieve the purposes for which it is offered. Militarily Turkey maintains large and relatively efficient armed forces, including one of the largest contingents committed to NATO of any of the countries in that organization. Turkey is one of the few countries allowing NATO missile sites on its territory. The Turkish armed forces also play a large role in literacy and practical education of large numbers of peasant conscripts, and are beginning to contribute men and equipment for road-building and similar economic development functions. In nonmilitary spheres, Turkey has the human and natural resource potential to use foreign aid to make as great and rapid advances in economic development as almost any other of the so-called "developing" nations. Equally important in American eyes should be the fact that a large number of Turkish leaders are determined to achieve these things through democratic means.

It is precisely because of these many material and ideological ties to the West that the United States has potentially great leverage in demanding the best possible use of its aid. The weapon so often used by developing nations, the threat to turn to the Soviet bloc, is of virtually no relevance in the Turkish case. History and ideology make it unlikely that, under present conditions, Turkey would succumb even to the most

[3] *New York Times*, May 28, 1960.

tempting Soviet offers. It is also highly improbable that Russia would offer terms of aid or support for Turkey for anything less than neutralization of the Straits, a point on which Turkey has said repeatedly that it would not even consider yielding.

Yet in an age of rapidly increasing realization of the importance of planning for optimum development, Turkey under Menderes remained planless. It was only through the International Monetary Fund, though with the strong backing of the United States, that in 1958 the Turkish government was finally persuaded to accept a Stabilization Plan. The revelations of the National Unity Committee about the size of the Turkish debt and the number of unfinished, unplanned, and unintegrated investment projects would have horrified any responsible American business executive, and should have had similar effect years earlier on those in Turkey charged with spending American public funds.

A concurrent complaint of the Turkish opposition to Menderes was that the United States did not use its leverage to persuade Menderes to ease his repressive political policies. In this area the line between legitimate American concern for Turkey's political health in order that development may take place most efficiently and effectively, and "interference in Turkey's internal affairs" is more imprecise than in the strictly economic sphere. Nevertheless, there is little evidence that the Menderes regime was nudged or urged to practice the democratic values that Turkey as a self-styled Western nation has preached.[4]

Opportunities as well as problems for the United States arose during the NUC period. From the American point of view civilian, multiparty politics is normally preferable to military rule. Yet there are possibly some distinct advantages of regimes that are not multiparty—military as well as civilian—in certain circumstances. Turkey, among other countries, has had difficulty for many years in achieving under a multiparty system some of the things that economists generally consider basic to enabling it to move from the "take-off" platform into a stage of increasingly domestic-generated development. Tax reform, for instance, was undertaken by the NUC, although for reasons discussed earlier it was not effectively implemented.

Admittedly the United States cannot look with benign approval on military usurpation of power from democratically elected governments. There are many cases, however, when the United States is either unable to prevent such an occurrence, or where the armed forces come to power for reasons that might be considered more acceptable, for example, overthrow of a government that is not democratic. Military regimes in

[4] One notable occasion when Western governments expressed an opinion on Turkish internal affairs was at the end of the Yassıada trials. There was praise for the handling of the proceedings, but also representations of several European governments for commutation of the death sentences passed on Menderes, Bayar, and others. See Chap. 2 above.

developing countries are of a wide variety: short-term transitional, long-term transitional, in search of merely administrative reform, revolution from bottom to top, liberal, totalitarian, or right or left wing. Research is beginning to show a variety of tasks that such regimes have attempted, either successfully or unsuccessfully, and that have had varying effects on such issues as popular participation in politics, the growth of interest groups, political parties, local government, and economic development.

The questions whether and to what extent the United States might encourage continuation of military or one-party governments beyond the period needed for the accomplishment of such minimal tasks as removing an oppressive or corrupt regime are extremely difficult ones, however. Little is as yet known about the comparative efficacy of military or civilian, multiparty or one-party regimes in achieving specific forward steps in development, nor are reliable criteria available for estimating whether a particular regime can attain its development aims. Neither do we have ways to determine whether a given military or one-party transitional regime will continue its movement toward multiparty government after it gets the feel of power. But to the extent that the United States gains knowledge and experience about the nature of such regimes, it may more effectively encourage progress toward multiparty governments committed to forward-looking economic and social policies.

APPENDIX A

A Note on Proportional Representation and Single-Member Constituencies in the 1961 Election Results

There was considerable debate in the Constituent Assembly about whether or not proportional representation was to be used in the election of deputies. It was unanimously agreed that the system under which the 1957 election was held—that a plurality in a province gave the winner that province's entire delegation—was not acceptable in terms of fairness. There was some talk, though, of single-member constituencies. In this connection it is significant that the results under proportional representation (PR) and under single-member provisions would have shown important differences. I have therefore made a rough attempt to determine the distribution of deputies under the latter form of election.

The analysis was done by dividing each province into as nearly equal, and geographically contiguous, constituencies as possible based on administrative districts, the unit next below the province. This compilation was not, of course, necessarily the one that would have been made if single-member constituencies had actually been used, but I believe that it comes close enough to what could reasonably have been expected so that the analysis is a plausible one.

Assembly Seats under PR and Single-Member Constituencies

Party	Seats Under PR		Seats in Single-Member Constituencies		Popular Vote	
	Number	Percent	Number	Percent	Number (in thousands)	Percent
JP..........	158	35.1	199	44.2	3,527	34.8
RPP........	173	38.4	135	30.0	3,726	36.7
RPNP.......	54	12.0	52	11.6	1,415	14.0
NTP........	65	14.5	64	14.2	1,392	13.7
Total......	450	100.0	450	100.0	10,060	100.0

The fact that there would have been hardly any change in the size of the RPNP and NTP groups is due to the primacy of the JP-RPP contest in many provinces. The tendency under PR to fragment the results and give exaggerated representation to small parties did not take place because of the fact that the number of parties in the race was only four. The peculiar pattern of division of anti-RPP voting results also played a part, keeping the two small parties out of areas in which the fact there was virtually a two-party race was the overriding fact.

This is illustrated in the case of the Aegean region, where neither the Nation nor the New Turkey Parties elected any deputies at all.

Assembly Seats under PR and Single-Member Constituencies, Aegean Region

Province	Deputies under PR		Deputies under Single-Member Constituencies	
	JP	RPP	JP	RPP
Aydın	6	2	8	0
Denizli	4	3	6	1
Izmir	10	7	15	2
Manisa	7	4	11	0
Muğla	4	1	5	0
Total	31	17	45	3

In this case PR accomplished precisely what it was designed to, i.e. to get the distribution of seats as close as possible to the distribution of votes. The application of PR on a province-wide basis, rather than single-member constituencies as used in elections to the lower house of the United States and some other countries, is in line with the statement in Article 76 of the Turkish Constitution of 1961, which states that "Members of the Grand National Assembly represent neither their constituencies nor their constituents, but the nation as a whole." This philosophy also explains the omission of a residence requirement as part of the qualifications for Assembly candidates.

APPENDIX B

Election Results 1957, 1961, and Referendum, 1960[a]

Province	1957 Election				1960 Referendum		1961 Election			
	DP %	RPP %	RPNP %	FP %	% Voting	% No	JP %	RPP %	RPNP %	NTP %
Adana	42.4	55.1	2.2	.3	75.7	44.8	51.3	43.9	4.2	—
Adiyaman	49.8	37.7	.3	12.1	84.5	33.4	2.9	37.5	10.7	48.9
Afyon	48.1	29.9	21.9	—	83.0	40.4	28.4	25.0	45.5	1.1
Ağri	50.2	41.4	8.4	—	88.3	17.1	11.0	32.4	34.3	22.3
Amasya	46.2	45.1	7.4	1.2	89.8	43.4	53.9	38.8	7.3	—
Ankara	37.3	45.8	13.4	3.4	81.3	31.6	19.8	38.7	35.6	5.0
Antalya	51.1	40.8	1.1	7.0	70.2	48.7	61.2	35.0	3.8	—
Artvin	49.7	39.9	.6	9.7	63.2	22.2	45.8	44.2	10.0	—
Aydın	60.5	35.0	2.2	2.2	83.0	56.0	64.4	30.9	3.8	.9
Balikesir	54.8	35.1	1.6	8.6	85.3	47.3	58.6	35.6	4.2	1.6
Bilecik	48.8	41.0	7.0	3.2	86.8	39.9	50.8	41.5	7.7	—
Bingöl	41.3	36.4	7.0	3.8	88.4	20.4	—	31.1	11.7	54.6
Bitlis	60.9	37.4	1.2	.4	87.1	33.5	—	30.8	22.3	46.9
Bolu	54.0	38.5	7.5	—	82.6	55.1	23.3	28.8	19.0	28.9
Burdur	33.4	30.6	.3	35.7	78.4	29.4	36.3	43.7	—	20.0
Bursa	58.1	29.0	5.3	7.5	85.0	52.8	63.1	29.3	5.6	2.0
Çanakkale	55.8	35.3	4.3	4.3	85.8	47.8	31.1	35.0	9.9	24.0
Çankiri	35.4	37.5	24.6	2.5	85.0	44.2	14.2	23.2	62.4	—
Çorum	45.5	34.2	17.7	2.5	87.5	52.2	52.7	29.6	16.1	—
Denizli	51.1	44.4	1.4	3.1	80.9	51.1	56.4	40.0	1.8	1.3
Diyarbakır	48.9	30.2	.8	20.0	84.7	26.3	19.2	32.8	5.2	42.8
Edirne	53.2	37.3	6.6	2.9	87.2	36.9	26.3	38.5	10.1	24.4
Elaziğ	41.6	44.5	3.7	10.1	76.5	36.6	42.2	35.3	21.9	.6
Erzincan	42.1	48.5	9.3	—	87.2	23.6	4.8	48.4	2.0	44.3
Erzurum	50.2	32.3	13.7	3.8	85.3	40.9	7.3	28.1	18.7	45.3
Eskişehir	52.1	37.0	4.8	6.0	86.3	34.6	37.4	35.2	24.7	1.8
Gaziantep	47.9	47.2	1.6	3.3	86.4	43.2	29.4	47.0	2.7	20.9
Giresun	43.9	42.6	9.9	3.6	65.4	38.1	2.8	34.8	23.4	39.0
Gümüşane	47.8	49.5	1.2	1.4	77.2	41.4	26.8	37.8	—	35.4
Hakkari	67.8	30.7	—	1.5	86.6	7.1	3.1	41.3	—	25.3
Hatay	45.4	47.0	2.0	5.6	79.0	40.3	21.7	37.3	3.6	34.0
Isparta	44.1	31.8	1.4	7.5	79.4	35.2	51.0	33.6	—	15.4
Içel	47.0	44.1	.7	23.4	70.1	46.1	55.5	41.2	3.3	—
Istanbul	52.2	41.1	4.2	2.4	75.1	22.6	41.7	38.2	12.4	3.3
Izmir	54.6	41.9	1.2	2.3	82.2	50.2	55.1	39.6	3.1	1.4
Kars	36.8	58.5	.8	3.9	85.9	7.2	21.8	47.8	—	30.4
Kastamonu	44.7	40.4	11.8	3.1	85.9	38.8	9.3	30.6	25.5	34.6
Kayseri	48.8	43.1	5.8	2.2	80.3	41.1	44.7	41.7	8.0	4.7
Kırklareli	52.8	38.4	4.2	4.5	86.1	40.2	14.4	40.3	8.6	36.7
Kırşehir	25.2	11.5	63.3	—	81.6	7.2	10.6	25.8	63.6	—
Kocaeli	50.7	39.2	5.9	4.2	80.4	41.3	44.7	38.8	14.1	2.4
Konya	44.3	40.9	10.4	4.4	79.2	37.8	23.2	34.8	25.3	16.7
Kütahya	53.4	31.9	14.1	.6	83.8	58.2	34.2	27.4	36.2	2.2
Malatya	32.8	65.3	.7	1.2	82.2	11.3	4.2	67.3	5.4	23.0
Manisa	56.9	33.2	2.5	7.5	84.3	56.1	59.9	32.6	7.0	—

Election Results 1957, 1961, and Referendum, 1960 (continued)

Province	1957 Election				1960 Referendum		1961 Election			
	DP %	RPP %	RPNP %	FP %	% Voting	% No	JP %	RPP %	RPNP %	NTP %
Maraş.......	42.1	45.1	12.8	—	74.5	48.8	51.0	38.9	6.0	2.0
Mardin......	46.2	53.1	.6	—	90.2	2.3	—	43.3	21.8	34.9
Mugla.......	54.9	43.1	1.1	.8	75.6	49.3	59.4	38.5	2.1	—
Muş.........	43.5	30.3	8.1	14.2	87.4	20.9	20.4	31.5	4.3	43.8
Nevşehir.....	42.3	28.8	28.9	—	80.3	30.5	32.6	31.9	35.5	—
Niğde.......	40.3	40.7	18.6	.4	79.8	41.0	29.6	30.8	35.5	4.1
Ordu........	43.1	51.4	4.3	1.2	78.8	39.9	24.6	40.5	6.9	28.0
Rize.........	50.6	30.9	18.5	.03	66.9	39.0	53.4	31.6	13.5	1.5
Sakarya.....	58.9	28.7	5.2	7.2	86.0	52.8	38.4	28.0	12.4	21.0
Samsun......	48.3	44.8	4.9	2.0	86.9	57.0	58.3	36.7	5.0	—
Siirt.........	49.5	43.4	.8	6.4	86.1	8.3	—	47.7	—	51.0
Sinop........	37.8	37.1	25.1	—	83.7	29.6	26.2	37.2	36.6	—
Sivas........	39.6	53.0	7.4	—	85.9	25.2	4.8	39.2	9.8	43.9
Tekirdağ.....	51.7	41.2	7.0	—	84.3	38.8	6.9	36.4	7.3	49.4
Tokat.......	45.0	48.7	4.4	2.0	89.3	42.9	16.0	38.2	5.7	40.3
Trabzon.....	47.4	43.4	7.1	2.1	55.3	40.4	51.4	39.5	6.8	2.3
Tunceli......	35.0	54.0	—	10.8	76.6	4.9	—	35.1	7.1	35.4
Urfa.........	45.3	52.0	2.5	.2	81.1	19.8	20.6	42.9	6.1	30.4
Uşak........	32.8	41.9	24.9	.4	72.1	24.5	20.7	41.7	37.6	—
Van.........	42.6	57.4	—	—	88.2	19.2	7.9	32.6	21.5	38.0
Yozgat......	43.8	32.7	23.3	.1	86.4	32.4	12.2	32.7	44.2	10.1
Zonguldak...	53.2	37.0	8.3	1.5	87.0	53.1	55.7	31.8	12.5	—
All Turkey...	47.9	41.0	7.7	3.8	81.2	38.2	34.8	36.7	14.0	13.7

Sources: 1957 Election: CHP Araştırma Bürosu Yayın No. 7, *Seçim Neticeleri Uzerinde bir Inceleme* Ankara, 1959.

1960 Referendum: semi-official figures as reported in Turkish newspapers.

1961 Election: official government figures.

[a] May not add to 100 percent due to rounding and to small independent vote in some provinces.

Index